T0399264

Sounds as They Are

OXFORD STUDIES IN MUSIC THEORY

Series Editor Steven Rings

Sounds as They Are

The unwritten music in classical recordings

RICHARD BEAUDOIN

OXFORD
UNIVERSITY PRESS

OXFORD
UNIVERSITY PRESS

Library of Congress Cataloging-in-Publication Data
Names: Beaudoin, Richard, 1975– author.
Title: Sounds as they are : the unwritten music in classical recordings / Richard Beaudoin.
Description: New York, NY : Oxford University Press, 2024. |
Series: Oxford studies in music theory | Includes index.
Identifiers: LCCN 2023033932 (print) | LCCN 2023033933 (ebook) |
ISBN 9780197659281 (hardback) | ISBN 9780197659304 (epub)
Subjects: LCSH: Sound recordings—Aesthetics.
Classification: LCC ML3877 .B415 2024 (print) | LCC ML3877 (ebook) |
DDC 781.1/7—dc23/eng/20230804
LC record available at https://lccn.loc.gov/2023033932
LC ebook record available at https://lccn.loc.gov/2023033933

DOI: 10.1093/oso/9780197659281.001.0001

Printed by Integrated Books International, United States of America

to my mother and grandmother,
whose conversations were music

Contents

Acknowledgments

A language was spoken in my childhood home that I did not understand. My mother, Ewa Beaudoin, and my grandmother, Stanisława Myślicki, immigrated to America from the small town of Gryfów Śląski, Poland. They did not teach me Polish, though they spoke it to one another. Wanting to understand their conversations, I became attentive to the pauses, intonations, and breaths that signaled their topic and mood. I am grateful for their expansive education in unwritten music.

I thank Philip Ewell and Stephanie Probst for their early commentaries on the first two chapters. Complete drafts took divergent forms and were guided by a core group of readers—Yves Balmer, Claire Chase, William Cheng, Orit Hilewicz, and Olivier Senn—to whom I am deeply grateful. Support from Dartmouth College was essential, especially from the Department of Music, the Leslie Center for the Humanities, and the Walter and Constance Burke Research Initiation Award. I thank all my Dartmouth colleagues, including César Alvarez, Victoria Aschheim, Charlotte Bacon, Jessica Beckman, Rebecca Biron, Miles Blencowe, Sophia Brelvi, Taylor Ho Bynum, Samantha Candon, Michael Casey, Marcia Cassidy, Filippo Ciabatti, Grant Cook, Theodosia Cook, Mona Domosh, Kui Dong, Bevan Dunbar, Jason Ennis, Crystal Fielding, Ash Fure, Gregory Hayes, Evan Hirsch, John Kulvicki, Iyabo Kwayana, Samuel Levey, Theodore Levin, Jodie Mack, Allie Martin, Annemieke McLane, Brian Messier, Ainsley Morse, Rowland Moseley, Sang Wook Nam, Sally Pinkas, Hafiz Shabazz, Elizabeth F. Smith, Steve Swayne, Emily Walton, Barbara Will, and Michael Zsoldos. Thank you to my students at Dartmouth, Harvard, and Brandeis for their enthusiasm, critique, and insight.

Friends and colleagues offered encouragement in many forms and I extend my appreciation to Knar Abrahamyan, Emily Abrams Ansari, Giulia Accornero, Martha Agostini, Arved Ashby, Joseph Auner, Daniel Barolsky, Nathaniel Barrett, Sarah Bassingthwaighte, Amy Blier-Carruthers, Sarra Braham, Lynne Broderick Byler, Glenn Brown, Velvet Brown, Dashon Burton, Joy Calico, Giovanni Cestino, Eric Chafe, Yu-Hui Chang, Eric Chasalow, Claire Chase, Andrew Clark, Suzannah Clark, Richard Cohn,

Colleen Conroy, Nicholas Cook, Annette Dasch, Colin Davin, Ginger Dellenbaugh, Kaye Denny, Emily Dolan, Michèle Duguay, Jonathan Dunsby, Nina Sun Eidsheim, yasser elhariry, Laura Emmery, Wolfgang Ernst, Susan and Chad Finer, Michael Finnissy, Rebecca Fischer, Alice Gomez, Estelí Gomez, Sumanth Gopinath, Andrae Green, Paul Griffiths, Tomie Hahn, Patricia Hall, Christopher Hasty, Áine Heneghan, Neil Heyde, Ellie Hisama, Jesse Holstein, Pavlo Hunka, Jennifer Iverson, Vijay Iyer, Heather Jackson, Yvette Janine Jackson, J. Daniel Jenkins, Alisha Lola Jones, Jenny Kallick, Andrew Kania, Van Kaynor, Tammy L. Kernodle, Lorenz Kilchenmann, David Hyun-Su Kim, Eva Kim, Mark Knoop, Aleksandra Kremer, Melle Kromhout, Edgar Laguinia, Frank Lehman, Liza Lim, Ana Llorens, Levy Lorenzo, Fan Lu, Olivia Lucas, Anabel Maler, Michał Matuszak, Peter McMurray, Eunice McMurray, Ingrid Monson, Joseph Moore, Klára Móricz, Nancy Murphy, Therese Muxeneder, Stanislas Nanchen, Ulrich Naudé, Drew Nobile, Marilyn Nonken, Mitch Ohriner, Senem Pirler, Ève Poudrier, Katherine Pukinskis, Kirstin Valdez Quade, David Rakowski, Frederick Reece, Alexander Rehding, Wolfram Rieger, Eva Moreda Rodriquez, Christian Rogowski, René Rusch, Paul Sanden, Stephanie Sandler, Rohan de Saram, Pauchi Sasaki, Janet Schmalfeldt, David Schneider, Nancy Shafman, Shahzore Shah, Caroline Shaw, Anne Shreffler, Geoffrey Silver, Peter Sheppard Skaerved, M. Lewis Spratlan, Inja Stanović, Loren Stata, Richard Stokes, Dominique Stutzmann, Mazz Swift, John Talbot, Camilla Tassi, Yosvany Terry, Mihailo Trandafilovski, Jeremy Tressler, Danick Trottier, Georgia Volioti, Rose von Schlegell, Daniel Walden, Mads Walther-Hansen, Brad Wells, Rachel Wong, and Linda Yan Zheng. In footnotes to the text, I acknowledge those who brought specific recordings to my attention; I extend apologies if I have failed to give credit where it was due.

This publication owes a great deal to the outstanding community at Oxford University Press. I offer my appreciation to senior editor Norman Hirschy, series editor Steven Rings, and project editor Rachel Ruisard. I would like to thank project manager Koperundevi Pugazhenthi at Newgen Knowledge Works, as well as the book's copyeditor Timothy DeWerff. Thanks also to Martin Cullingford for granting access to the *Gramophone* Exact Reviews archive, to Jeff Louie for assisting on the Granados transcription, and to Mykyta Tyshchenko for making the transliteration and English translation of the Ukrainian poem by Maksym Slavynskyi. Special thanks to Lee Cannon-Brown for editing the graphic and audio examples, and for organizing the

Philosophy and Music Interest Group session devoted to the book at the 2022 Society for Music Theory Conference in New Orleans.

Librarians were key allies and wise guides throughout my writing. I thank Memory Apata, David Bowden, and Craig Pallett at the Dartmouth College Library; Sarah Adams, Erin Conor, Sandi-Jo Malmon, and Kerry Masteller at the Eda Kuhn Loeb Music Library at Harvard University; Christina Linklater at the Isham Memorial Library at Harvard University; Liza Vick at the Otto E. Albrecht Music Library and Eugene Ormandy Music and Media Center at the University of Pennsylvania; Ann Maggs at the Morgan Music Library at Amherst College; and Marlene Wong and Janet Spongberg at the Werner Josten Library at Smith College. The proprietors of numerous bookshops and record stores were also invaluable resources, including and especially Sam Burton of Grey Matter Books.

Alongside the dedication to my mother Ewa and my grandmother Stanisława, I thank my father Richard, my sister Deborah and her family, and my relatives in China, France, Poland, and across the United States. Special thanks to my daughter Celia who researched critical reception of unwritten music, and to my son Louis whose invitations to throw the frisbee brought respite from the writing desk. The most significant and sustained inspiration for this book came from long walks in the Amherst hills with my wife Lea.

About the Companion Website

www.oup.com/us/SoundsasTheyAre

Oxford has created a companion website to accompany *Sounds as They Are: The unwritten music in classical recordings*. The companion website includes audio and video examples that enhance the discussions in the book and can be downloaded. Examples available online are indicated in the text with Oxford's symbol ⊙. To download the files individually, right-click (on a Mac: Control-click) on the audio or video player and save the file to your computer. You may need to select "Allow Download" if your browser asks permission to download the file.

The Spirit is the Conscious Ear –
We actually Hear
When We inspect – that's audible –
That is admitted – Here –

—Emily Dickinson (J 733 / F 718)

Introduction

Listening to Unwritten Music

Four octaves and one breath

Above is the opening of Fryderyk Chopin's Ballade in G minor, Op. 23. Three measures. Eighteen notes. (Thirty-six if you count the octaves.) You might be seeing this score for the first time. You might know it intimately. Whatever your relationship to this music, I ask that you re-enact with me a comparison that helped give rise to this book.

I first heard this ballade on Ruth Slenczynska's recording, which she made at the Pythian Temple Studio in New York in May 1960. The original Decca LP release did not credit the sound engineers by name. This is unfortunate, as engineers play a pivotal role in the content of a recording. Deutsche Grammophon's 2020 compact disc reissue partially rectifies this oversight, identifying the producer as Israel Horowitz, but credits the balance engineers only as "Decca Staff engineers." Whether or not we are able to identify everyone who contributed to the recording, we can study what there is to be heard on it. In the first measure of the ballade, Chopin notates four octaves: C, E-flat, A-flat, and B-flat. Thanks to Slenczynska, Horowitz, and the Decca Staff engineers, her recording of the first bar preserves just that: four octaves.

Sounds as They Are. Richard Beaudoin, Oxford University Press. © Oxford University Press 2024.
DOI: 10.1093/oso/9780197659281.003.0001

Years later, I encountered Emanuel Ax's recording, which he made at Walthamstow Assembly Hall in London in July 1985. The liner notes of his 1986 RCA compact disc credit the sound engineers—Jay David Saks assisted by Martin Atkinson—and even identify a separate editing engineer, Thomas MacCluskey. We are also told about their equipment. Ax was playing a Hamburg Steinway whose sound was captured by Schoeps and Neumann microphones, fed into a Sony 1610 digital recording system, and edited using RCA-Soundstream technology. What did this team and their gear capture? In Ax's recording of the ballade's first measure, we hear the four expected octaves. There is also an additional sound. Between the first two notes, Ax inhales sharply.

The point is not only *that* Ax inhales, but *when*. His audible breath coincides precisely with the third beat of bar 1, where the word *pesante* appears in the score. Ax's inhale, in effect, sounds the end of Chopin's tie. Its impression is non-trivial. Ax's breath alters the rhythm of the line. It suggests that the second note might be syncopated (which it is, though that will not be clear until later in the phrase).

Saying that Ax's track has an extra sound does not imply that Slenczynska's is missing one. Quite the opposite. Her recording more closely matches Chopin's notation. Ax's breath interpolates a non-notated sound, causing the rhythm to have a different profile from Slenczynska's. Her breath-*less* opening preserves a degree of metric ambiguity. This is by no means a critique. Some listeners might appreciate the metric hint provided by Ax's inhale. Others might feel that Slenczynska captures what Chopin was after. In any case, the piece has just begun. Both the meter and the tonality will take time to clarify. It is not until bar 3 that the melodic ascent reaches its peak and begins to fall. Later it will be revealed that the opening harmony was not the tonic after all, but its Neapolitan. At this early stage, what *is* clear is that these two recordings have a different number of audible events. At the end of the measure 1, it is Ax 5, Slenczynska 4.

Keeping count sounds like we are keeping score. But this is no competition. For the duration of this book, I will make the small but important request that like-versus-dislike opinions be set aside. The chapters that follow engage with recordings that some readers might find sublime, insightful, even revelatory. Other recordings might strike readers as irregular, unsatisfying, and (once or twice) even inappropriate. Whatever the response, it is fundamental to my music theory that tracks be appraised *as they are*. This means that recordings are not held up for examination vis-à-vis the score to judge whether a musician is "doing it right" or even "doing it well." On the contrary, the efforts of performers and sound engineers will be brought to the fore, or at least to an equal footing with the composers whose scores are being recorded. Tracks are artworks, and those who participate in their creation are my protagonists.

Defining unwritten music

This book studies non-notated sounds in recordings of notated music. I refer to these sounds as *unwritten music*, a phrase that I will apply in an intentionally limited way. Historically, most music can be classified as "unwritten." The quantity of music-making worldwide that forgoes score-based notation is so immense as to resist definition. Nino Pirrotta likened unwritten music to the vast, submerged portion of an iceberg (1984, 72). Reinhard Strohm surmised that "perhaps the biggest mystification would be to define 'unwritten music' as a specific kind of music at all" (1992, 229). Scholars have invoked the term *unwritten music* across a wide variety of musical, technological, and sociological contexts.[1] As this book is devoted to unwritten music, a working definition is necessary.

For the application that I have in mind, a useful understanding is found in Percy Grainger's 1915 article "The Impress of Personality in Unwritten Music." While I distance myself from some of Grainger's language (he refers to "primitive music"), I appreciate that he celebrates the magnificent complexity of folk music—much of it vocal—that has no referential score. Grainger was an avid investigator of folk music and made a series of hyper-detailed transcriptions with the aid of a phonograph. Discussing a singer that he identified as "an old Lincolnshire man (a perfect artist in his way)," Grainger writes:

> It would be difficult to exaggerate the extent to which such traditional singers embellish so-called "simple melodies" with a regular riot of

---

[1] For evidence of the variety of applications for *unwritten music*, compare its use in Jane Chesky "Indian Music of the Southwest" (1941, 9–12), Edith Gerson-Kiwi "Towards an Exact Transcription of Tone-Relations" (1953, 80–87), William Bascom "Verbal Art" (1955, 245–52), Maud Karpeles "The Distinction between Folk and Popular Music" (1968, 9–12), Kurt Blaukopf "The Sociography of Musical Life in Industrialised Countries—A Research Task" (1979, 78–86), Margaret Bent "*Resfacta* and *Cantare Super Librum*" (1983, 371–91), Leo Treitler "Medieval Improvisation" (1991, 66–91), and Rebecca Cypess "Evidence about the *Lira da Braccio* from Two Seventeenth-Century Violin Sources" (2007, 147–60).

individualistic excrescences and idiosyncrasies of every kind, each detail of which, in the case of the most gifted songsters at any rate, is a precious manifestation of real artistic personality; so much so that a skilled notator will often have to repeat a phonographic record of such a performance some hundreds of times before he will have succeeded in extracting from it a representative picture on paper of its baffling, profuse characteristics. (1915, 421–22)

The language that Grainger uses to describe the Lincolnshire singer mixes admiration and bemusement. Words such as "perfect" and "gifted" commingle with talk of "excrescences" and "baffling" characteristics. Even so, Grainger's thesis is perceptive. Recordings allow listeners to receive a profound impression of a musician's personality. While Grainger excludes notated works from his categorization, I co-opt the notion of unwritten music and redirect it toward classical tracks.

There lies an untapped energy in the idea that unwritten music allows the listener to glimpse the personality of the performer. Looking at classical recordings through this lens, it is startling to learn just how widespread is the silencing of personality-defining sounds such as inhales, exhales, grunts, and moans. The classical recording industry has been designed to valorize the composer (and their scores) while suppressing evidence of the musician in the effortful act of music-making. I forge a different relationship with these sounds and proffer an intentionally focused definition. In a recording of notated music, unwritten music will be any audible event that is not specified by the score being performed. Debates can be had about the phrase "specified by the score." If a composer writes an extended passage of physically engaging music, the score cannot be said to specify the audible heavy breathing that might result. The sounds that I study—sounds of breath, sounds of touch, sounds of effort, and surface noise—are not commonly designated in scores of classical music. In fact, they are the sort of sounds that composers, performers, and sound engineers have been keen to erase from recordings, when the technology allows it.

Why classical recordings?

I address classical music chiefly because it is the genre where the acceptability of non-notated sounds is *least* resolved. Following Andrew Kania, I take audio recordings to be "transparent, that is, that we hear things through them" (2020, 225) with the caveat that "if there is no original sound event captured on a 'recording' (e.g., in the case of a track produced purely electronically), then there is nothing for the recording to be transparent *to*" (2020, 247, italics in original). At the current historical moment, the acceptance of non-notated sounds *as music* is decidedly genre-specific. Film studies has already recognized the expressive nature of intimate sounds, as Carol Vernallis demonstrates in her study of the 2004 Michel Gondry film *Eternal Sunshine of the Spotless Mind*: "Much of *Eternal Sunshine*'s dialogue is close-miked voiceover, which draws attention to the soundtrack. More than in most films, close-miking here magnifies whispers, murmurs, breathing, sighs, and intimate features of a voice's grain" (2013, 105). The classical recording industry seems less comfortable with this level of sonic intimacy.

For a glimpse of mainstream attitudes toward unwritten music, consider Jeremy Denk's remarks about Glenn Gould, whose Bach recordings, like much of his recorded oeuvre, are replete with sounds that the composer did not notate, including breaths, vocalizations, and chair creaks. In a book review originally published under the title "The Pure and the Impure," Denk characterized Gould's humming as "extraneous noise," called his creaking chair "ridiculous," and concluded that "Gould immortalized his phobias, by grafting them onto Bach" (Denk 2012, 34). He implies that Bach's "pure" music is somehow sullied by Gould's body, whose sounds he considers byproducts of the pianist's "phobias." Garreth Broesche reports that "Jeremy Denk, for example, said to me that he prefers not to listen to 'Gould's Bach,' because when he listens to these recordings, 'his interpretations manifest his personality' rather than the work" (Broesche 2015, 171). Denk seems uncomfortable with the fact that Gould's recordings preserve the sounding body of the pianist. The contrast is made plain. Denk used the phrase "manifest his personality" as a pejorative. For Grainger, it was the highest compliment.

Disdain for unwritten music seems to make sense. Why would a listener want to hear a loud inhale or an effortful grunt while auditing a beloved work? It is worth questioning this logic. What if a performer needs to make such sounds in order to play well? And who decides which sounds are appropriate? Misgivings about inhales and grunts are less common in other genres. Music that does not rely heavily on elaborate staff-based notations maintains a healthy relationship to body and breath sounds. This is no doubt aided by the absence of exacting, notated scores that might tacitly (even insidiously) prescribe what is, and what is not, "the piece."

Jazz is exemplary. In Ray Brown's "Solo for Unaccompanied Bass," produced by Norman Granz and released on *Bass Hit!* (1957), Brown's vocalizing—including his whispered singing between 1:18 and 1:35—is integral to the track. As a young contrabassist, I recall transcribing Brown's solo and feeling compelled to capture his vocalizations alongside the bass notes. Popular music is likewise comfortable with these sounds. Hearing the outtakes from Bob Dylan's *Blood on the Tracks*—released in 2018 as *More Blood, More Tracks*—some listeners rejoiced at the authenticity created by the "audible clacking from the buttons on Dylan's jacket as they touched the back of his guitar" (Nainby 2019, 80). Within classical circles, however, the prizing of bodily silence around the presentation of a work still holds sway. The bandleader Dámaso Pérez Prado, popularizer of the mambo in the 1950s, was known to add emphatic vocalizations to otherwise instrumental tracks. In *Life on the Hyphen: The Cuban-American Way*, Gustavo Pérez Firmat writes that "Pérez Prado's grunts, however, were simply vestigial words. As he explained on several occasions, the sounds he made were slurred enunciations of the word *dilo*, with which he urged his musicians to give their all" (1994, 87–88). Grunts are powerful musical expressions. While rare in recordings of notated classical scores, they do occur. When they do, they deserve to be theorized as music. After all, as Pérez Firmat concludes, "One grunt is worth a thousand words" (1994, 88).

Music theory has begun to address the expressive nature of body and breath sounds. Jennifer Iverson studied the expressive nature of "wheezing" in Björk's song "Ancestors" (2016, 166). Kimberly Bain used her 2017 presentation at the Princeton Department of African American Studies Graduate Conference to highlight the role of breath in Rashida Bumbray's performance of "Lay Down Body" in the video version of Common's "Black Again America (featuring Stevie Wonder)." Bain said of Bumbray:

> She bears the heavy emotional toll required to perform, and it's audible. As she oscillates between call and response, she begins to run out of breath; words gaining a breathless quality. And then she gasps: in her second repeat of the chorus, between the phrases "Lay down" and "Lay down, body," she destabilizes the rhythm of the song with a gasp for air. (Bain 2017)

Music studies can learn a great deal from Bain's sensibility, in which there is no boundary between the notes that Bumbray sings and the inhales on which they rely. In *The Race of Sound* (2019), Nina Sun Eidsheim directs music studies to pay attention to "nonsonorous aspects" of the voice, including pronunciation, timbre, and breath (2019, 67). Victoria Malawey's *A Blaze of Light in Every Word* (2020) provides key categorizations for the study of paralinguistic sounds in popular singing. While body and breath sounds are accepted as part of the piece when they are notated by the composer, a theory of unwritten music has yet to be articulated. In the chapters that follow, I address the question: what analyses emerge when non-scored sounds in classical tracks are theorized as music?

Categorizing unwritten music

Accounting for unwritten music opens a Pandora's box. There are myriad non-notated sounds originating from numerous sources. A main preoccupation of this book—and part of its desired utility—is categorizing these sounds and theorizing their function. I have settled upon four large categories: sounds of breath, sounds of touch, sounds of effort, and surface noise. Each of these receives an analytical chapter. Within each chapter, subcategories are defined and illustrated via musical examples. Selected analyses incorporate audio examples available via an accompanying website, and a discography identifies the format and release date of each cited recording.

Chapter 1 unfolds the aesthetic and ethical aspects of unwritten music. I demonstrate the century-old practice of classifying non-notated sounds as unwelcome. Critiques range from record reviews to the development of breath-suppression software. Arguing for a widening of theory's lens, I invoke Arnold Schoenberg's views about non-harmonic tones and Suzannah Clark's democratic approach to the objects addressed by music theory. Recordings by Pablo Casals, George Walker, and Kim Kashkashian illuminate the reception of unwritten music, including the inequality between who is praised—and who is admonished—for making such sounds. A series of analogies link unwritten music to topics including the Barthian punctum, facial micro-expressions, the US Census, and paintings by Leonardo da Vinci, Johannes Vermeer, and Vincent van Gogh. Addressing the critical reception of unwritten music uncovers patterns of racial and gender bias. The chapter closes with a glimpse of the potential for unwritten music to provoke empathy.

Chapter 2 is devoted to sounds of breath. I begin with the field of medicine, which has precise nomenclature for "musical" and "non-musical" respiration. The field of psychology provides evidence for the impact of audible breaths on perceived mood. I present a categorization of inhales and exhales and gauge the expressive effect of their rhythmic placement. My typology spans breath as rhetoric, as anacrusis, as marker of expectation, as motive, as signal of climax, as phrase marker, and as narration. Establishing an analytical methodology that extends across the book, the visualizations in this chapter include score transcriptions, microtiming graphs, and annotated spectrograms.

Chapter 3 discusses sounds made by musicians as they touch their instruments. The analyses are organized as a north-south tour of the body, from fingertips to toes. I begin with the sound of finger*nails* as they relate to motive and meter. Finger*tips* are encountered via hammer-ons in string quartet music. Finger*falls*—the sound of fingers alighting on the fingerboard—are heard in solo cello playing. Moving to the hands, classical guitarists know well the squeaks that can accompany position shifts. I study the expressive nature of these sounds while simultaneously acknowledging the concerted effort of guitarists and engineers to remove them. Staying with the hands, I address the percussive clack of tuba valves. Moving to the posterior, a creaking piano chair registers the movements of a pianist's body. Finally, conductor podium stamps and the *sit-see* sound of the piano damper pedal offer opportunities to study sounds emanating from the feet.

Chapter 4 takes up sounds of effort, which is to say: grunts. These are among the most taboo sounds on classical recordings. I document their long history—Johannes Brahms grunted when he played—and note their similarity to sounds that can occur during sex. For some performers, such sounds are necessary. The negative critical response to grunting links classical musicians to tennis players, whose sport has undergone a similar reckoning. My categorization of sounded effort is divided into two subsets: climactic exertions and intimate ones. Within the first, I discuss exultant hollers, tense moans, and grunt lead. Within the second, I analyze subtle vocalizing, emphatic panting, and stifled grunting. A rare case of growling represents an extreme example of unwritten music. Sounds from the podium pinpoint moans as indicators of phrase. A closing section deploys Allyson Nadia Field's notion of an "archive of absence" to query who is, and who is not, allowed to audibly grunt on a track. This provokes an extended consideration of the role of grunts in one of classical music's most notorious scandals: the case of Joyce Hatto.

Chapter 5 treats the cyclic surface noise patterns heard on early recording formats as expressive music. I present a methodology of listening *with* surface noise (instead of listening *through* or *past* it). An analogy is drawn between the fierce swish of surface noise and a 1617 illustration of an optical drawing aid. My typology includes six modes of interaction between perceived meter and the pulse patterns of surface noise: *performance-centricity* (mode 1), *narrative asynchrony* (mode 2), *ekphrastic (non)coincidence* (mode 3), *expressive synchrony* (mode 4), *metaphoric development* (mode 5), and *surface-noise centricity* (mode 6). The sound of recording and playback machines is analyzed alongside the composition being recorded, theorizing the resultant totality as one music.

In Chapter 6, the lessons from the preceding chapters are distilled into a practical methodology called *inclusive track analysis* (ITA). Informed by the music and writings of Pauline Oliveros, I address attention as a foundational activity of both music and music theory and connect my practice to Walter Benjamin's notion of *reading what was never written*. I outline the framework of ITA and consider its relationship to the philosophical tradition of pragmatism, especially William James's idea of *theory-as-instrument*. I discuss ITA's applicability beyond classical recordings, first in popular music, then in recorded poetry readings, and finally in light of the psychological theory of Auditory Scene Analysis. The book closes with a short meditation on its title.

Five notes

A note on repertoire: the analyses in this book engage with recordings made between 1889 and 2023 of scores composed between 1720 and 2020. I refer to over 100 recordings, a subset of which are given their own musical examples as exemplars of my analytical categories.[2] My analyses encompass orchestral

---

[2] The musicians and ensembles represented in the graphic musical examples are the Alban Berg Quartet, Ana Archilés, Anton Arensky, Sheila Arnold, Roberto Arosio, Claudio Arrau, Emanuel Ax, Guido Balestracci, Sarah Bassingthwaighte, Johannes Brahms, Julian Bream, Velvet Brown, Dashon Burton, Enrico Caruso, Pablo Casals, William Chapman Nyaho, Claire Chase, Chicago Symphony Orchestra, Lucille Chung, Columbia Symphony Orchestra, Salvatore Cottone, Richard Goode, Glenn Gould, Enrique Granados, Bernard Greenhouse, Hélène Grimaud, Guarneri Quartet, Harlem Quartet, Valerie Hartzell, Anthony Hewitt, Janine Jansen, Kim Kashkashian, Keller Quartet, Evgeny Kissin, Anna Krushelnytska, Artina McCain, Zara Nelsova, Yannick Nézet-Séguin, Prades Festival Orchestra, Quatuor Debussy, Quatuor Mosaïques, Rotterdam Philharmonic Orchestra, Fazıl Say, Icy

music, string quartets, vocal works, pieces for flute, contrabass flute, tuba, guitar, violin, cello, pardessus de viole, and a great deal of piano music. The most recent track analyzed is Claire Chase and Senem Pirler's 2023 recording of Liza Lim's *Sex Magic*. The oldest recording that I analyze is the wax cylinder that captured, among other things, the sound of Johannes Brahms playing the piano in 1889.

A note on audio formats: the music analyzed in the forthcoming chapters was released on varied formats including wax cylinder, vinyl, compact disc, and streaming. Wanting my research to be replicable, the spectrograms that appear in my examples—made using the Lucerne Audio Recording Analyzer (LARA)—have in almost all cases been made from files taken from compact discs. While listeners might understandably prefer original formats, my choice of compact disc is designed to provide relatively stable objects of study. Sound engineers are central to my conception of a track's authorship. When discussing a recording of classical music, I credit sound engineers by name in the body of the text rather than a footnote. Unwritten music is an essential aspect of their purview, and they will be recognized alongside performers for their contributions to tracks.

A note on live recordings: when summarizing my research to friends and colleagues, a common question has been, Are you analyzing audience coughs? The implication is that non-notated sounds are primarily produced by people other than the performing musician. My answer, respectfully, is *no*. While they certainly classify as unwritten music, I leave analyses of coughs (as well as page-turns, ring tones, and airplanes flying over recording studios) to others. The sounds that I study are made by musicians in the act of recording as well as, in the case of surface noise, the sound of recording and playback media in action. While there are contextual differences between studio and live recordings, for the purposes of my research, they are

Simpson, Ruth Slenczynska, Georg Solti, Giambattista Valdettaro, George Walker, and Bruno Walter. The composers whose scores are represented in the graphic musical examples are Anton Arensky, J. S. Bach, Jean Barrière, Ludwig van Beethoven, Margaret Bonds, Johannes Brahms, Fryderyk Chopin, Claude Debussy, R. Nathaniel Dett, Gaetano Donizetti, Alice Gomez, Enrique Granados, Joseph Haydn, Zoltán Kodály, Liza Lim, Franz Liszt, Mykola Lysenko, Gustav Mahler, Chiel Meijering, Arnold Schoenberg, Franz Schubert, Robert Schumann, Alexander Scriabin, Francisco Tárrega, Pyotr Ilyich Tchaikovsky, and Edgard Varèse. The record labels whose tracks are analyzed in the graphic musical examples are Acis Productions, Albany Records, Alpha Classics, Audite, Auvidis Astrée, CD Baby, Champs Hill Records, Crystal Records, Decca, Deutsche Grammophon, Dynamic, ECM, Edition Zeitklang, EMI, Erato, Harlem Quartet Recordings, London, Marston, MSR Classics, Naxos Historical, New Focus Recordings, NM Classics, Philips, RCA, Sony Classical, Symposium, Vanguard, Velut Luna, Verlag der Österreichischen Akademie der Wissenschaften, and Warner Classics.

negligible. Occasionally, they are even misleading. I have encountered live recordings where there is no unwritten music, and studio recordings replete with sounds of breath, touch, and effort. For the purposes of this book, recordings are understood to preserve (at least in part) the sound of one or more people making music, be they unedited live captures, in-studio versions with splicing, or the many possibilities that lie in between.

A note on terminology: I use the term *classical* (lowercase "c") as a general adjective describing music that is connected to (mainly) European-derived notated traditions. I recognize that, for some, reading about Robert Schumann or Edgard Varèse in a book about "classical" music will chafe against more precise designations of these two as Romantic and Modernist composers, respectively. My usage is designed simply to allow a large group of music and musicians—for whom notation was (and is) an essential mode of communication—to be studied together. To avoid confusion, I avoid entirely using the term *Classical* (uppercase "C") in its era-specific form referring to late eighteenth-century compositional practice.

A note to the field of music theory: historically, theory's engagement with classical music has been primarily via reading, or *reading into*, scores. There are good reasons for this, one of which is that fixed notation is more amenable to written analysis. Another is that recordings and spectrograms are younger technologies than staff notation. Recorded sound is a form of writing, albeit an elusive one, and the complexity of analyzing it stems from multiple texts occurring simultaneously. A third reason is perhaps obvious: scores deserve close analysis because they are extraordinary documents of human imagination. Recordings are equally extraordinary and deserve equally close study.

It is perhaps uncontroversial to say that every score deserves to be analyzed. It is less common to suggest that every recording of a given score deserves the same. The statement implies that there are considerably more objects that the field of music theory must contend with if it is to adequately encompass its subject. It also suggests that theorists have a great deal of work to do. Take the Chopin ballade whose opening bars began this introduction. Examples of unwritten music can be found in nearly every one of the hundreds of recordings of this work. Hélène Tysman's 2013 recording on Oehms Classics, engineered by Céline Grangey, includes an intimate *sit-see* flicker of the damper pedal at 7:53 that coincides precisely with Chopin's marking of *sempre sotto voce* in bar 194. Valentina Kameníková's 1991 Supraphon recording, engineered by Stanislav Sýkora, avoids breath sounds entirely until Kameníková sounds a prominent inhale at 1:56, just before Chopin notates *agitato* in bar 40. Krystian Zimerman's utterance-rich 1988 recording on Deutsche Grammophon, produced and engineered by Helmut Burk, preserves the pianist's subtle, curving, vocal glissando at 5:53, which coincides with the apex of the pirouetting melodic climb toward Chopin's *più vivo* marking in bar 136, and which seems to somehow call forth the melody's subsequent, rapid descent. While this is the last time that I will mention Chopin's G minor ballade in this book, it testifies to the richness of unwritten music that a study could be devoted to non-notated sounds in recordings of this single piece.

Studying a score allows a theorist to state what is implied by the notation, but these conclusions are often challenged when the work is recorded. One must be prepared to encounter tracks whose unwritten music contradicts, or expands upon, what was suggested by the notation. Tracks that fit this description will be studied in the chapters ahead. When they appear, I have been careful not to deem them "wrong" or "right." A critic might protest that just because a recording *exists* does not automatically mean that the interpretation found there is "worthy" of analysis, especially in cases where the performer openly contradicts the composer's wishes. I would reply that recordings are works of art, not exams whose answer key is the score. Music theory isn't (or needn't be) a field that decides what is proper or correct about any given track. It is (or should) be a field that remains attentive to those who participate in music, and to the documents that record their effort.

Recordings of classical music preserve marvelous feats of composition, performance, and sound engineering. At their finest, all three occur simultaneously. Why focus, as I do, on sounds that the composer, performer, and sound engineer might gladly remove if they could? One reply would be to ask why a biologist studies protozoa instead of lions. Historically, music theory has spilled a great deal of ink on its larger mammals, even as the micro-level of audio recordings teems with less-studied life. This book pays attention to the smaller but no less essential members of the sonic ecosystem, whether their creators wanted them to be there or not.

1

The Aesthetics and Ethics
of Unwritten Music

Sound recordings as documents

In a letter written in Paris on January 8, 1674, Marie de Rabutin-Chantal, marquise de Sévigné, penned a memorable line: "We like no noise, unless we make it ourselves" (1811, 328).[1] The subject of her turn of phrase was not music, but rather a bit of palace intrigue. A high-ranking cohort was arriving at a grand residence, and the ladies of the house, accustomed to being waited on by servants, were perturbed at having to temporarily become servants themselves. The scene prompted Madame de Sévigné's observation that the appraisal of a given sound depends upon the listener's relationship to its producer. Critical reception of unwritten music follows a similar script. Certain listeners become uncomfortable when a breath, a tap, a moan, or a bit of surface noise interrupts their communion with a beloved composer's work.

In recordings of classical works, which sounds count as music? While events notated in the score are paramount, the sound of the performer breathing (or grunting) is generally regarded as peripheral, even undesirable. A century-long practice of admonishing musicians for making so-called extraneous noises has established widespread, unspoken norms encouraging recording artists to make their physical presence as inconspicuous as possible. When traces of sounded movements do find their way past sound engineers and onto commercial releases, they are routinely characterized as inappropriate. These attitudes extend back to the origins of recorded sound itself. Herman Klein's otherwise sterling 1929 review of Lotte Lehmann's recording of Robert Schumann's *Frauenliebe und -leben* makes the point explicitly: "Every sound stands out in bold relief; every syllable, every murmur, every tiny utterance, down to the particular sound whereof one would willingly hear less—I mean the constant hiss of the intake of breath—the only

---

[1] « On n'aime pas le bruit, si on ne le fait. » (Sévigné 1862, 358).

Sounds as They Are. Richard Beaudoin, Oxford University Press. © Oxford University Press 2024.
DOI: 10.1093/oso/9780197659281.003.0002

blemish upon the perfection of an exquisite achievement" (1990, 462).[2] To Klein, Lehmann's otherwise "perfect" recording is marred by her own breathing.

Klein's appraisal captures early twentieth-century anxieties regarding the intimacy of the microphone and summarizes apprehensions about its tendency to distort the sound of the human voice. His anxieties are again on display in his December 1930 article "The Distortions of Over-Amplification" from his series *The Gramophone and the Singer*: "I do not wholly blame that unconscious medium, the microphone. It has not yet become a perfect instrument, as no doubt one day it will; and when that day arrives I am sure it will, among other things, automatically refuse to aid and abet the chief culprit—to wit, the amplifier—in splitting our ears or transmuting the voice into something utterly unlike its original" (Klein 1990, 309). Such concerns about breath sounds are by no means outdated, nor are they unique to recordings of vocal music. Nearly seventy years later, Lionel Salter derided a member of the Guarneri Quartet for making intrusive sounds while recording music by Juan Crisóstomo Arriaga: "So, despite some reservations—one or two small flaws of intonation may be forgiven in view of the overall spirit and enthusiasm—this is an attractive issue. But I wish Philips had gagged whichever of the ensemble it is who grunts so audibly and so frequently" (1996, 68). Similar aversions can be found in contemporary responses to ASMR, whose intimacy likewise breaks cultural agreements about sonic proximities.[3] All this bad press prompts an analogy: if the notes prescribed by the score are considered flowers in the garden, then non-notated sounds made by the bodies of musicians are weeds that need pulling.

Music theory has generally overlooked non-notated sounds. The audible *sit-see* of the piano damper pedal, the *squeak* of position shifts on the classical guitar, the percussive *clack* of tuba pistons: the field of music analysis has neither categorized nor classified the musical function of these sounds. Pablo Casals's effortful grunt during a climactic phrase of the Schumann Cello Concerto might be beloved or reviled, but it is rarely theorized. The same

---

[2] Lotte Lehmann was singing an arrangement of Schumann's *Frauenliebe und -leben* for soprano and orchestra, conducted by Frieder Weissmann and recorded in Berlin on November 10, 1928. Klein listened to the recording on one of the four 10-inch, 78 rpm records that were released as Parlophone RO.20090-3. I listened to it on the 1994 compact disc, released as Pearl GEMM CD 9119, transferred by Mark Obert-Thorn from matrix nos.: Be 7601/8; issue nos.: Odeon O-4806/9.

[3] According to Jaime Lauren Keiles (2019), ASMR (Autonomous Sensory Meridian Response) is a term coined by Jennifer Allen to describe a pleasurable neurological response to hearing close-miked sounds.

holds true for Kim Kashkashian's audible inhales or the fingerboard taps made by cellist Zara Nelsova. Properly categorizing these sounds *as music* requires a new method of recording analysis. Nicholas Cook has encouraged musicologists to "exploit the potential of sound recordings as documents" (2009, 776), a recommendation he expands upon in *Beyond the Score* (2013). I propose a mode of analysis that includes non-scored sounds as part of a comprehensive appraisal of audible events. The expressive world unlocked by this new, hypervigilant mode of analysis turns out to be teeming with sonic life and meaning.

All sounds deserve recognition. I accept audio recordings as they are, and value their intermingled sounds coequally. From this methodology emerges a mode of recording analysis that acknowledges the sonic totality and classifies the musical function of all its constituent parts. I will ultimately refer to this pragmatic approach as inclusive track analysis, a methodology that makes frequent use of what Carolyn Abbate refers to as "the tactile monuments in music's necropolis—recordings and scores and graphic musical examples" (2004, 510). Useful across genres, inclusive track analysis equalizes the status of all sound events, whether they originate from instruments, bodies, or the playback medium itself. There is expressive information in these sounds, and they add meaningful content to a given track. Paying such close attention requires a form of media bilingualism wherein the analyst is fluent in reading both scores and spectrograms.

Studying recordings as documents allows music theory to gauge what philosopher Charles Sanders Peirce called "the total resultant Quality of Feeling presented in the work of art we are contemplating" (1998, 190). Peirce's phrase proves to be both instructional and inspirational. Music theory often confines itself to scores-as-artworks. In that endeavor, it is enormously successful. When we move beyond scores, questions arise. Do audible breath sounds count as music? How about effortful grunts, creaking piano benches, or the surface noise on wax cylinders? Expanding the frame of what counts as music, I propose a music theory based on tracks-as-artworks.

Alongside aesthetic considerations reside ethical ones, including how we collectively and individually feel about non-scored sounds, and why people expend such strenuous effort trying to erase them from recordings. The right of these sounds to appear at all—to be made by the performer during the act of playing, to be captured by the microphone in the studio or onstage, and to survive the editing process—is by no means a staid footnote. On the contrary, it is a lively area of commentary and debate. Tacit assumptions deserve reconsideration. Why precisely is it essential for musicians to silence themselves when recording classical music? Why should theorists pay attention to non-notated sounds at all, as such sounds were likely neither intended, nor desired, by the composer?

Questioning "intelligent suppression"

Across the classical music recording industry, producers, recording engineers, and performers have seemingly joined forces to present recordings where traces of the audible body are minimized. Influenced by both the market and the hegemony of a Western European "sanctity" for the composer's score as determinative of "meaningful content," the industry often caters to the belief that consumers desire the nullification of sounds made by the body of the performer. Listeners are evidently expected to want recordings to be audio representations of the compositions listed on the album cover, presented via the interpretive lens of the performer often pictured there, but without the "intrusion" of bodily sounds that might have been heard if the listener was with the musician at the moment of recording. A peculiar dynamic confronts performers and sound engineers of classical tracks. The two parties at the end of the production chain—composers and listeners—have the agency to make whatever sounds they wish. Performers and sound engineers, on the other hand, find themselves hemmed in. Owing to the acculturated norms of the genre, audible traces of performative effort are generally rejected as inappropriate, even when such sounds are physically necessary. Sound engineers have developed sophisticated techniques expressly to silence sounds that are not prescribed by the score. This practice generates significant aesthetic and analytical complexities. For example, sounds of inhaling and exhaling are commonly erased with the aid of studio techniques and related software. In their textbook on sound engineering, James Angus and David Howard place "breath noises" alongside "key clicks and page rustling" (2013, 473) in the category of "extraneous" sounds that are ripe for removal. It makes sense that a loud page-turn might be unwanted by an artist or engineer, likewise a prominent key click that obscures a pitch. But why is the sound of a musician breathing "extraneous"? Surely the musician is inhaling and exhaling when they are making the recording. Why then is their breathing subject to removal?

The history of classical music recording can be read as a search for methods to suppress sounds that are not found in scores. An arc can be drawn from wax cylinders to the "noise reduction" techniques invented by Dolby Laboratories to the digitally manufactured "silence" that envelops modern studio releases.[4] The enforced separation between "music" and "noise" has a long and contentious history within music theory, musicology, and the wider listening audience.[5] Without fully unfolding that debate here, the question of whether such a distinction should exist is an open one. A welcome view, which acknowledges the expressivity of audible bodies, is provided by Jennifer Judkins: "Musical sounds are generated through rhythmic physical motions or air pressure applied to an instrument, and instruments (and humans) are noisy things" (2014, 14). Owing to a reverence for composers and their notations, the recording industry has historically gone to great lengths to suppress traces of the mechanical (surface noise), the instrumental (sounds of pedals, bow crossings, guitar string squeaks, creaking chairs), and the corporeal (singing, grunting, even breathing).

Quelling such "noises" turns out to be a lucrative business. The Magix Computer Products International Company has an unsettling name for their proprietary breath-suppression tool: "Spectral Cleaning." Another software plugin, this one from Wave, is called "DeBreath." This product is advertised with a teaser that is equal parts comic and tragic: "Singers insist on breathing—even when it spoils a perfectly good take!" A widely used audio restoration software suite—iZotope's RX 7—offers a "breath control module plug-in" that "reduces tedious, seek-and-destroy editing to one click with intelligent suppression." It seems disturbingly Orwellian to apply the phrase "intelligent suppression" to the sound of someone breathing.

Everything that sounds simultaneously

Arnold Schoenberg articulated, for his time, rather liberal feelings about which sounds should be recognized by music theorists. He argued *against* the existence of non-harmonic tones, and his language for doing so is

---

[4] The ongoing search for silence within the field of sound engineering is discussed in Jonathan Sterne (2003), Andre Millard (2005), Susan Schmidt Horning (2015), and Melle Kromhout (2021).

[5] Investigations of the distinctions between music and noise include Jacques Attali (1985), Karin Bijsterveld (2008), Paul Hegarty (2007), Mack Hagood (2011), Greg Hainge (2013), Michel Chion (2016), Wolfgang Ernst (2016), and Marie Thompson (2017).

instructive: "Before anything else, then, [let us affirm that] the non-harmonic tones do form chords (*Zusammenklänge*), hence are not non-harmonic; the musical phenomena they help to create are harmonies, as is everything that sounds simultaneously" (Schoenberg 1983, 309, translated by Roy E. Carter).[6] The idea that "everything that sounds simultaneously" should be part of theory's harmonic purview was, in Schoenberg's contemporary milieu, an inclusive stance. I see my methodology as a logical extension of this idea. My analyses incorporate many audible events—some with fixed pitch, some without—that *sound simultaneously* with the music denoted by the score. Such an extension requires that Schoenberg's statements about "non-harmonic tones" be applied to "non-scored tones." Repurposing and altering his language, one might say that non-scored tones generate harmonies, even if those harmonies do not match those in the score of the work being performed. It will be necessary to redefine what counts as music within the objects that we are studying. In this endeavor, Schoenberg's inclusivity proves inspirational.

Carl Dahlhaus situates Schoenberg's aesthetics as a rejection of ornament, writing that "Taken strictly, his assertion that non-chordal notes, notes without harmonic influence, do not exist is an aesthetic postulate, rooted in the opposition to all things ornamental and without function, rather than a description of musical reality" (Dahlhaus 1974, 210–11). Motivated in no small part by his compositional thinking, Schoenberg opposed the notion of non-harmonic tones and non-functional objects within (what he considered) masterpieces.[7] In sympathy with Schoenberg's aesthetic position, I aim to account for everything that is audible within a given recording and seek to understand its expressive function. The rapid intake of breath, the exhausted exhale, the grazing of an open string, the effortful grunt at a climactic arrival, the hiss of a wax cylinder: none of these are ornamental

---

[6] „Vor allem also: die harmoniefremden Töne bilden doch Zusammenklänge, sind also nicht harmoniefremd, sondern die durch ihre Mitwirkung entstehenden Ereignisse sind Harmonien wie alles, was gleichzeitig klingt" (Schoenberg 1922, 373).

[7] Stephen Peles summarizes a theoretical divide between Schoenberg and Heinrich Schenker on the subject of what counts as a musical event: "True enough, the aesthetic credo that 'masterworks' contain no irrelevant events was not under dispute; both men subscribed to *that* belief (and thus did Viennese aesthetics make strange bedfellows). More importantly, this was a dispute over what counts as an event and what counts as relevant. Each man was concerned with a wholly different *explanandum*. For Schoenberg, the entities with which the discipline of harmony is concerned are simultaneities; for Schenker harmony is the study of *Stufen* and their progression, and the underlying psychology. Simultaneities and *Stufen* are different kinds of things, and the two are incomparable: not all simultaneities are *Stufen*, and not all *Stufen* are (literal) simultaneities" (2010, 167, italics in original).

nor are they without function. This mode of analysis requires taking a proper census of the sound events in an audio recording, applying the (extended) Schoenbergian notion that musical phenomena include "everything that sounds simultaneously," and charting the relationships created by the totality of sounds working together.

Suzannah Clark offers another way of framing analyzable events. In a 2019 article that investigates the limitations of Heinrich Schenker's hierarchic tendencies, Clark brings up the idea of tones having "equal rights." Analyzing Schubert's "Auf dem Flusse," Clark contrasts Schenker's view with David Lewin's, in particular their divergent readings of the modulation to G-sharp minor within Schubert's E major setting of Wilhelm Müller's poem. For Lewin (1986), Schubert's move to the mediant is the linearization of a major triad, an idea that is unavailable within Schenkerian theory. Schenker, on the other hand, goes to great lengths to suppress the notion that the tonic triad is being linearized, lest it express a *Bassbrechung* that moves through the mediant. Clark frames Schenker's reading in vividly political terms: "But presumably Schenker felt his effort to hide [the mediant] was worth it: the omission preserves *Diatonie* at the background level—that level apprehended only by the genius. Schenker's 'aristocracy of genius' permits no democracy of tones, no 'equal rights' for musical tones" (2019, 148). Clark's invocation of "equal rights" can be extended from tones to the unwritten music produced during (and by) the act of recording. Extending the political analogy, I advocate that music theory recognize the entire population of audible events on a given recording, not just the sounds granted citizenship via the score.

An unwritten note

Pablo Casals recorded J. S. Bach's Cello Suite in D minor, BWV 1008, at Abbey Road Studios in London on November 25, 1936. As he makes clear, his recording captures a unique interpretation: "My way of performing a work does not last for longer than the actual playing of it: that is to say, I don't know, and cannot know beforehand, if I shall not introduce modifications when playing it afresh" (Corredor 1958, 210). Example 1.1 presents the notation of mm. 21–24 of the Sarabande, which unfolds a cadence in D minor. The bass motion of the compound line moves through scale degree 7 in m. 22, through scale degrees 3, 4, and 5 in m. 23, and ultimately resolves both motions via the D3 to D2 octave in m. 24.

Example 1.1 J. S. Bach, Sarabande from Cello Suite in D minor, BWV 1008, mm. 21–24.

The first time Casals plays through this passage, the music is played as notated. In keeping with his notion of "modifications," Casals's second pass includes something rather unexpected: he plays a note that does not appear in Bach's score. At 3:45, the open G string of Casals's 1733 Gofriller cello vibrates briefly as he shifts between the cadential D octaves in m. 24. As seen in Example 1.2, this G2 is clearly audible and acts as a kind of inadvertent ornament. The open G was possibly caused by Casals releasing his finger from the D3 on beat 1, or it was activated by the cellist's bow as he moved toward the D2 on beat 2. Throughout this book, my primary interest is studying the sounds as they appear on the track, rather than using the sounds to decipher the physical act that produced them. Whatever caused Casals's G string to vibrate, the pitch that is added is the subdominant within the local key. Had the sound been the open A string, it would have implied an arpeggiation of a D minor triad and preserved an untroubled tonic resolution. Had the sound been the open C string, it would have been more disruptive, the subtonic disturbing the resolution and creating a cross-relation with the C-sharp in the preceding bar. As subdominant, the G adds a softening warmth to Casals's cadence.[8] The nomenclature here matters. It is *Casals's* cadence that we are discussing, as Bach did not write that note in that bar.

I do not consider Casals's grazed G as an "error" or a "misreading" of the notation and see no reason to call out an artist for creating a sound that does not explicitly appear in the score that they are playing. Treating sound recordings as documents means that their authorship is, by design, shared. Most recordings include sounds that are not designated, nor even implied, by the score being performed. The practice of music theory often (though not always) begins with realities of the score and subsequently proffers insights according to hierarchic principles. My framework begins with *tracks* (based,

---

[8] A millisecond-level transcription of Casals's 1936 recording of the Sarabande from BWV 1008 is discussed in Beaudoin (2023, 133).

Example 1.2 J. S. Bach, Sarabande from Cello Suite in D minor, BWV 1008, mm. 23b–25.1b, with a spectrogram of 3:38–3:48 from the 1936 recording by Pablo Casals. See ⊙ Audio Example 1.1.

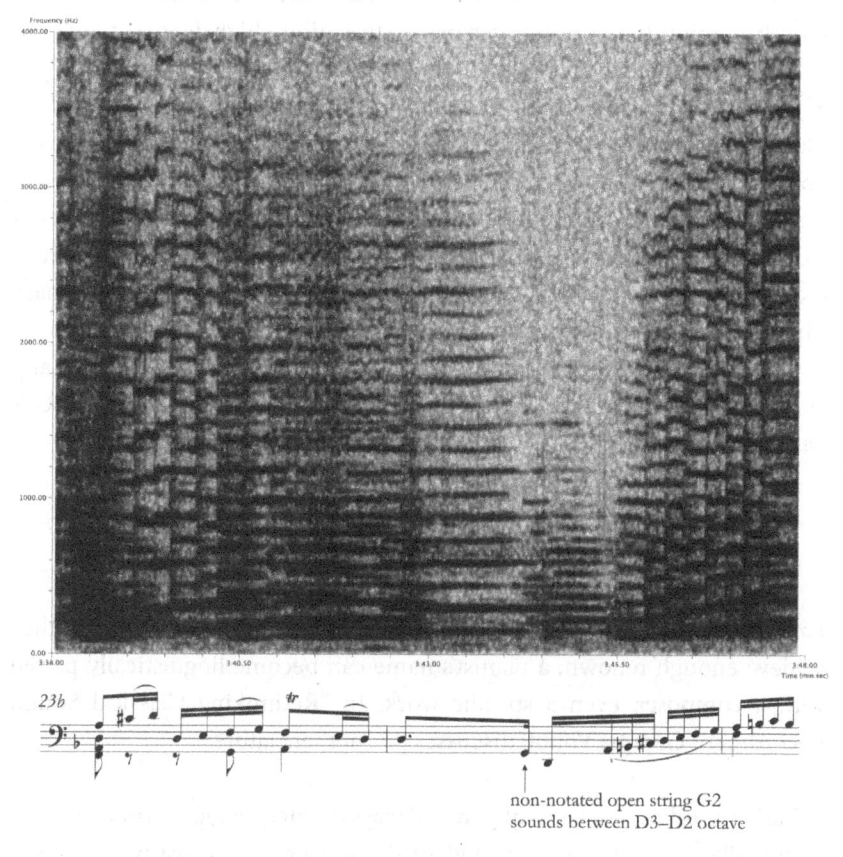

non-notated open string G2
sounds between D3–D2 octave

to be sure, on scores) and accepts all sonic additions made during the act of recording. While it is oversimplified to say that the former is reductive and the latter is additive, the fact remains that accepting Casals's open G stands in opposition to score-based theory's implied dismissal of it.

Once unwritten music—not only added notes like Casals's G, but also breaths, grunts, fingertaps, and surface noise—are accepted as equal to the melodies, harmonies, and rhythms that surround them, the expressive importance of these so-called extraneous sounds can be theorized. Paul Sanden has written about "corporeal liveness," which he defines as "liveness invoked by music's connection to an acoustic sounding body, usually that of a human performer" (Sanden 2009, 9). Sanden's categorizations include "liveness of fidelity," wherein "the further a recording or performance deviates from 'true' (acoustic) performed sounds, the less live it is" (Sanden 2013, 35). For example, when a recording of vocal music captures the sound of a singer's mouth opening, the recording can be said to exhibit a high degree of "liveness of fidelity." Sanden does not create a theoretical methodology for the analysis of unwritten music. He does, however, instinctively recognize the need for music theory to acknowledge and codify these sounds: "An account of corporeal liveness in recordings, in other words, recognizes recorded music as a form of communication in which the *performer* (and not just the composer's work) holds great significance, even if this communication is made indirect by the mediation of technology" (Sanden 2013, 53, italics in original). My methodology constructs just such a systematic theoretical framework. It recognizes the "great significance" of performer-generated sounds and creates terminology that classifies their musical function. Casals's open G is part of the music heard in his 1936 EMI recording. The sound counts.

A series of enigmatic clicks

Landowska's Bach, Solomon's Beethoven, de Larrocha's Albéniz. Once they achieve enough renown, a pianist's name can become linguistically paired with a composer, even a specific work. In "Rethinking Classical Sound Recordings," Georgia Volioti discusses this nomenclature:

> Early recordings, in particular, reveal ways of interpreting scores that are radically different from our modern-day practices, and clearly show us that the performance of Western art music actually adheres much less to composers' scores than we would like to maintain. This rich aural evidence also attests to performers' central roles in the transmission of Western art music and their frequently close association with a composer's work, as listeners identify compositions—even composers' names—with particular performers' interpretations on record: Cortot's (Chopin) Berceuse, Grainger's (Grieg) Concerto, Backhaus's "Brahms," Gieseking's "Debussy," and so on. (Volioti 2021, 61)

Volioti is correct that many recordings "adhere much less" than one might expect to composer's scores. In the case of unwritten music, however, it is a question not so much of *adherence* as it is of *augmentation*.

Example 1.3 Fryderyk Chopin, Étude in G-flat major, Op. 10, No. 5, mm. 41–44.

In 2004, George Walker was making a recording of Fryderyk Chopin's Étude in G-flat major, Op. 10, No. 5.[9] His recording was captured by a Nagra D-2 at 24/96 using Neumann TLM-170 R microphones. When Walker's recording was released a year later by Albany Records, the track was suffused with clicking sounds occurring across its entire 1:57 duration. At first listen, these clicks sound somewhat like an analog metronome, but their location is not metronomic. They ebb and flow in time that is seemingly connected to Walker's left-hand motions. Example 1.3 presents mm. 41–44 from Chopin's score, a virtuosic prolongation of D-flat major marked by *molto perpetuo* sixteenth-note triplets in the right hand.

While Walker's recording includes all the notes in Chopin's score, it adds dozens of additional sounds in the form of prominent clicks. Example 1.4 shows a spectrogram of 0:50–0:56, corresponding to mm. 41–44 of Chopin's étude, and marks the location of these enigmatic clicks.

What is the source of the clicks on Walker's track, and what proper studio would "allow" such sounds to remain part of the mix? Leaving the first question intentionally unanswered, I address the second.[10] There *was* no "proper studio" for Walker's 2005 Chopin recording. He made the master in his home in Montclair, New Jersey. According to the album's recording engineer, Jeremy Tressler:

---

[9] Walker recorded Chopin's Étude in G-flat major, Op. 10, No. 5, three times: in 1997 on Albany TROY 252, in 2001 on Albany TROY 411, and in 2005 on Albany TROY 697.

[10] The source of the clicking sounds is difficult to verify, though they are likely produced by the pianist's fingernails, a subject I address in Chapter 3 in relation to recordings by William Chapman Nyaho and Claudio Arrau. Readers interested in such sounds are encouraged to study Walker's 2005 recording of Liszt's *Valse oubliée*. A compendium of unwritten music, the track includes sounds of breath, sound of touch, and sounds of effort.

Example 1.4 Fryderyk Chopin, Étude in G-flat major, Op. 10, No. 5, mm. 41–44, with an annotated spectrogram of 0:50–0:56 from the 2005 recording by George Walker. See ▶ Audio Example 1.2.

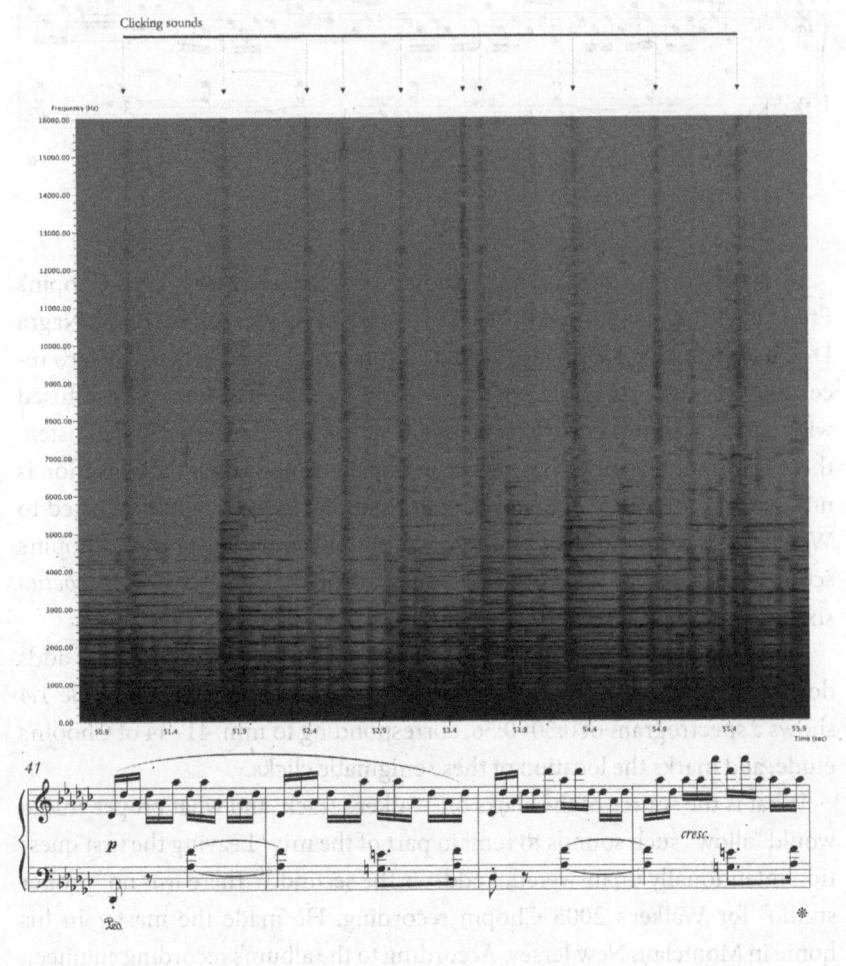

This was one of Walker's self-recorded projects. He did the recording entirely by himself in his own home and with his own equipment, then he brought the Nagra D to my studio where we downloaded the recording data for editing within my system. There was a time when George had a Bösendorfer, however, I am almost entirely certain that he had since sold this piano thus everything thereafter would have been done on his Steinway D. (personal correspondence, December 2, 2020)

The engineer was not present during the recording session. As a result, Tressler himself was not able to identify the source of the clicking sounds, but he did provide a rather insightful answer when asked about their origins:

> Interesting, it almost sounds like a metronome. I don't know what it is. The clicking is not completely metronomic but very much so. George was resistant to help or input with his home recordings, so I accepted them as they were. We experimented with subtle mastering effects such as EQ and Ambience, however, George typically preferred the sound completely unchanged from what was captured by his Nagra. (personal correspondence, December 2, 2020)

If the clicks were a byproduct of Walker recording in his own home, why was he recording there in the first place, and alone? The answer to these questions highlights the intersection between identity and unwritten music. In an interview with Mickey Thomas Terry, Walker makes plain the reasons for his working outside of a studio:

> *Terry*: Albany Records has released five recordings of your music and piano playing. Has this helped to make you better known?
>
> *Walker*: I produced four of the five Albany recordings because no record company was willing to release any of my music even when I provided the tapes. Peter Gelb, the president of Sony Records, informed me that my music would not sell. Yet, white composers with far less significant works have exclusive recording contracts. (Terry, Monson, and Walker 2000, 379)

The unwritten music on Walker's Chopin recording documents a disadvantage: racially motivated exclusion from major labels forced him to make recordings not only outside the studio system, but outside the studio itself. Working from his house in Montclair, Walker's Nagra-D picked up the clicking sounds as part of his performance. These sounds could not be removed by sound engineer Tressler and, even if they could, Walker preferred the sounds as they were. This track not only captures *Walker's Chopin*, it also records the reality of his situation: a celebrated Black musician making records in his house.

A decisive inhale

Imagine the scene: Kim Kashkashian is at the American Academy of Arts and Letters in New York, holding her Stefan-Peter Greiner viola and preparing to record the Gigue from Bach's Suite in C minor, BWV 1011. As seen in Example 1.5, the time signature in Bach's score reads 3/8, and the movement begins—as do all the gigues in Bach's unaccompanied cello suites—with an eighth-note pickup. The recording's Tonmeisterin, Judy Sherman, awaits. Kashkashian plays the pickup G, and the Gigue is off and running.

Not so fast. The pickup note is not followed by the E-flat that appears in Bach's score, but rather by a rhythmically decisive intake of air. This inhale extends the duration of the anacrusis so dramatically that the gesture sounds not as an eighth note, but as a quarter note that is subdivided into two parts: G plus inhale. The spectrogram in Example 1.6 illustrates the novel sound object created by Kashkashian's anacrustic breath, which is as substantial as the viola note that precedes it.

Kashkashian's recording includes hundreds of these audible inhales, and critical reception of them runs the gamut. Two reviews present extremes of acceptance and aversion. In certain circles, Kashkashian's breaths are understood as fascinating, knowing, even inviting gestures:

> Meanwhile I am hearing her breathe through her nose. Her breathing is not what you will buy the record for, but it is not beside the point. Sometimes it marks off modular units of music—four-measure segments, say—or appears when a motive is restated through paraphrase. But more often she is following her own map of accents, and the really impressive breathing happens during emphatic climbs or peaks, before a downbeat. The best one in the second prelude happens in measure 42, amid three big steps upward. In her inhaling she is giving herself energy to keep playing the music, and marking gestures she finds valuable. She is also gathering the listener closer into the music, whether or not she intends to. (Ratliff 2019)

Example 1.5 J. S. Bach, Gigue from Cello Suite in C minor, BWV 1011, mm. 1–4, transcribed for viola.

Example 1.6 J. S. Bach, Gigue from Cello Suite in C minor, BWV 1011, mm. 0–1, transcribed for viola, with a spectrogram of 0:00–0:02 from the 2018 recording by Kim Kashkashian. See ⊙ Audio Example 1.3.

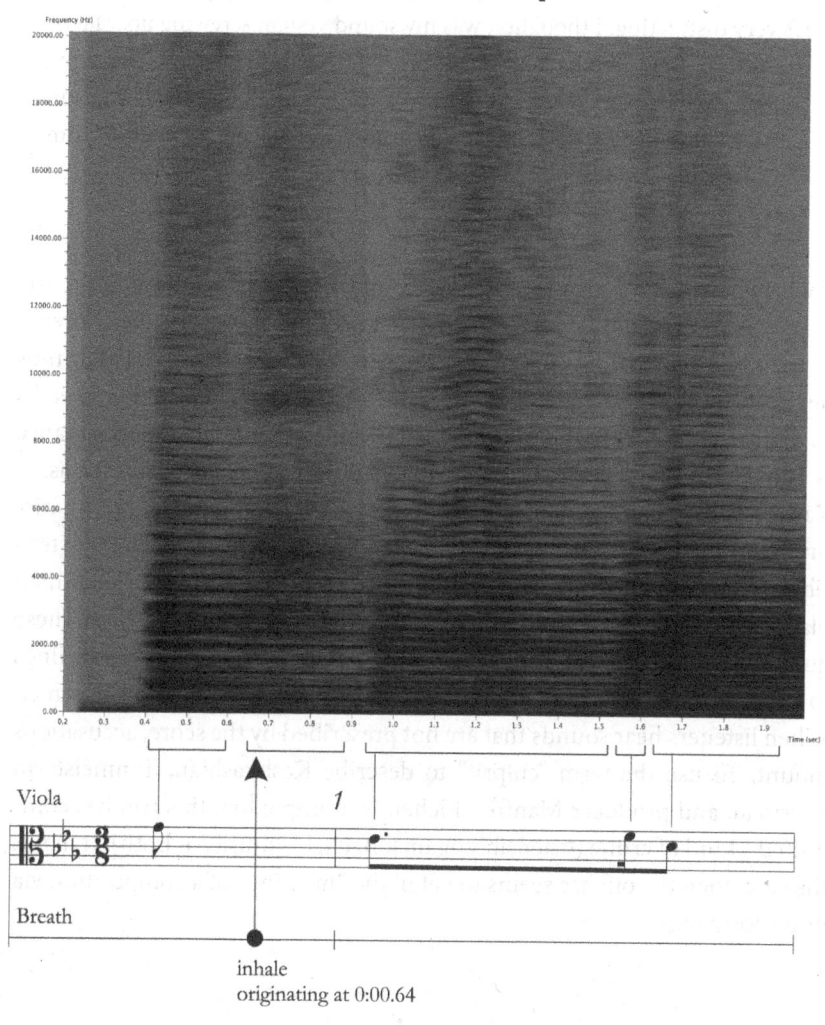

inhale
originating at 0:00.64

By contrast, the following critique offers an unvarnished, dismissive response to the same recording:

Like I said great music, great recording but something must have been overlooked by other listeners. You don't even have to listen carefully. I understand sometimes in a performance there are extraneous sounds emitted from an instrument, chair, etc. The culprit here is the performer or the mic placement, take your pick. Constant loud breathing is evident throughout, especially in the second disc. I'm sure many people will say get over it. Sorry, it's very distracting. I thought it was my sound system screwing up. Maybe the disc player rubbing on something. Maybe the furnace was having trouble. No, I'm sorry. A great performance is ruined by this. If you can get past this constant noise, more power to you. (Review by "jdej" of Kim Kashkashian, *J. S. Bach: Six Suites for Viola Solo* BWV 1007–1012, ECM New Series ECM 2553/54, Amazon.com, December 4, 2018)

Each review has its own internal logic, and I am fascinated by both. The former is effusive about Kashkashian's breaths, singling out the "best" breath in the same way that one might choose their favorite chord. The latter finds her "constant" breathing to be "distracting." The former hears her breaths as "gathering the listener closer," the latter thinks that "a great performance is ruined" by them. In both cases, her breathing engenders questions. If Kashkashian inhales audibly when she records Bach, then why are we disturbed when those sounds appear on her recording? If the listener has ostensibly purchased, borrowed, or clicked on this recording to hear Kashkashian play Bach's Gigue, why do they take offense at hearing her do just that? These questions pinpoint what is at stake. Some listeners use classical recordings to "hear the piece," as if such a thing were possible without the performer. When listeners hear sounds that are not prescribed by the score, accusations mount. To use the term "culprit" to describe Kashkashian, Tonmeisterin Sherman, and producer Manfred Eicher, is to imply that this trio has committed a kind of crime (ostensibly against Bach, his music, or both). If that is the case, then the offense seems to entail the "marring" of a composition via its performance.

Five analogies

A series of intentionally kaleidoscopic analogies ricochet the notion of unwritten music off photography, psychology, government, and two modes of painting. While all analogies are intrinsically incomplete, I invite the reader to loosen disciplinary boundaries to allow ideas to intermingle despite contextual differences. Roland Barthes's concept of the photographic punctum, the psychological category of facial micro-expressions, and the mechanism of the US Census all rhyme in meaningful ways with the recognition of non-notated sounds. Analogues for the authorial tensions created by unwritten music are found in the *craquelure* of paintings by Johannes Vermeer and Leonardo da Vinci, and in the contributions of insects and fingerprints to paintings by Vincent van Gogh.

Unwritten music and the photographic punctum

Reflecting on photography in *La chambre claire* (*Camera Lucida*), Roland Barthes formulated the now-classic contrast between the studium—the term he invokes to define the factual contents of a photograph—and its punctum. His definition of the latter is rather vibrant: "This second element which will disturb the *studium* I shall therefore call *punctum*; for *punctum* is also: sting, speck, cut, little hole—and also a cast of the dice. A photograph's *punctum* is that accident which pricks me (but also bruises me, is poignant to me)" (Barthes 1981, 27, translated by Richard Howard).[11] Barthes isolates precisely which aspect of a photograph operates as its punctum, citing a woman's "strapped pumps" in James Van Der Zee's "Family Portrait" (1981, 43–44) or a child's "bad teeth" in William Klein's "Little Italy, New York" (1981, 45–46). Barthes recognizes the punctum's peculiar duality: "Last thing about the *punctum*: whether or not it is triggered, it is an addition: it is what I add to the photograph and *what is nonetheless already there*" (1981, 55, translated by Richard Howard).[12] The audible creaks of Glenn Gould's piano chair are classic audio puncta. The creaks provide glimpses into the corporeality of a performative moment, the sense of *the pianist at the piano*. Transposing the punctum from photographs to audio recordings reveals differences in each medium's experiential temporality. Non-notated sounds inspire many of the same (often contradictory) reactions that Barthes experienced while looking at photographs. The chair creaks annoy, disturb, and break cultural agreements, while at the same time arousing sympathy, fascination, and a sense of intimate connection.

---

[11] « Ce second élément qui vient déranger le *studium*, je l'appellerai donc *punctum*; car *punctum*, c'est aussi: piqûre, petit trou, petite tache, petite coupure – et aussi coup de dés. Le *punctum* d'une photo, c'est ce hasard qui, en elle, *me point* (mais aussi me meurtrit, me poigne). » (Barthes 1980, 49)

[12] « Dernière chose sur le *punctum*: qu'il soit cerné ou non, c'est un supplément: c'est ce que j'ajoute à la photo et *qui cependant y est déjà*. » (Barthes 1980, 89).

Unwritten music becomes expressive when we rescue the act of listening from public admonitions that such sounds are "insignificant" or "distracting." Barthes's ultimate point is that puncta *are* distracting, in the most expressive sense of the term. This distraction can be viscerally attractive, as Barthes demonstrates in his paean to cinematic sound at the conclusion of *Le plaisir du texte* (*The Pleasure of the Text*):

> In fact, it suffices that the cinema capture the sound of speech *close up* (this is, in fact, the generalized definition of the "grain" of writing) and make us hear in their materiality, their sensuality, the breath, the gutturals, the flesh-iness of the lips, a whole presence of the human muzzle (that the voice, that writing, be as fresh, supple, lubricated, delicately granular and vibrant as an animal's muzzle), to succeed in shifting the signified a great distance and in throwing, so to speak, the anonymous body of the actor into my ear: it granulates, it crackles, it caresses, it grates, it cuts, it comes: that is bliss. (Barthes 1975, 67, translated by Richard Miller)[13]

Jonathan Dunsby has called upon music studies to pay closer attention to the expressivity of performative sounds. He characterizes close listening as valuably discomforting: "The more that kind of critical response may make us squirm, may render us coyly objective, the more it may be that post-structuralist criticism knew something which current musicology would do well to reinvent for itself" (Dunsby 2009, 131). Cinematic sound brings the listener not only closer to the declaration, but closer to the mouth of the declarer. Transposed onto music, Barthes's image implies a microphone embedded in "*le museau humain*" (the human muzzle)—the projecting part of the face including the nose, mouth, and jaw—that picks up every click of the tongue against the teeth, every glint of saliva between the lips, alongside the sound of the words, be they sung or spoken. "Muzzle" has several meanings, some more disturbing than others, including: as a noun, a covering for the mouth used to prevent biting, something that prevents expression, or the open end of an implement such as the discharging end of

---

[13] « Il suffit en effet que le cinéma prenne de très près le son de la parole (c'est en somme la définition généralisée du "grain" de l'écriture) et fasse entendre dans leur matérialité, dans leur sensualité, le souffle, la rocaille, la pulpe des lèvres, toute une présence du museau humain (que la voix, que l'écriture soient fraîches, souples, lubrifiées, finement granuleuses et vibrantes comme le museau d'un animal), pour qu'il réussisse à déporter le signifié très loin et à jeter, pour ainsi dire, le corps anonyme de l'acteur dans mon oreille: ça granule, ça grésille, ça caresse, ça râpe, ça coupe. Ça jouit. » (Barthes 1973, 105).

a weapon; as a verb, to gag, restrain, or restrict. While these meanings are frighteningly present within social history and global politics, I seek to retain Barthes's term here in its primary sense as a physical descriptor.

I was initially resistant to equate the musician's muzzle to that of an animal. However, the beauty and complexity of both human and animal mouths redirects the comparison away from dehumanization and toward something more natural, fascinating, and praiseworthy. My own muzzle is a place of interest as a locus of my speaking and (amateur) singing, and audio recordings provide listeners with rich traces of muzzle- and lung-based activity. They not only preserve notes sung in certain rhythms, but capture glottal stops, plosive pops, and the sounds of breathing. Barthes makes a perceptive distinction: the detail that interests him "does not necessarily attest to the photographer's art; it says only that the photographer was there, or else, still more simply, that he could not *not* photograph the partial object at the same time as the total object" (1981, 47, translated by Richard Howard).[14] The recordings analyzed in this book—themselves exemplars of thousands yet unstudied—are "total objects" whose sounds provide evidence that the musician "was there."

Unwritten music and facial micro-expressions

Unwritten music is analogous to facial micro-expressions. The topic originated with the research of Haggard and Isaacs (1966). According to Paul Ekman (2003), micro-expressions—and the related categories of "slight" and "partial" expressions—are the facial gestures that we witness, or make, when listening or speaking. These rapid facial motions deliver expressive and often crucial information that would not be recorded in a written transcript of a given conversation. Just as facial micro-expressions offer valuable and often revealing information that enhances the meaning of spoken words, the placement and density of breaths, grunts, fingerfalls, and other non-scored sounds represent audio traces of physical activity. Ekman suggests that micro-expressions reveal "concealed emotions" (2009, 3451) and that they "may occur when the inhibition of expression occurs outside of consciousness"

---

[14] « . . . il n'atteste pas obligatoirement l'art du photographe; il dit seulement ou bien que le photographe se trouvait là, ou bien, plus pauvrement encore, qu'il ne pouvait pas ne pas photographier l'objet partiel en même temps que l'objet total. » (Barthes 1980, 80).

(2003, 220). The involuntary, expressive aspect of micro-expressions is analogous to sounds made by musicians in the performative moment.

The analogy between unwritten music and micro-expressions extends into the realm of discourse analysis, a subfield of linguistics that analyses speech itself, including "small pauses, slight hesitations, subtle changes of sound, pitch, rate, and loudness, as well as close synchronizations between speakers" (Gee 1999, 88). Recordings that succeed in capturing every nuanced inhale or exhale of a performer provide the theorist with an event-rich object of study, one in which sonic micro-expressions are intermingled with the sounds derived from notation. Sounds created by recording and playback media—such as surface noise—preserve historically specific information that situates the performative act within its available contemporary technologies. In a tantalizing hypothetical future that sees music and linguistics departments fuse into one, unwritten music could form a bridge.

Unwritten music and the census

As currently constituted, the US Census must necessarily make an "actual Enumeration" (Kassinger 1999, 68) of the number of persons in each state. The belief is that counting all people, rather than all citizens, allows lawmakers to make more intelligent political decisions. Transposing these ideas onto music theory, the notes and rhythms inscribed by composers have unquestionably achieved "citizenship" within theory's published literature, at the exclusion of many other sounds and sound sources. By contrast, non-notated sounds are treated by music theory as "non-citizens." Within classical music recordings, unwritten music is repeatedly denied entry by a self-reinforcing feedback loop between critics, sound engineers, performers, and consumers. Such sounds have been tacitly understood to exist *apart* from the music, even while being enmeshed in tracks since the dawn of recording technology. In the recording studio, removing or suppressing these sounds can, in some cases, deprive the listener of unique types of intimacy and musical understanding.

This analogy recalls Suzannah Clark's notion that musical tones might be granted "equal rights" (2019, 148), extending calls for equality within the *field* of music theory—set forth by Loren Kajikawa (2019), Philip Ewell (2020), and Ellie Hisama (2021)—into the realm of *sounds themselves*. In solidarity with these notions, my methodology operates according to census-like tenets whereby the "complete population" of a recording *counts*. For a recording analysis to be inclusive, sounds of breath, touch, effort, and surface noise must be part of the "actual Enumeration." The prerequisite is audibility, and "citizenship" is not tied to the existence of a marking in a score. Unwritten music has always been plainly audible in classical recordings, and music theory must orient itself toward the relationship between sounds *without exclusion based on their origin*. Echoing the rationale of the US Census, music theory is only well informed when all sounds are counted. Whether in a governmental census or an audio track, recognizing the totality provides the data necessary for more educated analytical conclusions to be reached.

Unwritten music and craquelure

The surface of an oil painting is a place of great activity. Brush strokes fix the painter's materials to a foundation, leaving evidence of movement and age. Over time, the paint and varnish can develop a network of fine cracks called *craquelure*. When craquelure is relegated to the corners of an image, its expressive effect is minimized. When it appears centrally, such as on the face of a portrait, it can alter the viewer's sense of the what the painting is expressing.

A recording, too, has a surface. The patterned hissing imparted by early capture and playback devices is, after all, called *surface noise*. Like craquelure, surface noise confounds notions of agency and authorship. When we listen to a wax cylinder recording, the machine that captured the sound contributes, sometimes mightily, to the soundscape. There is surface noise in paintings as well and, like early recordings, the "author" of a painting's craquelure is not the painter, but the medium reacting with the environment over time.

The Renaissance offers vivid examples of expressive craquelure. Figure 1.1 presents Leonardo da Vinci's *Portrait of an Unknown Woman (La Belle Ferronnière)*. In his catalogue raisonné of Leonardo's paintings, Frank Zöllner (2011, 228) gives the medium as oil on walnut and suggests that the painting's nickname—*La Belle Ferronnière*—might be related to the band that the sitter wears around her head, which was called a *ferronnière* and which was popular in Milan when the painting was made. *La Belle Ferronnière* has inspired numerous commentaries regarding its intriguing composition. Stefano Zuffi writes: "The fairly usual placement of the head and upper body against a neutral dark background derives intense vitality from the young

Figure 1.1 Leonardo da Vinci, *Portrait of an Unknown Woman (La Belle Ferronnière)*, ca. 1490–1495, oil on walnut, 63 cm × 45 cm, Paris, Musée du Louvre, Inventory number 778, public domain.

woman's charged and sympathetic facial expression and accentuated rotation" (2019, 148).

Elements of *La Belle Ferronnière* contradict Zuffi's appraisal. Figure 1.2 provides a close-up view of Leonardo's painting. The oil paint and the varnish atop its walnut surface has, over centuries, reacted to form a set of cracks

Figure 1.2 Detail from Leonardo da Vinci, *Portrait of an Unknown Woman (La Belle Ferronnière)*, ca. 1490–1495, oil on walnut, 63 cm × 45 cm, Paris, Musée du Louvre, Inventory number 778, public domain.

that propagate across the subject's face. Comparing *La Belle Ferronnière* to two other paintings by Leonardo, Zöllner writes: "A very fine craquelure is apparent in particular in the areas of the flesh, whereby it differs from the craquelure found in the *Cecilia Gallerani* and *Mona Lisa* in the unevenness of its distribution" (2011, 228). When I show this close-up image to friends, one recurring response is that the sitter looks ill. The cross-hatching of craquelure across her visage seems at odds with Zuffi's notion of "vitality," suggesting instead its opposite.

Zöllner compares the craquelure of *La Belle Ferronnière* with the *Mona Lisa*. Unlike *La Belle Ferronnière*, the *Mona Lisa*—whose formal title is *Portrait of Lisa del Giocondo*—was painted on poplar and thereby exhibits a different pattern of "surface noise." A detail from the face of the *Mona Lisa* appears as Figure 1.3. The craquelure in this case forms trenches and channels that are reminiscent of subway maps, electrical grids, or a parched desert.

Attending to the skin at this level of detail alters my feeling about the painting. From a distance, I am taken by the poise of the subject. She looks rather calm. Up-close, the surface of her face—of the painting—crackles with

Figure 1.3 Detail from Leonardo da Vinci, *Portrait of Lisa del Giocondo (Mona Lisa)*, 1503–1506 and later, oil on poplar, 77 cm × 53 cm, Paris, Musée du Louvre, Inventory number 779, public domain.

energetic mark-making. While these dark channels were not individually inscribed by Leonardo during the act of painting, the combination of his activity, his materials, and the passage of time leaves us with an artwork that has layers of contradicting elements. The same holds true of audio recordings. Certain analyses in the forthcoming chapters reveal music that is serene at a distance and vigorously unsettled (and *unsettling*) when analyzed close-up.

The specific patterns of craquelure in *La Belle Ferronnière* and the *Mona Lisa* relate in part to their respective foundations. The former is painted on walnut, the latter on poplar. Canvas can also be the base for craquelure. Take, for example, Johannes Vermeer's *The Guitar Player*, a detail of which can be seen in Figure 1.4. Executed in oil, the painting depicts a seated woman in a fur-clad garment playing a five-course guitar. A network of fine cracks blanket the surface of the painting, altering the image and reminding the viewer of the material reality of the artwork. One craquelure pattern in *The Guitar Player* seems to emanate from a point on the musician's sternum, radiating out like a spider's web. Cascades of cracks cross boundaries between the player's hands and the body of the guitar, contradicting their separateness within the painted scene.

Looking at these paintings *as they are*—inclusive of the sensations created in the viewer by the interaction of the aging paint, varnish, and foundation—is precisely the mode of inquiry demonstrated across this book, including and especially in the study of surface noise in Chapter 5. I set aside common notions of listening *through* surface noise and instead present a practice whereby we listen *with* it. Doing so allows us to appraise what the recording-as-document is expressing in its current (and continually developing) state.

Unwritten music and painting *en plein air*

A different sort of unwritten mark is memorialized in an oil painting that hangs in the Kröller-Müller Museum in Otterlo, The Netherlands. The painting is Vincent van Gogh's *Olive Grove*, July 1889, an oil on canvas executed outside of the asylum in Saint-Rémy-de-Provence during a period when the artist's attention was drawn to planted fields, dark cypresses, and olive trees. According to research by Nicole R. Myers, Margje Leeuwestein, and Muriel Geldof, the painting was produced in three phases: an initial sketch followed by two painting campaigns. The initial sketch involved priming the canvas and outlining basic compositional elements. The two

Figure 1.4 Detail from Johannes Vermeer, *The Guitar Player*, ca. 1672, oil on canvas, 53 cm × 46.3 cm, English Heritage, The Iveagh Bequest, Kenwood, Inventory number 88028841, public domain.

campaigns were undertaken "with enough time elapsing between each session for the underlying paint layer to completely dry" (2021, 102). While the final phrase seems to have been completed in the painter's studio, the preparatory phase and the first campaign seem to have taken place outdoors. The evidence is compelling: "There are several indications that this first painting campaign, including the initial preparatory phase, was painted *en plein air* in an olive grove. Traces of an insect walking through the wet paint of the first painting session have been found in two locations" (2021, 102).[15]

Van Gogh was working outside, and his wet canvas captured the painterly imprint of a creature taking a short stroll.[16] Since he allowed the paint to dry between the first and second campaigns, these marks remain part of the artwork to this day. This is not the only evidence of nature found on the canvas: "Several examples of plant material—a possible seed and pieces of what might be a stem or blade of grass—and grains of sand were also found embedded on the surface" (Bakker and Myers 2021, 102–3). Again, there is a kinship with surface noise. A pattern is embedded into the final artwork that was not placed there by the artist and which, in effect, *records the act of recording*. Canvas is a recording medium. Van Gogh was painting in an olive grove in Saint-Rémy-de-Provence. There, in July 1889, an arthropod author contributed, however subtly, to the work.

The analogy with surface noise is imperfect, but it need not be the only analogy we draw from van Gogh's paintings from summer 1889. Another in the same series—*Olive Trees*, completed in November of that year—preserves two separate fingerprints, likely those of the artist.[17] The fingerprints foreshadow my analyses of fingernail clicks on tracks by William Chapman Nyaho and Claudio Arrau in Chapter 3. In the case of van Gogh, the traces are visual; in the case of Chapman Nyaho and Arrau, they are sonic. In all cases, they record the artist in the act of making: the painter at the easel, the pianist at the piano. The cross-disciplinary nature of this analogy reveals a meaningful difference in *value* between recordings and paintings. Fingernail clicks are considered extraneous largely because they are not part of (and seemingly interrupt) the interpretation of a composer's score. They are often

---

[15] A photomicrograph of the insect's contribution to the painting appears as Figure 49 in Bakker and Myers (2021, 102).

[16] These insect-canvas interactions were not always temporary. Embedded in *Olive Trees*, June 1889 [F715, JH1759, Nelson-Atkins Museum of Art in Kansas City, Missouri] are the remains of a grasshopper, specifically its "disarticulated body fragments (head and hind leg)" (Bakker and Myers 2021, 91).

[17] A photomicrograph of these fingerprints appears as Figure 73 in Bakker and Myers (2021, 131).

removed by producers and sound engineers. By contrast, it is unlikely that curators would attempt to remove van Gogh's fingerprints from his canvas.

The reception of unwritten music

Critiques of unwritten music have both logic and validity. Why would anyone want emphatic inhales, creaking piano chairs, or hissing surface noise to intrude across a beloved recording? At times, I share this sentiment myself. But music theory is not about cherry-picking which sounds we want to pay attention to; it is about reckoning with the comprehensive totality of audible events and their relationship to one another. Moments such as Kashkashian's inhales have long gone untheorized, even "unheard." Whether such sounds elicit affection or revulsion, their existence opens a space to discuss what recordings of classical music represent in the eyes of music theory. While recordings can be beautiful and expressive with or without such sounds, the classical recording industry seems to encourage artists to efface their corporeality and diminish their sonic presence.

The erasure of body and breath sounds is often enacted in the name of sonic "perfection." The front cover of all sixteen discs of Bayer Dacapo's 1990 collection *Enrico Caruso: Complete Recordings*—which features their proprietary NoNoise-System—advertises that the tracks are presented "in digital perfection." Attempts to remove noise are energetically displayed. The set includes a disc devoted entirely to five presentations of the same two-minute excerpt from Caruso's November 1902 recording of Ruggero Leoncavallo's "Vesti la giubba." Each track offers a different level of sound processing: Original, *Erste Filterung*, Denoised Version, Declicked Version, and *Endfilterung*.

While "noise" is understood to the enemy of "perfection," this characterization is not universally accepted. In *Flaming? The Peculiar Theopolitics of Fire and Desire in Black Male Gospel Performance*, Alisha Lola Jones powerfully redirects the notion of perfection. Discussing the hybrid music genre of gospel go-go, Jones coins the term *sounded convergence*: "The process of sounded convergence is musicians' untidy negotiation of musical and sociotheological change as gospel and go-go cocreate gospel go-go" (2020, 130). Jones's verb—*cocreate*—applies equally to classical recordings. Written and unwritten sounds cocreate classical tracks. Even so, notated and non-notated sounds are not valued equally. Jones goes on to describe the sonic erasure of go-go music's integral (and "noisy") characteristics when it was blended with gospel: "When insider participants subsequently hear go-go beats performed in Christianized pop music, the product lacks the intoxicating or grimy qualities" (2020, 131). The "grimy qualities" of go-go music are *toned down* when blended with gospel for mass consumption. Analogous acts have been perpetrated on the liveness of non-notated sounds in classical tracks.

Jones's notion of *sounded convergence* argues in favor of go-go's "grime." She rescues the notion of "imperfection" in a bold recharacterization: "Sounded convergence is an aesthetic that asserts performed acoustic imperfection is holy and just" (2020, 130). Leaving aside whether classical tracks are "holy," I am compelled by Jones's description of acoustic imperfection as "just." She opens a valuable category for the study of classical recordings. Breaths, grunts, and touch sounds are widely perceived as "imperfections." My inclusive methodology does not argue that such sounds are necessary (or desirable), but when they appear, I follow Jones's example and argue that they should be considered as both just and justified. The mainstream consensus within the classical music industry has been that unwritten music mars perfection. When notated and non-notated sounds *converge* in classical tracks, so-called imperfections should be recognized and theorized, even if they are erroneous in the eyes of their creator and unwelcome in the ears of the listener.

Unwritten music often creates unease. Glenn Gould's tracks are replete with sounds that do not appear in the scores of the works he is performing. These sounds range from his infamous singing to the creaking, cracking, and clicking made by his loose-jointed piano chair. Reception of these sounds has ranged from infatuation to annoyance. When the recordings were originally released, their status was precisely characterized. On the back cover of Gould's 1965 album of Beethoven's Op. 10 piano sonatas, producer Thomas Frost wrote explicitly about Gould's chair and its sound-making tendencies. The passage represents the tacitly accepted viewpoint of many listeners and theorists and opens several avenues for my inquiry:

> For some years now, Gould has been merrily fugueing [*sic*] his way through the keyboard works of Bach, Beethoven and Schoenberg to the accompaniment of the strange creakings and groanings of an old, beloved friend— his piano stool. This object of endearment, decrepit and moth-eaten as it is (having reached retirement age long ago), apparently has learned to swing

and sway so perfectly with Glenn Gould's body motions that he has stubbornly refused to part with it in spite of all counsel and advice—and an offer from the Smithsonian Institution. It has come to this: Columbia Records has decided to call upon the powers of science to construct a facsimile of the famous chair which will have the same swayability without the noise. Until then: Glenn Gould refuses to give up his chair. Columbia Records refuses to give up Glenn Gould. And we hope that you, the consumer, will refuse to be discomforted by some audible creaks that are insignificant in light of the great music-making on this disc. (Frost 1965, back cover)

Frost deems the audible creaks of Gould's chair to be "insignificant" and his rhetoric consciously separates them from the "great music-making" that he otherwise celebrates. He explicitly requests that the listener (whom he tellingly refers to as "the consumer") do the same. Is Frost's distinction a useful one? What is gained and lost when we prioritize notated sounds over non-notated ones? Reversing Frost's distinction, what about listeners who are *not* discomforted by such sounds, but instead are energized and fascinated by them? Certain listeners have confessed that some of their favorite moments in the recorded literature are, for example, Arturo Toscanini's humming (Russell Platt 2017), Pablo Casals's grunting (Audrey Davis 1960), and Gould's singing (Tom Service 2012). Frost's disclaimer about the "extraneous" nature of Gould's chair creaks clarifies his position on unwritten music. For Frost, it is a nuisance, one that risks critically undermining the commercial success of a recording.

Gould's chair creaks are just the beginning. The pianist's now-legendary vocalizations are a focal point for harsh reviews and musicological diagnosis. Kevin Bazzana makes clear that Gould's vocal elaborations were not an attention-seeking public affectation, since they are heard on his commercial releases and private recordings alike. While record executives clearly objected to these sounds, Gould himself felt they were *not under his control*. Bazzana quotes Gould as saying of his singing: "I can't do without it. I would if I could. It's a terrible distraction. I don't like it . . . I can only say that I play very much less well if I don't indulge in a few vocal elaborations" (2004, 248, ellipsis in original). Gould admits that such sounds can be distracting, but accepts them as an unavoidable aspect of his way of playing. His frank self-evaluation makes clear that his vocalizing (and his chair creaks) could not be disambiguated from the physical act of playing (or playing "well"). Dana Gooley makes a similar point about Franz Liszt, whose "excessive" bodily motions provoked criticism and prompted contemporary critics including

François-Joseph Fétis and Pierre Alexandre Specht to call for their suppression: "These critics assumed that Liszt had control over his bodily motions, that he *could* stop them, that they were indeed subordinate to his sovereign will" (2004, 46, italics in original). The same holds for Gould. His process of playing "well" was inextricably entwined with his physical need to vocalize. Gould's playing involved the production of both written and unwritten music. Exhortations for non-scored sounds to be removed from Gould's recordings are, at root, a request for integral aspects of his physicality to be erased because they obscure the musical thought of the composer.

Distinctions about who is *allowed* to audibly breathe, moan, or grunt while playing classical music are often drawn along lines of race and gender. Critics can be observed lauding unwritten music when the performer shares their identity and rejecting it when they don't. Within the archive of reviews published in *Gramophone* magazine extending back to January 1983, non-scored sounds including breaths and grunts are routinely disparaged. The following excerpts are representative:

> One member of the Borodin Trio, I am not sure which, either suffers from asthma or has a habit of taking deep gulps of breath in roughly the same places that a singer would if these were vocal compositions. I have frankly never heard heavy breathing rendered with quite such startling realism on record, and I found it quite distracting, in the slow movements especially.
> —Michael Oliver (1985, 1243) reviewing the Borodin Trio's Erato recording of chamber music by Dmitri Shostakovich

> Finally, if he is to make any more recordings he should be encouraged not to grunt audibly at moments of stress: the opening of the *Gwendoline* Overture is only one of several passages thus marred.
> —Roger Nichols (2000, 57) reviewing conductor Yutaka Sado's Erato recording, with the Lamoureux Orchestra, of music by Emmanuel Chabrier

> Only a couple of niggles: like the Wanderer Trio, the string players apparently ignore the *con sordino* instruction in the finale (at 7'09"), and in the Passacaglia, at 1'54", there's a very prominent exhalation from one of them—bothersome enough to make one wonder why it was left in.
> —Harriet Smith (2005, 77) reviewing Boris Berezovsky, Dmitri Makhtin, and Alexander Kniazev's Warner recording of Shostakovich's Piano Trio No. 2

The recorded sound has impressive depth, but every singalong grunt from the podium is luridly audible.

—Philip Clark (2009, 85) reviewing Mikhail Pletnev's
Pentatone recording, with the Russian National Orchestra, of
Shostakovich's Symphony No. 15

If you are allergic to grunting and sniffing, be warned that Aimard evidently isn't. This is music that sensitises the ear to tiny nuances of colour, and odd groans that might be intensely involving in the concert hall can be equally distracting on disc.

—David Fanning (2018, 25) reviewing Pierre-Laurent
Aimard's Pentatone recording of Olivier Messiaen's
Catalogue d'oiseaux

Eventually the initial shock and awe subsides, and Say's titillating expressive touches wind up sounding as predictable as the vocal groans, grunts and grimaces accompanying nearly every crescendo. The net result is a highly calculated and calibrated pianism that draws more attention to Fazıl Say than to the composer he purports to serve with 300 pens at the ready.

—Jed Distler (2020, 65) reviewing Fazıl Say's Warner
Classics recording of the complete
Beethoven piano sonatas

Non-scored, body-generated sounds are characterized as "distracting," "detracting," and "lurid" events that mar the music. Harriet Smith wonders aloud why an exhalation was "left in." Michael Oliver complains that a member of the Borodin Trio "suffers from asthma." (One wants to ask, in reply, why having asthma should prevent a musician from recording music.) David Fanning makes the intriguing distinction between groans in the concert hall ("intensely involving") and those on recordings ("distracting"). Some reviews are more cutting. Roger Nichols's appraisal of Yutaka Sado's grunting goes so far as to recommend *that Sado not release any more recordings*. Fazıl Say, who claimed to have annotated his Beethoven scores with 300 different colored pens, is criticized harshly by Jed Distler, who suggests that Say is a *servant* (of Beethoven) and, in that role, has no right to grunt.

On the surface, *Gramophone* reviews provide information about which releases their readers might want to purchase—often at considerable expense—and warns them about recordings that intermingle composer-designated sounds with those of a working, perspiring musician. Digging deeper, the archive betrays a more divisive reality. Many of the harshest critiques are levied against performers of color, while rare positive appraisals are extended to white, male musicians. (It also helps to be famous.) The following excerpts extol the virtues of unwritten music. Note the difference in tone, and their correlation to the subject of the review:

> I'll end by adding that even if not told who the cellist was throughout these three discs, you'd guess at once: without all those little grunts and groans at moments of heightened intensity, Casals would not have been Casals.
> —Joan Chissell (1994, 69) reviewing Pablo Casals's Philips recording of Beethoven's piano trios and cello sonatas

> To play like this while still a teenager; to play like this at any age! The recordings are adequate to the occasion; an assortment of wheezes and grunts and what sounds like a crashing plate in the *Liebestraum* add to the almost palpable exhilaration.
> —Bryce Morrison (1997, 88) reviewing Evgeny Kissin's Revelation Records recording of music by Franz Liszt and Robert Schumann

> Toscanini's audible singing (you hear it throughout the set) is further proof of his ecstatic involvement.
> —Robert Cowan (1999, 105) on Arturo Toscanini's BBC Legends recording, with the BBC Symphony Orchestra, of music by Ludwig van Beethoven, Wolfgang Amadeus Mozart, and Luigi Cherubini

> Tony Faulkner's close-set engineering captures plenty of inner detail (and Sir Colin's grunts and groans add to the sense of involvement), but ambient glow is in short supply.
> —Andrew Achenbach (2003, 41) reviewing Colin Davis's LSO Live recording, with the London Symphony Orchestra, of Antonín Dvořák's Seventh Symphony

Instead of suggesting that some sonic "crime" has been committed, these reviewers applaud their subjects for making sounds not notated in the scores that they are recording. Witness Bryce Morrison writing that Evgeny Kissin's wheezes and grunts add an "almost palpable exhilaration" or Andrew Achenbach's judgment that Colin Davis's grunts and groans "add to the sense of involvement." Across the *Gramophone* archive, I find few instances of performative grunts made by women or people of color that are commended in this way. If we take Joan Chissell at her word when she claims that, without his grunting and gasping, "Casals would not have been Casals," then would it not also be true to say that, without his grunts and gasps, Say would not be Say? Madame de Sévigné's observation—"We like no noise, unless we make it ourselves"—remains in effect. Similar sounds are heard differently based on the identity of their producer.

One of the reasons that the classical recording industry seeks to delete non-notated sounds is because *they were not made by the right person*. They rival and interrupt a listener's appreciation of the composer's art. This explains why jazz and popular music (to name just two) are more comfortable with sounds of breath, touch, and effort. In those genres, the composer and the performer-as-track-maker are often one in the same. In general, there is no preexisting document, no urtext, to violate. In her book *Marginalia: Readers Writing in Books*, H. J. Jackson provides a perceptive gloss: "Annotation combines—synthesizes, I should say—the functions of reading and writing. This fact in itself heightens the natural tension between author and reader by making the reader a rival of the author, under conditions which give the reader considerable power. The author has the first word, but the annotator has the last" (2001, 90).[18] With just a few media-related substitutions, Jackson's words can be transformed to state one of the basic tenets of my methodology. Tracks synthesize the functions of reading a score and hearing a (recorded) performance of that score. This fact in itself heightens the natural tension between composer and performer by making the performer the rival of the composer, under conditions which give the performer considerable power. The composer has the first word, but the performer—it would be more precise to say *the track*—has the last.

---

[18] For more on the expressive nature of marginalia—including the pictorial, the scatological, and the comic—see Michael Camille *Image on the Edge: The Margins of Medieval Art* (1992).

The empathetic dimension

In certain circles, unwritten music can inspire a more constructive response. Body and breath sounds can evoke empathy. Violinist Jesse Holstein, a founding member of the Providence String Quartet, shared with me that a teenage experience of hearing breath sounds had inspired him to become a musician. The breaths, he recalls, were preserved on the Borodin Quartet's 1989 recording of the first movement of Claude Debussy's String Quartet in G minor, Op. 10. Holstein heard the piece on compact disc at Greenwood Music Camp in Cummington, Massachusetts, and—some thirty years later—remembers the listening experience in detail, including the precise location and impact of the breath sounds:

> When the opening theme returns after the cascading scales, I heard something that drew me in even further. I heard the quartet breathing and sniffing together between gestures. This was an added dynamic element to the music-making that I found thrilling and gave me the tingles for the first time. It was the sound of the quartet's total commitment to the music, even with their bodies. I skipped back to that moment on the recording over and over that week. (personal correspondence, July 9, 2021)

Holstein is referring to the passage beginning at 0:56 in the 1989 Borodin Quartet recording, which corresponds to the upbeat into m. 28 in Debussy's score. The inhale might have come from first violinist Mikhail Kopelman, or from one of his colleagues: Andrei Abramenkov, Dmitri Shebalin, or Valentin Berlinsky. Whoever produced it, the breath sound exists, and it made a significant expressive impact on a young listener. The Borodins are not the only ones that Holstein might thank for this sound. The inhale was captured and preserved by producer John H. West and balance engineer Mike Hatch, in accordance with their own sensibilities as well as the refinement (and limitations) of their recording and editing equipment. Credit for the sound must also be shared with the acoustic itself: the recording was made at St Martin's Church in East Woodbury, Berkshire, United Kingdom.

Sound engineers and producers are co-protagonists in this book, their creative agency summed up by Rick Altman: "Far from simply recording a specific story of a specific sound event, the sound engineer actually has the power to create, deform, or reformulate that event" (1992, 25). Hearing these inhales provided Holstein with access to the effortful reality of a performer in the act of performing and inspired him to become a violinist. The Borodin Quartet's recording not only intensified Holstein's love for Debussy's quartet, it engendered empathy toward Kopelman, Abramenkov, Shebalin, and Berlinsky. Unwritten music, in all its forms, has the potential to build connections between performers and listeners (some of whom will go on to become performers themselves).

A more complete picture of a track as a musical document emerges when we rescue the act of listening from the implied admonitions that unwritten music is—in the unsettling language of iZotope's audio editing software—a candidate for "intelligent suppression." Music theory benefits when scholars widen their analytic lens to account for events that they find expressive, even if earlier scholars deemed them trivial. Dissolving the implied separation between "significant" and "insignificant" sounds, I accept so-called extraneous noises as coequal to the pitches surrounding them.

My methodology takes inspiration from pivotal moments in the history of music theory when scholars felt the need to pay attention to what their forebears ignored. Kofi Agawu argued for the centrality of structural highpoints in Schumann's *Dichterliebe* (events deemed rhetorically insignificant by Schenkerian scholars at the time), writing: "A hierarchy of dimensions derived from late eighteenth-century practice—with, for example, melody, harmony and rhythm as primary, and texture, dynamics and register as secondary—is no longer tenable here" (1984, 165–66). The field of music theory should widen its scope to include all sounds contained in a recording. Repurposing and redeploying Agawu's rhetoric: the hierarchy of dimensions within recording analysis—with, for example, tempo, rubato, and tuning as primary, and sounds made by the bodies of musicians, their equipment, and the recording apparatus as secondary—is no longer tenable.

Recognizing recordings of classical music as independent artworks—whose content is guided by, but not limited to, the score being recorded—allows for an expanded definition of what *counts* as music, and who does the counting. The ear recognizes non-notated sounds and registers when they appear and subside. They are an integral part of the interpretive act we engage in when we listen. Friedrich Kittler gets it right when he identifies the threshold of intimacy crossed by the invention of recorded sound: "The 'sound of music in my ear' can exist only once mouthpieces and microphones are capable of recording any whisper" (1999, 37). I see no reason to consciously and actively *hear past* the "whispers" and other aural evidence of the performer's body—be it Casals's added tone, Walker's enigmatic clicks, or Kashkashian's breaths. These events are expressive and deserve to be analyzed. The result is a mode of listening that reckons with a complete census of all sounds on a given recording. Non-notated sounds are integral elements of classical recordings. They provide a window into the humanity of music-making and are themselves music.

2
Sounds of Breath

Breath sounds as music

Inhales can be drawn, gasped, gulped, sucked, sniffed, or taken. Exhales can be expelled, expired, exuded, huffed, issued, or vented. Either can be secreted or sounded prominently. When breaths are audible, they carry expressive information. Each pitch produced by a singer is made possible by an unpitched inhale. Inhales are, in fact, the *unsung partners* of melodies, since every sung melody is, at a fundamental level, an intoned exhale. The same is true in instrumental music. Discussing wind playing, Tomie Hahn observed: "So we have the inhale and then the note and the end of the phrase. . . . The breath . . . is what each phrase is built upon. And in between each phrase we have silence and then the taking in of the breath. This is actually the pace of all the units and how they connect all the little phrases that build up the piece into a larger rhythmic form" (Hast, Cowdery, and Scott 1997, 101, ellipses in original). With so many types of air sounds, and so many musical circumstances where they can appear, a categorization will be useful. Using a series of exemplars, I catalog the manifold roles that breath plays within recordings. Each example probes a different aspect of the expressive, rhetorical, and rhythmic impact of audible breathing.

The fact that respiration is essential to the homeostasis of every musician underlines its importance to music theory. All musicians inhale and exhale when they make recordings. Whether their breath sounds reach the ears of listeners is another matter, one that is related to genre, era, instrument, cultural norms, and the sensibility of those that act as gatekeepers of a recording's content. In popular music, breath sounds are often controlled and sculpted in post-production. In classical recordings, the inclusion of breath sounds is often kept to a minimum, with traces of breathing appearing mainly at moments where it is cumbersome or (currently) impossible to delete them without also removing integral aspects of the sounding notes. Some purveyors of audio equipment treat audible breaths as a sign of quality. In his liner notes for the LP *Acoustic Research Demonstration Record*, Volume 1: *The*

Sound of Music Instruments, Martin Borish characterizes clarinetist Julio Pañella's audible breathing in his recording of Igor Stravinsky's *Three Pieces for Clarinet* as a selling point: "Practiced hi-fi enthusiasts will surely want to point out how their equipment makes it possible to hear the artist breathing" (1976, 1). Norms differ by instrument. While the breath sounds of pianists and string players can be rendered imperceptible by microphone placement and judicious editing, those of vocalists and wind-players are more difficult to erase, their melodies being a highly controlled form of exhalation.

Breath sounds are already considered "musical" by physicians, at least when they exhibit identifiable pitch.[1] Relying on Forgerac's nomenclature, Andrew Bush defines "wheeze" to be "a musical, polyphonic expiratory noise" (2019, 6). Fouzas et al. include a range of poetic characterizations for breath, citing stridor, wheeze, and rhonchus as "musical sounds" and crackles, mixed sound, pleural friction rub, voice-transmitted sounds, grunt, snuffle, ruttle, and snore as "non-musical sounds" (2019, 36–45). One of the main differentiators between "musical" and "non-musical" breaths seems to be their continuity of pitch. Within the field of pulmonary disorders, so-called adventitious breath sounds "are primarily divided into musical, continuous sounds and non-musical, discontinuous sounds" (Fouzas et al. 2019, 34). Hasse Melbye characterizes *normal tracheal sound* as "hollow and non-musical," *wheeze* as "musical, high-pitched, heard on inspiration, expiration, or both," *coarse crackle* as "non-musical short, explosive sounds; heard on early inspiration and throughout expiration," and the onomatopoetic *squawk* as a "mixed sound with short musical component (short wheeze) accompanied or preceded by crackles" (2019, 76). In clinical terms, the breath sounds studied in this chapter will be "non-musical" inhalations and expirations. In the context of my analyses, however, they will be treated as emphatically musical.

The clinical perspective sits alongside the psychological one. How fast or slow a person respirates is a potential signal of their state of mind. Take the bass solo that proclaims the first vocal iteration of the "Ode to Joy" theme in

---

[1] Janina Wellmann offers a historical perspective on *auscultation*, or the act of listening to sounds of a patient's inner organs: "Toward the end of the eighteenth century, the physiological anchoring of musical rhythm placed the relationship of music and medicine on a new foundation. The topos of the body's musicality now became the linchpin for both the theoretical explanation of music as a representation of life and the new science of physiology itself. In both domains, rhythm played a similar role, as the underlying structure of a flowing movement and the guiding principle of development. This is why physiological arguments and terminology so often feature in the musical debates of the period: rhythm as the inner organization of music corresponds with rhythm as the inner organization of organic nature" (2017, 69).

the last movement of Beethoven's Symphony No. 9, Op. 125. Recording the passage with the NDR Sinfonieorchester under Gunter Wand, bass Roland Hermann can be heard to inhale rapidly, and prominently, between each poetic couplet:

> Freude, schöner Götterfunken,
> Tochter aus Elysium, [*inhale*]
> Wir betreten feuertrunken,
> Himmlische, dein Heiligtum. [*inhale*]
> Deine Zauber binden wieder,
> Was die Mode streng geteilt; [*inhale*]
> Alle Menschen werden Brüder,
> Wo dein sanfter Flügel weilt.[2]

By contrast, when bass Theo Adam recorded the same passage with the Staatskapelle Dresden under Herbert Blomstedt, his inhales are barely audible.[3] These two interpretations exhibit a myriad of differences beyond the audibility of breath, including in tempo and timbre. Even so, Hermann's emphatic inbreaths give a nervous air to the passage in the Wand/NDR Sinfonieorchester recording, whereas Adam's inaudible inhales lend the Blomstedt/Staatskapelle Dresden passage a greater resolve.

While all musicians breathe while they play, lung capacities differ, as does the composition of the air available to them, which can range from oxygen-rich to polluted. Such variances generate individual physiological differences. They also record social inequalities that are amplified by racism, classism, and political geography. Literature on the affective possibilities of breath sounds has mainly focused on singing. Writing about paralinguistic sounds in the context of the popular singing voice, Victoria Malawey relates breath to embodiment: "Breath, brought to the fore through close-miking, signifies aliveness and humanity, and thus the embodiment of the singer" (2020, 137). Nina Sun Eidsheim has refined the language that our field uses to address vocal sounds, highlighting the voice's "nonsonorous aspects" (2019, 67). Within classical singing, the age-old norm calls for discreet (if possible, inaudible) breathing. The vocal pedagogue Richard Miller writes encouragingly of the singer's goal as the "*immediate and silent renewal of breath*"

---

[2] Roland Hermann's performance can be heard on Gunter Wand (1986/2018).
[3] Theo Adam's performance can be heard on Herbert Blomstedt (1980/2020).

(1997, 37, italics in original). Meribeth Bunch Dayme provides a more flexible appraisal of the expressive realities of breath sounds, based in part on her reading of Paul J. Moses's *The Voice of Neurosis* (1974):

> As indicated earlier, breathing patterns can give clues to personality and feelings. Moses noted that shallow-rapid breathing showed excitement or agitation, and slow controlled breathing denoted calmness and confidence. An extremely tense or excited person will have shallow (high chest) breathing patterns, or seem not to breathe at all, and will run out of breath in the middle of sentences and phrases. By contrast, an angry person will manifest intensity by taking very few breaths and by running sentences together. The person who is balanced in his speech and his emotions breathes deeply and evenly. (Dayme 2009, 51)

The expressive power of breath is not only the domain of singers. It is possible for instrumentalists to create expectation with an inhale (or a series of them).

A prominent inhale can indicate anticipation. It can also function as a signal. A rapid suck of air by a violinist during a calm passage might prefigure the arrival of a dramatic gesture or change in tempo. Whether or not such a change arrives is beside the point. The breath itself creates anticipation. Inhales often work in tandem with passages of harmonic expectation, such as the prolonged dominant chord that often precedes the recapitulation in sonata form. Take, for example, the C dominant seventh chord in bars 107–11 of the first movement of Mozart's String Quartet in F major, K. 590. In a 1972 recording by the Quartetto Italiano, these measures include no breath sounds. By contrast, a 2004 recording by the Hagen Quartett includes at least three inhales. Marrying harmonic anticipation with audible inbreaths lends an additional dimension of expectation to the Hagen Quartett's recording of this heightened moment in sonata form.

Breath sounds possess the same diversity, complexity, and expressivity that music theorists associate with chords. My categorization of their musical function begins by establishing their essential rhetorical function via an exchange between pianists Richard Goode and Alim Beisembayev. From there, I discuss breath-as-anacrusis in Guido Balestracci's recording of Jean Barrière's Sonata No. 4 in G major for Pardessus de Viole and Basso Continuo. Breath and expectation are illustrated by the Quatuor Mosaïques recording of the last movement of Joseph Haydn's String Quartet in E-flat major, Op. 33, No. 2, "The Joke." Breath-as-motive is addressed via recordings of Claude Debussy's String Quartet in G minor, Op. 10, by the Debussy, Harlem, Keller, and Alban Berg Quartets. Breath-as-climax is demonstrated by Sarah Bassingthwaighte's recording of Edgard Varèse's *Density 21.5*. Two final categories address breath sounds across larger musical forms. Kim Kashkashian's recording of the Gigue from J. S. Bach's Suite in C minor, BWV 1011, acts an exemplar of the influence of audible breaths on phrase rhythm, as well as their capacity to function as Baroque ornaments. Dashon Burton's unaccompanied recording of "He Never Said a Mumberlin' Word" inspires an extended meditation on the role of breaths within the presentation of a lyric.

The examples create a continuously expanding frame, from single measures by Beethoven and Barrière, to phrases by Haydn and Varèse, to complete sections and movements by Debussy and Bach, and finally to the level of the complete track in Burton. In all these examples, breath sounds will be visualized along a continuum of detail. In the case of Goode, Balestracci, and the Debussy, Harlem, Keller, and Alban Berg Quartets, the breath sounds will be symbolized by arrows: up for inhale, down for exhale. The breaths in Bassingthwaighte and Kashkashian necessitate specialized diagrams to capture their precise duration in milliseconds. Finally, the Burton analysis uses spectrograms to peer inside individual breaths and reveal the delicate mouth sounds embedded there. All musicians breathe when they make recordings. The following analyses theorize their audible inhales and exhales as music.

Breath as rhetoric

On July 30, 2018, at Le Hameau in Verbier, Switzerland, Richard Goode gave a master class to Alim Beisembayev on the first movement of Beethoven's Piano Sonata in D major, Op. 10, No. 3.[4] The setting was neither a concert performance nor a studio recording, but a moment of teaching. In the excerpt, Goode never mentions breathing. However, his use of audible breath—and, by contrast, his emphatic *withholding* of it—forms the subtle, intentional, and unspoken crux of his lesson. The wisdom that Goode imparts is never fully verbalized, only made explicit by his playing. It is a joyful fact that Goode begins his lesson by making a direct analogy between Beethoven's narrative

---

[4] I am grateful to Jenny Kallick for drawing my attention to this example.

dramaturgy and the lifting of the stylus of a record player. In doing so, Goode illuminates the rhetorical impact of an inhale.

To situate Goode's exchange with Beisembayev, Example 2.1 presents the Beethoven passage that they are discussing: mm. 113–33 of the first movement of Op. 10, No. 3, which encompasses the end of the exposition and the beginning of the development. Over a tonic pedal in the local key of A major, Beethoven reduces the texture to a series of call-and-answer motives between the right and left hands that are based on a fragment of the first subject. The effect serves the dual function of the exposition's close. Since this passage includes the repeat sign that sends the music back to the opening, bar 124 connects the end of the exposition with the start of the piece and, the second time round, ushers in the development, which in this case serves to continue its melodic and rhythmic pattern. Beethoven is no stranger to this type of blurring between the end of the exposition and the opening of the development; such masking is found in an analogous location in the first movement of the Sonata in C major, Op. 53, "Waldstein." However, unlike

Example 2.1 Ludwig van Beethoven, Piano Sonata in D major, Op. 10, No. 3, first movement, mm. 113–33, incorporating Richard Goode's characterization of the notated silence between mm. 123.4–124.3. See ⓟ Audio Example 2.1.

the "Waldstein" retransition, the passage in Op. 10, No. 3, is marked by a notated silence. From mm. 123.4 to 124.3, Beethoven writes four beats of rest in both hands of the piano. It is this notated silence that Goode takes up in the master class.

To set the scene: Beisembayev is positioned to Goode's right, and each pianist has a nine-foot Steinway grand piano before him. Beisembayev plays mm. 125–26, then Goode makes the following remarks, interspersed with playing:

> You probably don't remember long-playing records very well *[laughs]* but, one would put the, take the arm off *[lifts his arm, as though removing the stylus from the record, sings mm. 121.4–123.3, pauses in silence, then lowers his arm]* and put it back on.
>
> So, this place always seems to me like that, because this is a perfectly blank place. And kind of wonderful, wonderfully strange. *[plays and sings mm. 119–126.3]* So, I would dramatize the fact that nothing's happening there—the music simply stops in the middle *[plays mm. 121.4–125.1]*—by just being quite quiet on the piano. *[plays and sings mm. 121.4–126.3]* And then it goes backwards, and it goes backwards with a different note.
>
> So, if you do this *[plays mm. 121.5–125.1 sounding an audible inhale during m. 124]* or something like that, it's not the effect of the music at all. There's some silences where you move, you move over them, but here is when you just simply stop *[plays mm. 121.4–127.3, but this time takes no breath at all during m. 124]* and resume. *[plays mm. 113–114.3]*
>
> Yeah, what I think I'm sort of asking you to do a lot, in this, is dramatize whatever is happening in the music. Even overdramatize it, so you make it clear for yourself. (Goode 2018)[5]

Goode likens Beethoven's notated silence to "a perfectly blank place" and uses the analogy of a record stopping as soon as the stylus is lifted. Upon reading this transcript or watching the film, one might assume that Goode's teaching topic is Beethoven's use of notated silence. And it is. However, a careful consideration of the totality of Goode's sound-making allows his lesson to become clear. While he never mentions it, Goode is demonstrating the usefulness and rhetorical effect of audible breath via what one might call

---

[5] Audio Example 2.1 presents the excerpt from Goode's master class with Beisembayev transcribed above.

audible non-breath. The salient moment occurs when Goode demonstrates the phrase surrounding m. 124 in two different ways. The sounds emanating from the piano are nearly identical in both of his versions. He first performs the passage unsatisfactorily (adding an audible inhale) and then satisfactorily (with no inhale). Goode describes the moment at m. 124 as "when you simply stop." It is not a question of phrasing the descending scale differently, nor is it a question of volume, nor touch.

The difference between Goode's two versions is that, in the former, he takes a large, audible inhale during Beethoven's notated silence, and in the latter, he holds still. Without ever saying so in words, Goode teaches Beisembayev that an audible breath during the silence in m. 124 ruins the effect of the music. The difference that Goode incorporates into his dramatization of "stopping still" is to withhold any breath sound during the notated silence. While Goode describes this moment as "being quite quiet on the piano," he demonstrates to Beisembayev that it is also *the pianist* who must be "quite quiet."

Goode is making a point about interpretation, about "dramatizing" this "perfectly blank place" that bridges the exposition and development of Beethoven's movement. And yet the only audible difference between Goode's two versions of Beethoven's notated silence is his own inhalation. Goode suggests that the notated rest in m. 124 as analogous to the sudden lifting of the stylus on a record player. Of course, Beethoven never knew record players, and Goode himself suggests that Beisembayev is too young to remember them. Even so, the lifting of the stylus arm is an effective and memorable analogy. Goode characterizes the four beats of notated rest as a moment where "nothing's happening." His contrasting readings set up implications. The first is an intentional failure and the second is a qualified success. Goode characterizes the failed version as "not the effect of the music at all." The withholding of breath is precisely what Goode is teaching Beisembayev to practice. It is part of what Goode considers a dramatic and impactful performance of this moment in this work. To be sure, Goode practices what he preaches or, more specifically, performs what he teaches: his own 1991 studio recording of Op. 10, No. 3, made at the Academy of Arts and Letters in New York City and engineered by Max Wilcox, betrays no unwritten music whatsoever at this moment in the score—no breaths, no singing, no creaking of the piano bench.

What is the deeper rhythmic and gestural point invoked by Goode's advice? Put another way, what dramatic tension is lost or spoiled if the pianist breathes audibly in m. 124? The answer lies in the repeated four-note figures that begin in bar 113, and in the way the notated silence in bar 124 creates rhythmic suspense. This moment of silence exerts its dramatic effect during both passes through the form. Bar 113 inaugurates ten consecutive four-note scalar motives—all but one of them descending. These gestures are in dialogue with the four downbeat iterations of the low A2, and the listener is thereby entrained into a metric environment where scalar motives initiated on beat 4 become the local norm. Coming after the ten iterations of the four-note motive, the quarter rest at m. 123.4 vividly breaks this pattern. There *should* be a sound here, but there isn't. On the first pass through the form, the pianist returns to the opening of the piece, which re-enacts yet another version of the scalar motive. The second time through, the development begins by continuing the cascade of four-note descents that flow toward the emphatic arrival to the octave A-naturals on the downbeat of m. 132. Goode's (and Beethoven's) dramatic (and silent) bar 124 becomes a pivotal expression of *doubt*. As Goode says: "So, I would dramatize the fact that nothing's happening there. The music simply stops in the middle." Of course, something *is* happening there, and Goode knows this. That something is *nothing*, and that *nothing* is critical.

Beethoven's notated rest across the repeat sign is full of rhythmic and metric import. It is a sounded silence, and Goode is teaching Beisembayev that "being quite quiet on the piano"—and indeed within the respiratory system—is not only the right way to play the music, but the right music to play. Beethoven regularly harnessed the dramatic energy of grand pauses for rhetorical impact. Discussing the composer's piano music as "oration," George Barth writes: "As for [Beethoven's] handling of oratorical or pathetic accent, it evidently depended on combinations of greater length, a higher dynamic, and, where appropriate, evocative silence" (1992, 131). The notated silence in m. 124 of the first movement of Op. 10, No. 3, might be likened to a taut string, and the sound of the pianist's breath would undesirably relax its tension. Such a moment exemplifies the rhetorical device of *aposiopesis*, which connotes breaking off a phrase, leaving it unfinished and palpably uncontinued: "An aposiopesis gives an utterance the texture of real speech— the sound of thinking happening rather than a record of thoughts already had. The speaker stops to grope for words, to start a digression, or to think better of what he had planned to say" (Farnsworth 2011, 182). Goode's advice makes clear that an audible breath of any kind at this moment would break Beethoven's rhetorical spell and create the impression not of suspenseful thinking but of an unwelcome relaxation of drama. Farnsworth adds that a "speaker may use an aposiopesis to stop half-falsely. The interruption invites the audience to plead that the concealed thing be said after all, which it typically is" (2011, 187). Beethoven's phrase is just such a "half-false" pause, in that it momentarily interrupts the series of scalar fragments. It also satisfies the notion that such a break "invites the audience to plead that the concealed thing be said after all," doing so in two ways. The first time through the exposition, the expected event is the repeat of the opening bars; the second time, the "concealed thing" is the beginning of the turbulent development and its forthcoming breakthrough into B-flat major. For the silence of m. 124 to be rhetorically effective—for it to operate as an *aposiopesis*—it cannot be punctured by an audible breath.

The Goode example demonstrates that a single breath can meaningfully impact the music around it, and that the audibility of breaths is integral to music-making. While Goode framed his example around a withheld inhale, there exist numerous instances of breath sounds—both inhales and exhales—that are both expressive and effective. My study of unwritten music is not framed within a dichotomy of correct versus incorrect, desirable versus undesirable, good versus bad. Audible respirations are studied as component parts of tracks. Recordings are largely dictated by the scores that are being performed, but my analyses are enacted with an ear toward providing a proper census of all sounds that are present. I will not shame musicians for making them, nor will I criticize engineers for including them. I will also refrain from applauding when they are repressed or deleted. On any given track, I am interested in what there is to be heard.

Breath as anacrusis

When a breath sound is audible, it can commonly be found before an opening downbeat, where it acts as an anacrusis. This is true even though these breath sounds are among the easiest for recording engineers to remove since they emerge from silence. Breath-as-anacrusis is often used to create a shared sense of tempo within an ensemble or as part of a solo musician's preparatory gesture. Such sounds were rarely notated before the twentieth century, as such requests would ostensibly require a composer to begin the piece with a breath mark. Even so, the opening moments of recordings provide numerous examples of inhales—and, more rarely, exhales—in action.

The reasons for the prevalence of inhales versus exhales are threefold. First, exhales are generally executed more quietly, and often through the mouth, whereas inhales are often taken through the nose and are therefore more prominent in the soundscape. Second, inhales often occur in otherwise silent moments of cueing, whereas exhales are often coincident with instrumental sounds. Third, audible exhales are relegated to recordings by pianists, percussionists, and string players, since vocalists and wind-players use their exhaling breath to produce the notes themselves.

A single recording—Guido Balestracci's disc of Barrière's Sonata for Pardessus de Viole and Basso Continuo No. 4, Book V, in G major—provides a mini-compendium of anacrustic breath strategies. The four movements of this work—an *Adagio* in common time, an *Allegro* in 2/4, a second *Adagio* in 3/4, and a closing Aria in 3/8—provide a catalog of the differing functions of preparatory inhale-exhale combinations at opening gestures. The recording was made between February 9 and 15, 2015, under the direction of Bruno Cocset and producer Hugues Deschaux, and is notable throughout for its close-miking, and by the refusal of the creative team to erase the sounds of breath, to rather vivid effect.

Example 2.2 displays four types of audible pre-downbeat breath types, as heard in the opening of each movement of Balestracci's recording. The four types are (1) a (rather rare) inhale-exhale pair preceding the downbeat; (2) a double anacrustic inhale; (3) an anacrustic inhale with downbeat exhale; and (4) a (rather common) anacrustic inhale.

In the opening *Adagio*, Balestracci's exhale seems to breathe the opening G major triad into being. The downbeat is preceded by a sounded anacrusis provided by Balestracci's breath (perhaps commingled with the inhales of his continuo partners Emmanuel Jacques, cello, and Bertrand Cuiller, harpsichord). This trio of sounds—inhale, exhale, chord—has an almost cinematic effect. Balestracci's pre-downbeat inhale vividly registers as an anacrusis. His exhale, however, does something entirely different. It arrives *before* the opening chord and continues after the chord arrives. When the sonata's opening G major triad appears, it is enveloped in Balestracci's exhale. Images of a personified West Wind come to mind, putting air in the sails of tall ships, and it seems no coincidence that the cover image for Balestracci's recording is a detail from Claude Joseph Vernet's 1775 painting *A Grand View of the Sea Shore Enriched with Buildings, Shipping, and Figures*. Balestracci's breath both prefigures and accompanies the tonic chord during its first annunciation.

Example 2.2 Jean Barrière, Sonata for Pardessus de Viole and Basso Continuo No. 4, Book V, in G major, the opening of each movement with annotations of the breath patterns in the 2015 recording by Guido Balestracci. See ⏵ Audio Example 2.2.

Opening of I. Adagio
inhale-exhale pair

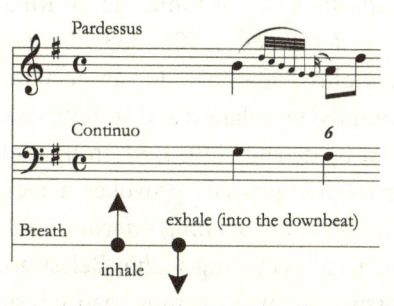

Opening of II. Allegro
double anacrustic inhale

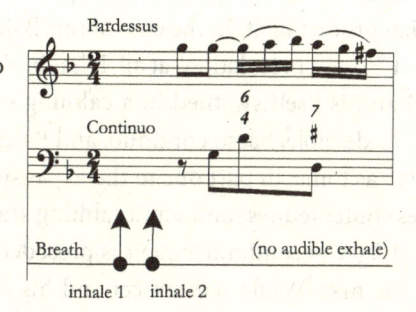

Opening of III. Adagio
anacrustic inhale and downbeat exhale

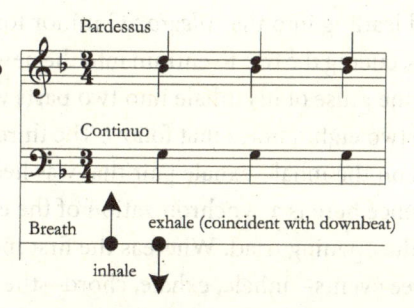

Opening of IV. Aria
single anacrustic inhale

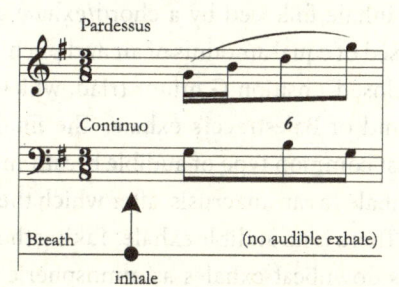

I hear the exhale that accompanies the opening chord as not only a signal of tonic function—a kind of corporeal "home"—but also as part of the tonic itself. Summarizing historical perspectives on whether opening consonant triads are heard as tonic, Steven Rings (2019, 121) invokes Schenker's "*Egoismus des Tones*" (1906, 333), Lerdahl's pitch-space (2001, 194), and Richard Cohn's view that "for an acculturated listener, a major or minor triad, sounded in isolation and without prior context, signals the tonic status of its root by default" (2012, 8). In light of these perspectives, Balestracci's chord-enveloping exhale provokes a reckoning. A hypothetical granular transcription of the opening *Adagio* would record the sounding notes of the G major triad occurring *within* Balestracci's exhalation. Cohn's argument tacitly assumes that an opening triad appears without the breath sound of the musician producing it. In the case of this Balestracci track, the opening triad does not "sound in isolation" at all. It has both "prior context" (the anacrustic inhale) and is itself swathed in a calming exhale. The commingling of the pardessus de viole, basso continuo, and Balestracci's audible respiration flag this triad as tonic, in part due to the expansive qualities of his breath, which radiates contentedness and sets a calming seal on the opening chord.

The *Allegro* second movement is preceded by a prolonged dominant that closes the first. While Balestracci and his cohort create a silence between movements, the second movement proper begins with a prominent breath sound leading into the *Allegro*'s G minor tonic. This inhale has two distinct pulses, cueing the trio to entrain into the new tempo. The pardessus de violist splits the pulse of his inhale into two parts whose timing matches the speed of the two eighth notes that follow. The third movement *Adagio* offers a variation on the inhale-exhale pair that was heard at the outset of the first. The difference here is a synchronization of the exhale to be precisely coincident with the opening triad. Whereas the first movement began with a sequence of three events—inhale, exhale, chord—the opening of the third movement has an inhale followed by a chord/exhale synthesis. The opening chord is composed of equal amounts of air and pitch. An inhale prepares the entrance of the closed-position G minor triad, which, when it arrives, is coated with the sound of Balestracci's exhale. The final movement's 3/8 Aria presents the most common type of audible breath in recorded music. Balestracci audibly inhales as an anacrusis, after which the trio of musicians attack the first chord. There is no audible exhale. Taking the four tracks together, Balestracci deploys downbeat exhales as atmospheric enhancements to the two slow movements and withholds audible exhales in the two faster ones.

Breath as expectation

It is delightful to arrive at a point in a piece of music when one fully expects something specific to happen. Such moments are ideal places for composers to deliver something else entirely. The *locus classicus* of such cleverness is the close of the last movement of Haydn's String Quartet in E-flat major, Op. 33, No. 2, "The Joke." It is a passage wherein several games are being played with tempo, topoi, and expectation. Gretchen Wheelock has written extensively about Haydn's manifold methods of creating humor in his chamber music. Her analyses repeatedly invoke the hypothetical experience of the work in the mind of both eighteenth-century performers (as readers of the score) and eighteenth-century listeners (as viewers and auditors of early performances), and her inquiry points up valuable distinctions between the two. Wheelock's work can be re-read and reconsidered by comparing her conclusions with a modern recording that includes prominent audible breath sounds: the 1996 recording of Op. 33, No. 2, by the Quatuor Mosaïques. The members of the quartet heard on this recording are Anita Mitterer, Andrea Bischof, Erich Höbarth, and Christophe Coin. Their recording was made in Kufstein, Austria, in 1995, engineered by Thomas Gallia.

The humor of the closing pages of the last movement Op. 33, No. 2, stems from Haydn's elaborate use of notated silence. The piece ends with the opening motive being isolated and repeated, with an altered phraseology that creates doubt and ambiguity, and which generates the intended amusing effect. Wheelock writes: "In this movement Haydn engages the listener in a game of second-guessing about when the piece will end and, in the event, whether in fact it has. His ploy is to offer progressively less stable conclusions—and in the end no conclusion at all" (1992, 5). Her reading opens avenues for our recognition of breath sounds by the Quatuor Mosaïques. Though Haydn's joke will ultimately occur at the close of the movement, it is set up by the opening phrases. Seen in Example 2.3, the opening eight measures are a picture of regular phrase rhythm. The example denotes the first two audible breaths on the Quatuor Mosaïques recording, which appear as anacruses to bars 1b and 9, respectively.

What is the role of audible breaths in the playing out of Haydn's clever jest? Example 2.4 presents the final *Presto* of the movement, transcribing the audible inhales that form a vivid component of the 1996 Quatuor Mosaïques track. There are five inhales within the passage, in mm. 152, 156, 160, 164, and

Example 2.3 Joseph Haydn, String Quartet in E-flat major, Op. 33, No. 2, "The Joke," last movement, mm. 1–8, annotating the first two audible inhales in the 1996 recording by the Quatuor Mosaïques. See ⓑ Audio Example 2.3.

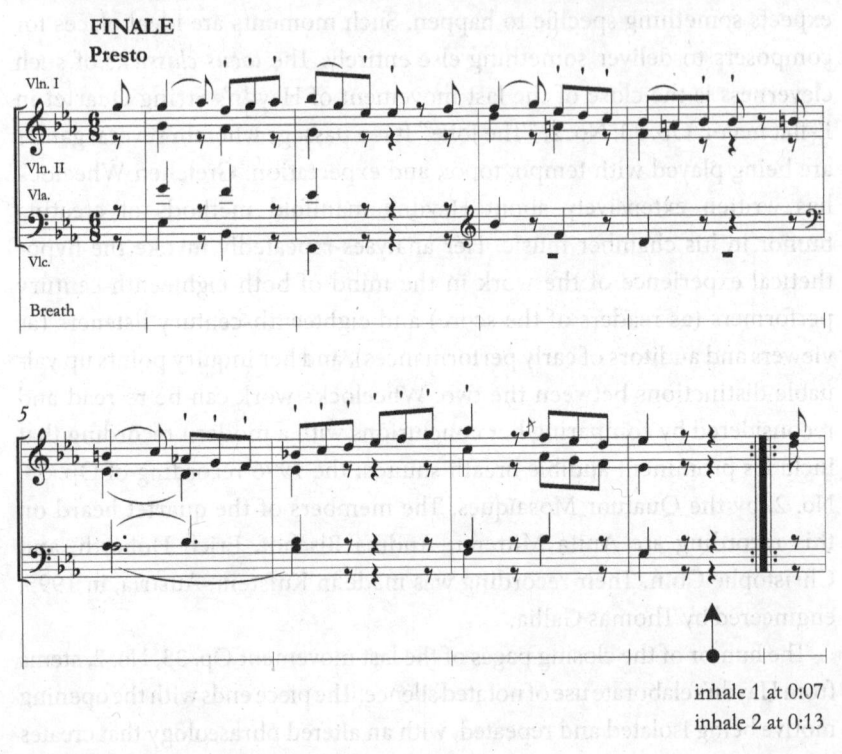

inhale 1 at 0:07
inhale 2 at 0:13

170. These breath sounds appear where one might expect: as anacruses to the two-measure fragments of the theme. Of particular interest is inhale 5, which precedes the final fragment, and "inhale 6" whose designation in quotes hints at the fact that it never arrives. Inhale 5 sets up the joke. The *Presto* has thus far created a pattern: inhale, two measures of music, two measures of silence, inhale, two measures of music, two measures of silence, and so on. This pattern is broken when Haydn extends the length of the silence in mm. 167–70. Wheelock's reading asserts that, during the silent m. 167, the listener is expectantly awaiting two measures of music. In the Quatuor Mosaïques recording, each of these two-measure fragments is anticipated by an audible inhale. Such inhales not only signal that the fragments are coming, they fuse with the fragments themselves.

Example 2.4 Joseph Haydn, String Quartet in E-flat major, Op. 33, No. 2, "The Joke," last movement, mm. 153–72, annotating a series of inhales in the 1996 recording by the Quatuor Mosaïques. See ⊙ Audio Example 2.4.

The close of the movement—if it can be said to have one—exemplifies the role of breath sounds in the creation of dramatic suspense. Haydn's notated drama extends past the double bar, where I have labeled "inhale 6." In an echo of the Goode/Beisembayev master class discussed earlier, breath sounds can impart drama via their absence as well as their presence. In the case of "The Joke," their consistent appearance before each phrase fragment makes their absence conspicuous. The role of audible inhales in the

Quatuor Mosaïques recording augments Haydn's attempt to compose non-finality. Placing us at the moment of the quartet's first reading, Wheelock writes:

> In a first reading of the quartet in 1782, four string players in private chambers might have been confounded before they were amused by the extended rests in their individual parts. (Perhaps they first blame an inattentive copyist, then question the attention of the other players. Ultimately, they might even be reminded that trust in one's partners is a first principle in playing chamber music.) Still, it is in playing the work before others that the joke finds its point. The standard notational convention of a final double bar confirms the end for the performers, but, "in play," the seeming denial of closure assumes auditors catching themselves in the act of listening. Here the ending that is defined by notational convention for the players, but suspended "indefinitely" for other listeners, provokes awareness of the various dialogues that engage listeners and players. Seen thus, Haydn's is a strategy of inclusion, one that invites his audience to become self-conscious participants in completing the jest. (Wheelock 1992, 8)

Such a marvelous exegesis of the psychological and aural ellipsis in Haydn's score can be extended to the activity of listening to the Quatuor Mosaïques recording. Wheelock's sense of the work in performance—her term is "in play"—leads her to feel that the "seeming denial of closure assumes auditors catching themselves in the act of listening." Listening for what? In the case of this recording, *listening for the inhale of breath that will prove that the work is not finished.*

Sometime after the final notes prescribed by Haydn's score are done ringing, the listener is searching for the next sound, a sound that—if it arrives at all—will begin not as notes sounded by string instruments, but by an inhale. To the credit of the Quatuor Mosaïques and their sound engineer Gallia, there is a full seven seconds of silence at the end of the track, long enough for the mind of the listener to remain in a state of suspense. Seeking an inhale that never comes, listeners become hyper-aware of their role as "self-conscious participants in completing the jest." Paying attention to the granular soundscape of the Quatuor Mosaïques recording, a listener awaits a breath sound and, in its absence, perceives (to borrow Wheelock's apt phrase) "no conclusion at all."

Breath within motive

Musicians sometimes embed an audible breath within a specific motive, thereby presenting the listener with a recurring pitch-plus-breath object. The implication of recognizing such objects as new motives is somewhat staggering. When one considers how much analytical literature is devoted to motivic transformation within scores, it is startling to think about the multiplicity of analytical possibilities created by the inclusion of body and breath sounds in the definition of new motives, ones that can undergo parallel or independent transformations. Consider the opening measures of Debussy's String Quartet in G minor, Op. 10. Example 2.5 compares the first four measures of the quartet alongside transcriptions of audible breath sounds in two recordings, one by the Quatuor Debussy, the other by the Harlem Quartet. The members of the Quatuor Debussy are Christophe Collette, Marc Viellefon, Vincent Deprecq, and Fabrice Bihan. Their track was recorded at Espace Monod in Vaulx-en-Velin, France, in December 2012 under the artistic supervision of Roger Germser, with the balance and editing by Christophe Germanique, and the recording was released in 2014 as Timpani 1C1207. The members of the Harlem Quartet heard on this recording are Ilmar Gavilán, Melissa White, Jaime Amador, and Felix Umansky. Their track was recorded in March 2019 at Oktaven Audio, New York, engineered by Ryan Streber, and was released in August 2020 on the album *Cross Pollination*.

Example 2.5 Claude Debussy, String Quartet in G minor, Op. 10, first movement, mm. 1–4, annotating the breath sounds in the 2014 recording by the Quatuor Debussy and the 2020 recording by the Harlem Quartet. See ⓟ Audio Example 2.5.

The Quatuor Debussy recording includes two audible inhales, the first of which subdivides the first beat of the first measure, the second of which divides the last two quarter notes of m. 2. The Harlem Quartet recording includes no breath sounds in these measures. The motivic implications of these breath sounds are significant. The lack of audible inhales during the second half of m. 1, beat 1, in the Harlem Quartet recording allows the opening G minor sonority to feel "held" (almost in suspense), finding release only in the half-diminished chord on beat 2. The fact that Debussy marks beat 2 with a down-bow highlights the rhythmic tension implied at the outset of his score, with the downbeat triad acting as a strange sort of upbeat (and up-bow) anacrusis to beat 2. By contrast, the prominent inhale in the Quatuor Debussy recording inserts itself emphatically *between* the two opening chords. The result punctures the rhythmic tension of the chord pair. Not only does the audible breath in the Quatuor Debussy recording sap a degree of energy from the held anticipation within beat 1, it also provides the listener with what will become—across the entire track—a *reliable* subdivision of this beat within this motive. The Quatuor Debussy's breath sound delivers important information about the meter before we even reach the second beat of the piece.

There is yet more sonic life within these two measures. While the Harlem Quartet remains breath-less during the second bar, the Quatuor Debussy recording includes a second inhale between beats 3 and 4 of m. 2. This inhale has rhythmic and motivic implications. Firstly, it rhymes with their breath in m. 1, as both inhales bisect gestures where the entire ensemble plays two consecutive quarter notes. Moreover, inhale 2 does something rather unexpected. Whereas inhale 1 stabilizes the meter, inhale 2 complicates and unsettles it. The location of inhale 1 shines a rhythmic light on the second beat of the bar, whereas inhale 2 shines a light on beat 4. The Quatuor Debussy's second inhale directs the ear to hear the last beat of m. 2 as—and *only* as—upbeat to m. 3, whereas the Harlem Quartet's lack of breath leaves open the notion that the last beat of m. 2 is the conclusion of the motive that began the piece.

Such comparisons are only the introduction to a deeper study of embedded breath sounds within (and as) motive. A single audible breath is not enough to globally redefine a motive. Redefinition requires repetition. When a pitch-plus-breath object is repeated, it creates a memorable event that can undergo development across an entire recording. Put another way, pitch-plus-breath motives can reappear *sans* breaths and the attentive listener will register the change. Along the way, sonic objects generate new layers of narrative possibility. We can judge what is added—and what is lost—when breath sounds become embedded within motives.

The iconic first measure of Debussy's Quartet—in which all four musicians articulate the principal motive—returns in an altered format sixteen times during the movement. Taken together, these seventeen ensemble iterations tell varied stories: harmonic, registral, notational, and durational.[6] Example 2.6 presents these seventeen iterations alongside the location of audible breath sounds in recordings by the Keller Quartet and the Alban Berg Quartet.[7] The members of the Keller Quartet heard on this recording are András Keller, János Pilz, Zoltán Gál, and Ottó Kertész. Their track was recorded at Salle de Musique de la Chaux de Fonds, Switzerland, in November 1993. It was released in 1994, engineered by Jacques Doll and produced by Martine Guers-Fernoux. The members of the Alban Berg Quartet heard on this recording are Gerhard Schulz, Günter Pichler, Thomas Kakuska, and Valentin Erben. Their track was recorded in April 1984 at the Ev. ref. Kirche, Seon, Switzerland, engineered by Johann-Nikolaus Matthes and produced by Gerd Berg, and released in 1986.

The Keller recording is breath-rich, while the Alban Berg recording is nearly breath-less. Comparing the two sheds light on the developmental life of a breath-inclusive motive. Continuing a sensibility that extends across this book, I limit value judgments about which interpretation I find preferable. Put another way, I am interested in both recordings and my exposition of their differences is not calibrated to produce a "winner," but simply to register the contrasting narratives created by the sounding corporeality of the Kellers as opposed to the relative quietude of the Bergs.

Example 2.6 synthesizes the journey of the opening motive across two complete recordings of the movement. The Keller Quartet embeds an audible breath during all seventeen iterations. In eleven cases—mm. 3, 4, 5, 26, 29, 30, 32, 33, 34, 141, and 142—the breath occurs between beats 1 and 2. Four other iterations—mm. 1, 36, 138, and 140—present the breath as an

---

[6] These presentations of the opening motive involve all four musicians annunciating the gesture simultaneously. They are distinct from appearances in a single voice, such as in m. 122, where the motive is played only by the violist. The only iterations that do not involve all four parts in rhythmic unison on beats 1 and 2 are mm. 3–4, where the upper three strings present the opening gesture over the cello's held G.

[7] The reader is invited to compare the complete recordings by the Keller Quartet (1994) and the Alban Berg Quartet (1986).

Example 2.6 The seventeen full-ensemble iterations of the opening motive in the first movement of Claude Debussy's String Quartet in G minor, Op. 10, annotating the breath sounds in the 1994 recording by the Keller Quartet and the 1986 recording by the Alban Berg Quartet.

anacrusis. In the remaining two appearances—mm. 28 and 75—the breath is coincident with the downbeat.

The unfolding of these breath-infused motives follows its own exposition-development-recapitulation pattern. Bars 3, 4, and 5 establish the breath as occurring between beats 1 and 2, a position reinforced by the same embedding in bars 26, 29, and 30. When the motive appears in bars 75, 138, and 140, the breath is either on or before the downbeat. It is both poetic and genuinely recapitulatory that the last two appearances of the motive—in bars 141 and 142—reinstate the breath to its normative, expository position between beats 1 and 2.

Compared to the Keller Quartet's regularly placed breaths, the Alban Berg Quartet's presentation of these same seventeen motives reads rather like a null set. Their entire movement is nearly without audible breath sounds.[8] Faint inhales can be heard in mm. 26, 28, 29, and 30, which are the only appearances of the motive played at a *piano* dynamic. The track does not capture breath sounds within the initial iterations of the motive. For all intents and purposes, the motive in the Alban Berg Quartet's recording is a *different sound object* from the one heard in the Keller recording. The interior suspense is not the same. The Keller's version of the motive is intertwined with inhales, the majority of which fill the space between beats 1 and 2 with a rapid suck of air. The Alban Berg Quartet's version of the motive maintains a suspenseful silence between the first two beats. It is not a question of wishing the Kellers were quiet or that the Bergs were breathy, but simply that there is a difference in what Peirce called "the total resultant Quality of Feeling" presented in these two tracks.

Breath as climax

Works that contain extended, effortful climaxes make significant physical demands on musicians. Anyone who has attended a performance of Iannis Xenakis's *Tetras* or Michael Finnissy's *The History of Photography in Sound* can attest that the act of performing complex music can leave musicians breathing heavily. An example of a just such a demanding, prolonged climax occurs in Edgard Varèse's *Density 21.5*. Analyses of the score have focused on its motivic plasticity (Kresky 1984), its rhythmic patterning (West Marvin 1991), and its semiological nature (Nattiez 1982). Candace Brower writes: "No twentieth-century work has inspired more metaphorical description than Edgard Varèse's *Density 21.5*" (1998, 35). The latest frontier

---

[8] An exception occurs at the very end of the movement, in bar 191, when an inhale is heard during the notated rests.

of theoretical attention paid to this iconic solo flute work includes a foundational study on expressive timing by Mitchell Ohriner (2019). Ohriner compared twenty recordings of the piece and provided insights into the varied duration of specific motives. He asks, "to what extent do performers agree on the relative lengths of events in the opening of the piece?" (2019, 384). Ohriner's analyses, however, do not classify breath sounds as events, and I am unaware of any published analysis of *Density 21.5* that grants musical "citizenship" to audible inhales, even as they appear in virtually every commercial recording of the work.[9]

Sarah Bassingthwaighte's 2006 recording of *Density 21.5* entangles the climactic phrase with a series of emphatic inhales. Bassingthwaighte's recording was made at the Brechemin Auditorium of the University of Washington's School of Music, engineered by Allen Goldstein and Stephen Bangs. Their recording exhibits a high degree of "fidelity of liveness." Reading the totality of this recording opens the possibility of re-reading Marion Guck's 1984 analysis, to see what her study and Bassingthwaighte's recording might say to one another. Guck's close reading of the linear and harmonic drama of *Density 21.5* acts as a resonating board for an understanding of the expressive rhythm in Bassingthwaighte's recording, one that is inclusive of her breath sounds.

The registral and structural highpoint of the score of *Density 21.5* begins when the flute reaches the high D7 in bar 46. Guck describes the energy of the passage in metaphorical terms:

The oscillation between B and D in measures 46–50/2 is the culmination of the piece. The energy absorbed by the soundstream in the first 28 measures and then alternately frantically released and reabsorbed is expended here in a final carving out of new registral space. Due to the time spent on this oscillation, which is the longest in the piece, there is a sense that the achievement of this extreme is also limiting—as if the stream is beating against the boundary set by the high D without being able to break it. This effect may be created by the relative durational emphasis of D and enhanced by the fortissimo, which creates the most raucous timbres in the piece. (Guck 1984, 344)

---

[9] Within the first fourteen measures of Varèse's *Density 21.5*, seven inhales are heard in the 1984 recording by Lawrence Beauregard (at 0:11, 0:21, 0:27, 0:33, 0:36, 0:43, and 0:48), five are heard in the 2013 recording by Claire Chase (at 0:11, 0:20, 0:25, 0:41, and 0:45), seven in the 2018 recording by Emmanuel Pahud (at 0:11, 0:20, 0:27, 0:32, 0:37, 0:43, and 0:47), and six in Chase's 2020 recording (at 0:11, 0:19, 0:25, 0:30, 0:41, and 0:45).

Example 2.7 Edgard Varèse, *Density 21.5*, mm. 46–50, annotating the duration, in milliseconds, of each pitch and inhale in the 2006 recording by Sarah Bassingthwaighte. See ⊙ Audio Example 2.6.

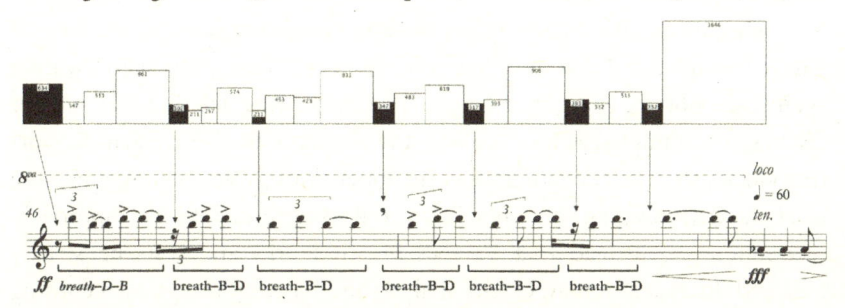

Example 2.7 presents a micro-temporal analysis of mm. 46–50 of Bassingthwaighte's recording, providing a score excerpt alongside a diagram illustrating the duration of the interonset intervals [IOI] between all audible events, including her seven inhales, which are shaded in black. The duration of each sound event can be judged both by the relative height of each square, and by the number inside each square, which tallies the IOI in milliseconds.

Bassingthwaighte's seven breaths isolate a rising B6–D7 motion as a motivic object, a construct that is by no means obvious in Varèse's score. On the page, Varèse's rests and notated breath marks suggest four segments: D–B–D (rest) / B–D–D–B–D–B (breath mark) / B–D–B–D (rest) / B–D–D. Bassingthwaighte's breaths generate something different: a segmentation into seven objects, five of which begin with the rising B–D shape: (breath) D–B–D / (breath) B–D–D / (breath) B–D–B / (breath) B–D / (breath) B–D / (breath) B–D / (breath) D. Bassingthwaighte's breaths highlight the rising B–D motive even at moments when Varèse's notation does not. Her effortful inhales provide an ideal rendering of Guck's characterization of the passage as the moment in which "the energy absorbed by the soundstream in the first 28 measures and then alternately frantically released and reabsorbed is expended here in a final carving out of new registral space." Bassingthwaighte's breaths physicalize and dramatize the attainment of the D7, making known not only the effort required for the *flutist* to make those sounds at that moment, but the effort that the *piece* has demonstrated in its iconic ascent to the climax.[10] A standard microtiming analysis of this

---

[10] The immediate after-effect of this climactic D7 is a precipitous fall to A♭4, calling to mind the climax and aftermath of the *Andante* from Ruth Crawford Seeger's String Quartet (1931), which Daniel M. Grimley narrativizes: "The climax at the apex of Seeger's Andante might appear

climactic area would measure IOIs between pitches. Such an approach would not properly account for the role of audible breaths as one of the recording's integral expressive elements.

Bassingthwaighte's recording generates an arresting sonic illustration of Guck's metaphorical description of mm. 46–50 as the soundstream "beating against the boundary set by the high D without being able to break it." Her inhales, intermingled as they are with the climactic B6–D7 oscillation, portray Guck's story of the line finding its upper limit. I can well imagine flute teachers discouraging students from a Bassingthwaighte-like approach, recommending instead that Varèse's breath marks and rests be strictly followed. Be that as it may, Guck's analysis and Bassingthwaighte's recording sing to one another. The flutist's prominent inhales sonically corporealize Guck's metaphoric reading of Varèse's score. Paying attention to unwritten music allows a theorist to investigate sounds as they are, without policing them against the scores that they animate. Unwritten music redefines the very object commonly understood to be under analysis.

Breath as phrase marker

Kim Kashkashian's 2018 recording of J. S. Bach's Six Cello Suites, BWV 1007–1012, in a transcription for viola—first glimpsed in Chapter 1— exemplifies the impact of audible breaths on phrase rhythm. Her recording invites what Olivier Senn, Lorenz Kilchenmann, and Marc-Antoine Camp have called an "inverse interpretation," wherein "performance analysis can study the characteristics of a performance in order to discover those structural features of the composition which are highlighted in the interpretation" (2012, 31).[11] Following their example, I will not seek to unveil insights into Bach's work generated by Kashkashian's breathing—such a stance would reinforce the unwelcome hierarchy which places the composer "over and

---

to be a negative point of formal articulation—a sudden inability to speak or maintain coherence, a gesture of frustration or rage. But it might also be heard as a site of liberation, the moment at which the movement's form breaks down and uncovers a new set of potentialities, one that could permit the emergence of a different register or voice" (2019, 363). In the context of the climax in Bassingthwaighte's Density 21.5 recording, the inhales permit the emergence of the flutist's breath as a new, prominent "voice."

[11] Senn, Kilchenmann, and Camp carefully define the parameters of their methodology, writing: "it must be emphasized that inverse interpretation never claims to reconstruct the intentions or thoughts of a performer. Rather, it tries to argue, from an observer's perspective, why a performance makes sense with respect to the score" (2009, 108).

above" the performer—but instead recognize the recording as a creative *interaction* between composer and performer. In case there is any doubt about Kashkashian's belief in both the act of breathing and its sonic capacity, consider her advice to violist Yu-Ting Hsu in a recorded master class on the Sarabande from BWV 1012: "If you were to watch a wind player, you would see that they have to breathe—it's part of the music. I believe a string player should also breathe" (Niles 2019).

David Ledbetter begins his analysis of the C minor Gigue with a frank pronouncement: "This movement has caused some puzzlement" (2009, 226). His bemusement extends to other scholars, as there seems to be little agreement about the phrasing of this movement. Ledbetter suggests that the opening twenty-four bars are a single unbroken phrase. Rowland Moseley (2018, 87) reads the first period as comprising *six four-bar unit counts* that begin at mm. 1, 5, 9, 13, 17, and 21. Moseley's groupings superficially concur with the analysis by Meredith Little and Natalie Jenne, who write that "in spite of the imbalances introduced in this piece, the underlying harmony is that of eight-measure phrases" (2009, 152). The score of mm. 1–24 of the Gigue is seen in Example 2.8, alongside Moseley's six four-bar unit counts.

From the perspective of phrasing, Kashkashian's 2018 recording tells a different story, one in which Bach's notes (there are no notated rests in this movement) are interwoven with a series of audible inhales. Whatever Kashkashian

Example 2.8 J. S. Bach, Gigue from Cello Suite in C minor, BWV 1011, mm. 1–24, transcribed for viola, noting the six four-bar unit counts described in Moseley (2018).

herself might think of theories regarding the phraseology of this gigue, her recording—inclusive of its unwritten music—contradicts Ledbetter, Moseley, and Little and Jenne. In discussing the difference between scholarly and performance-related notions of phrase, I am amplifying a distinction drawn by Janet Schmalfeldt: "Moreover, for scholars of a broad range of musical styles, the concept of phrase is inextricably bound to ideas about musical grammar, syntax, cadence, accent, rhythm, meter, and form. By contrast, performers—music-makers of any status, amateur or professional—are centrally concerned with *phrasing*, the expressive and dynamic act of shaping 'phrases'" (2019, 295–96, italics in original). A study of Kashkashian's audible breaths only heightens Schmalfeldt's distinction.

To gauge just how interruptive Kashkashian's audible breaths are, it will be useful to take a close look at one of them. Example 2.9 charts the duration of each measure in mm. 1b–10b (Kashkashian's second pass through the opening period, between 0:23 and 0:34 of her 2018 recording). Bar 7 lasts 1,359 milliseconds, whereas the average measure duration in the surrounding measures (mm 1–6 and mm. 8–10) is 950 milliseconds. As such, bar 7 is 43 percent longer than the average bar length in the rest of the passage. The reason for the extended duration of this measure is Kashkashian's prominent inhale after the G3, which creates something quite different from the music seen in, or implied by, Bach's score. At the moment one expects the beginning of bar 8, one hears instead an inhale whose length contributes to a sense of conclusion. The effect is neither slight nor subtle. As seen in the square notation above the staff, which represents the duration of each

Example 2.9 J. S. Bach, Gigue from Cello Suite in C minor, BWV 1011, mm. 1b–10b, slurs removed, annotating the interonset interval (in milliseconds) between each downbeat in the 2018 recording by Kim Kashkashian. See ⏵ Audio Example 2.7.

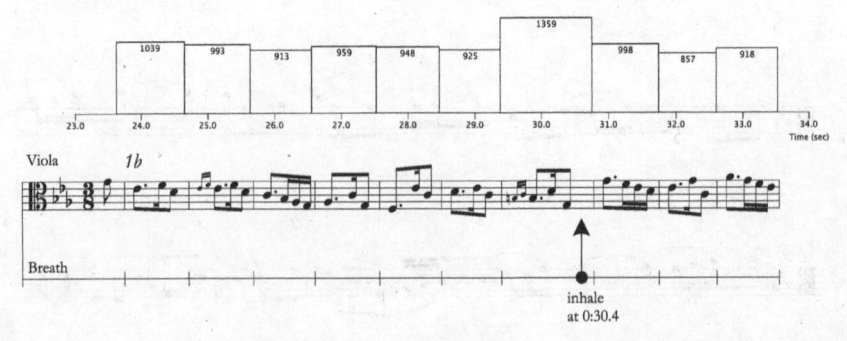

measure, Kashkashian's inhale makes bar 7 longer than any other in the phrase. When bar 8 finally does arrive, the music sounds less like a conclusion to the opening phrase than as a new beginning whose arrival has been delayed by a breath. Kashkashian does not inhale at this moment during her first time through the form, though she does insert a substantial pause, suggesting that she feels this measure naturally deserves extension. Her emphatic inhale during the second pass, at 0:30.4, produces a breath that has an ornamental, even interruptive function. It is, to my ear, a moment of energetic sonic storytelling, all the more because it cross-cuts—and powerfully contradicts—Moseley's "four-bar unit counts" and Little and Jenne's "eight measure phrases."

Having made plain the rhythmic impact of Kashkashian's breaths, we can register their role in the overall phrase rhythm of the passage. The first period of the Gigue from BWV 1011 spans twenty-four measures. Kashkashian's recording generates enormous tension between the harmony and phrase rhythm. Two points must be made about Kashkashian's inhales in this opening strain. First, they have a rapid, expectant quality, as though the sound of her breath is a smokescreen out of which the subsequent note emerges. Second, her breaths are both longer and more prominent on the repeat than they are on the first time through the strain. Since she also adds grace notes during her repeat, the character of her inhales opens a category of breaths-as-ornament.

Moving to the whole of the first period, we can appreciate the formal groupings created by Kashkashian's breaths. Example 2.10 transcribes 0:23–0:46, representing the repeat of the first period. The breath sounds after m. 7b, m. 11b, and m. 14b imply an irregular phrase rhythm, which is labeled in the example. The phrase structure is at odds with any feeling of four- or eight-bar phrases. Instead, the groupings reveal her sensitivity to motive as a generative phrase initiator. Inhale 1 sets off mm. 8b–11b as a "four-bar unit count" (to be sure, one that contradicts the placement of Moseley's). Inhale 2 rhymes with that of inhale 1 and reinforces the role of bar 15 as the beginning of a new motivic group. Inhale 3 sets off m. 15b as a strong agogic accent and moment of both tonal and metric arrival, and the absence of an audible breath before bar 17b supports its interior repetition of the rhythm of bar 16b as a recursion. Inhales 4 and 5, respectively, generate a motivic parallelism that creates two *three-bar* counts in mm. 15b–17b and mm. 18b–20b. Little and Jenne refer to these six bars as "a set of two triple 'mega-measures' in which the 'sautillant' figure seems transported to the measure level" (2009, 152).

Example 2.10 Transcription of 0:23–0:46 of Kim Kashkashian's 2018 recording of J. S. Bach's Gigue from Cello Suite in C minor, BWV 1011, mm. 1b–24b, slurs removed, annotating the location of her six inhales and their impact on meter and phrase rhythm. See ▶ Audio Example 2.8.

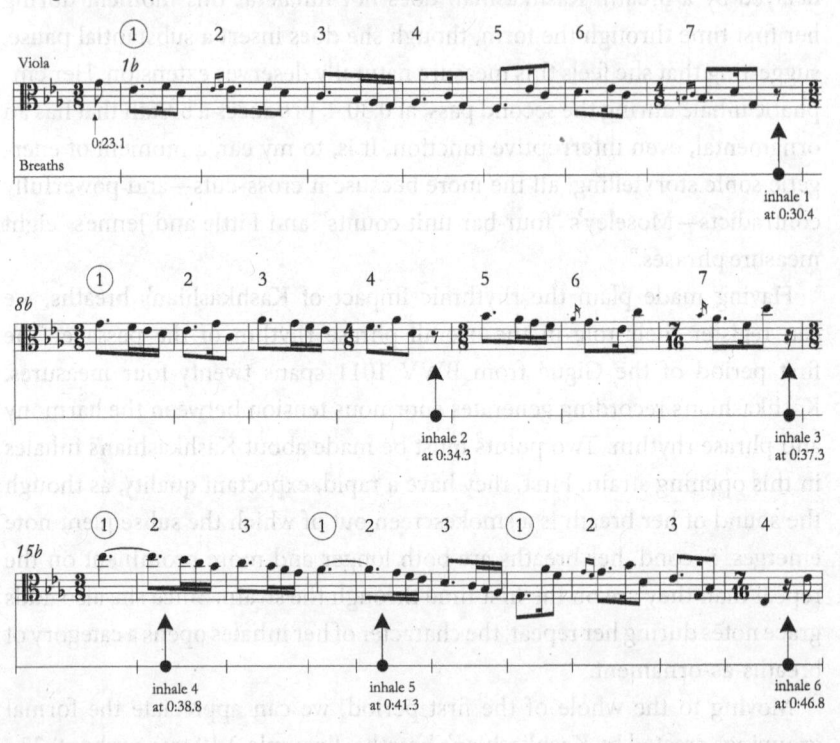

Inhales 4 and 5 concur with Little and Jenne's notion of "two triple mega-measures," as Kashkashian's breaths both reinforce and illuminate the pair of three-bar groups that highlight Bach's sequence of descending thirds across the six-bar phrase.

The contrast between score and recording is stark. According to Moseley's score analysis, bar 17 initializes a new unit count. According to Kashkashian's recording, this same measure is *the weakest metrical event in the entire period*, representing the last unit in a series of two three-bar groupings. The final inhale in the passage—inhale 6—reinforces the cadence and clears the air before the violist sets off into the second section of the gigue.

The totality of sounds in Kashkashian's recording work together to create a decidedly unique narration of Bach's decidedly unique gigue. The preceding analysis is not meant to present an irreconcilable rift between Kashkashian's recording and published analyses of Bach's score. It is not a question of who gets it wrong or who gets it right. Two truths emerge: (1) the phrase groupings generated by the interaction between notes and breaths might never have occurred to a theorist who was only studying Bach's score, and (2) Kashkashian's emphatic inhales in mm. 1b–24b illustrate that repeated sections offer an opportunity for her not only to insert ornamental *melodic* figures, but to embellish the passage with her *breath*. Kashkashian's recording beautifully problematizes the implied regularity of Bach's score. Moseley read the opening twenty-four measures of Bach's score as an 8 + 8 + 8 grouping. Kashkashian's recording, inclusive of her inhale location, suggests 7 + 7 + 3 + 3 + 4. Her unwritten music creates irregularity in a passage that, in the leaf, looked to be regular.

I would encourage the reader to compare Kashkashian's recording with other recordings of the Gigue from BWV 1011. They will likely find no other musician who approximates the breath placement and overall timing of Kashkashian's repeat of the first period. This study is not enacted to call out Kashkashian for producing a meter-distending inhale only to compare it to another, less breath-infused recording in an effort to prove which interpreter is more Bachian, more "musical" or "better." On the contrary, this breath-inclusive analysis is intended to recognize and emphasize the expressive rhythm of all the sounds on her recording, even those which are neither present in, nor implied by, Bach's notation. Kashkashian's breaths are unpredictable to the theorist accustomed to analyzing Bach's score. Her inhales remind us of the myriad interpretations generated by this kaleidoscopically fascinating gigue, and one might smilingly characterize her respiratory ornamentation as "breathtaking."

Breath as narration

In my experience, performing musicians are more attuned to the presence and location of breath sounds than are theorists. Speaking in a 1961 audio interview with Arnold Michaelis, Bruno Walter alludes to both the expressive and *pedagogical* aspects of audible breath sounds. The subject of their conversation is the fact that Walter's life—he was born in 1876—spanned the birth of sound recordings:

Michaelis: Well, it's particularly significant that you do live in this era, the electronic age. If you had lived a few generations back, we wouldn't have the benefit of the many recordings that you've conducted.

Walter: No, this is, I am really very happy about this idea that the *disappearance* of all the traces of our lives as performing musicians is not any more to be feared. That we really, in some sense, can live on with our best efforts. I imagine it began with the records of Caruso, for instance, which have preserved the beauty of his voice for coming singers, who can study his voice production, and see how he sang on this vowel and attacked this phrase—where he took his breath—and all these things. So, it's a kind of school, even. (Walter 1962/1994, 0:18)

I consider myself a student in the "school" that Walter describes. Paying attention to the interaction between phrasing and breath sounds is an education not only for singers, but for the field of music theory writ large.

Upon first consideration, it might seem that breath sounds play a categorically different role in recordings of vocal music than instrumental music. In the context of this study, the difference is minimal, perhaps even nonexistent. Singers' breaths are functionally and musically equivalent to those taken by wind players. Having categorized both inhales and exhales in terms of rhetoric, anticipation, expectation, motive, climax, and phrase rhythm, I turn now to address the accumulation of narrative meaning across an entire recorded track. My final example involves a decidedly subtle sound: a single, audible breath taken by Dashon Burton two and a half minutes into his recording of the song sermon "He Never Said a Mumberlin' Word," which appears on his 2015 album *Songs of Struggle and Redemption: We Shall Overcome*.[12] Tammy L. Kernodle designates the spiritual as a "praxis of Black postmodernism" and makes clear that personalized versions of spirituals—such as found in the oeuvres of Undine Smith Moore and Margaret Bonds—"served as the core part of Black concert artists' repertoire for decades" (2020, 774). My emphasis on the micro-temporal listening experience represents an intentionally slowed-down documentation of Burton's singing, his breathing, and the interaction between the two. It is less a matter of interaction than of integration. His breathing *is* his singing.

---

[12] The designation of "He Never Said a Mumberlin' Word" as a song sermon is given in Roland Hayes (1948, 121). Burton acknowledged that this categorization also applies to his own version (personal correspondence, July 2, 2020).

Burton recorded "He Never Said a Mumberlin' Word" on the stage of the Concert Hall at Drew University in Madison, New Jersey, on August 22, 2013. According to Burton's sound engineer, Loren Stata, the singer was standing stage left, with a piano to his right. The piano was not used on this track but remained in place, as the session mainly involved Burton performing with pianist Nathaniel Gumbs. Burton's voice was preserved by a set of six microphones: a pair of Milab DC-196 microphones (set to cardioid) were placed about a foot behind his music stand; for the main room sound, a pair of Schoeps Mk2S microphones were spread three feet from one another on a high stand behind him; finally, alternate room sound was captured via an AEA r88 stereo Blumlein ribbon microphone placed at center stage. Stata edited the audio using the sound engineering software Magix Sequoia 12, whose "Spectral Cleaning" function was discussed in Chapter 1. While Stata reports using the software to alter the audibility of certain breaths, each remains audible, some vividly so.

It is necessary to clarify the lyrics of "He Never Said a Mumberlin' Word" as sung by Burton on this track, as they differ from the liner notes that accompany Burton's disc.[13] Below is a transcription of the lyrics as Burton recorded them. I have kept editorial punctuation to a minimum to stay as close as possible to the sung text:

> Wasn't it a pity and a shame
> And he never said a mumberlin' word
> Wasn't a pity and a shame
> And he never said a mumberlin' word
> O not a word, not a word, not a word
>
> They nailed him to the tree
> And he never said a mumberlin' word
> They nailed him to the tree
> And he never said a mumberlin' word
> O not a word, not a word, not a word

---

[13] The liner notes in Burton's disc reproduce the lyrics as they appear in Roland Hayes's 1948 arrangement, and Hayes's score was one of the sources for Burton's version. Prior to Burton's version, arrangements of the work were published by J. Rosamond Johnson (1925), William Arms Fischer (1926), and John W. Work (1940). Johnson's arrangement, titled "Crucifixion," appears in James Wheldon Johnson and J. Rosamond Johnson (1925, 174–76) and is dedicated to Roland Hayes. Fischer's arrangement, titled "The Crucifixion (He Never Said a Mumbelin' Word)," appears in William Arms Fischer (1926, 1–3). Work's arrangement, titled "He Never Said a Mumblin' Word," appears in John W. Work (1940, 103).

> They pierced him in the side
> And he never said a mumberlin' word
> They pierced him in the side
> And he never said a mumberlin' word
> O not a word, not a word, not a word
>
> The blood came a-twinkalin' down
> And he never said a mumberlin' word
> The blood came a-twinkalin' down
> And he never said a mumberlin' word
> O not a word, not a word, not a word
>
> He bowed his head and died
> And he never said a mumberlin' word
> He bowed his head and died
> And he never said a mumberlin' word
> O not a word, not a word, not a word

The poetic form of these twenty-five lines is structured around a series of intensifying events, each of which is answered by resolute, meaningful muteness. Purposefully leaving aside the religious connotation of the song, the actions of the five stanzas relate the story of a man being killed, and the first lines of each stanza present the death scene as a series of five related, escalating actions: (1) feeling; (2) nailing; (3) piercing; (4) bleeding; and (5) bowing/dying. These stages summarize the narrative trajectory, whose developing story of torture and death is answered at every turn by a powerful non-action: the steadfast silence of the dying man. The poetic form of the lyric draws its power from the tension between an intensifying arc of violence and the dying man's nonviolent stoicism. The pronouns in each stanza draw a narrative trajectory that plays out across Burton's performance. Taken as a whole, the lyric posits four agents: the narrator, those listening to the narrator, the killers, and the man being killed. These four groups—narrator, listeners, killers, and killed—are invoked differently across the five stanzas. Stanza 1 includes no pronouns; it simply states that the scene is, unequivocally, "a pity and a shame." Stanzas 2 and 3 shift the focus to the killers themselves. The plural pronoun "they" that begins stanza 2 instantiates the existence of both the violent actors and the narrator-as-onlooker. The narrator stands separate from the violent acts and reports them. The opening line of stanza 4 withdraws again from pronouns and centers on the body of

Example 2.11 Duration, in milliseconds, of the five stanzas in Dashon Burton's 2015 recording of "He Never Said a Mumberlin' Word."

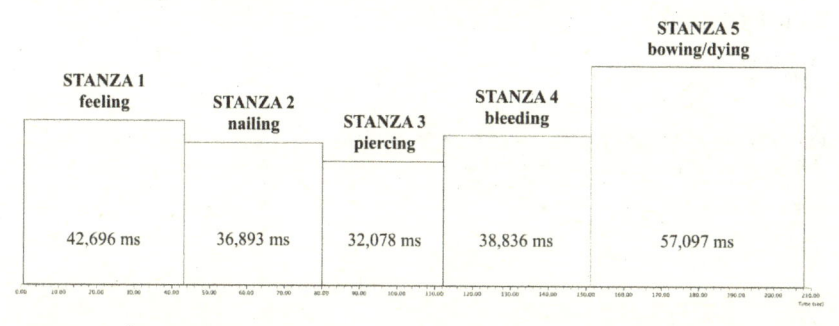

the dying man. The "twinkalin'" of the blood is described factually, recalling the earlier "pity" and "shame." Stanza 5 ("He bowed his head and died") culminates the lyric and focuses the gaze. It demonstrates the outcome of the preceding violence: nailing, piercing, and bleeding have brought about dying.[14] This final stanza also resolves the pronoun conflict that has marked those before it. Stanza 5 refers neither to the killers ("they"), nor to the listeners, nor to the narrator; the entire drama converges on the man who is dying and, by the end, has died.

As Burton sings a nearly identical melody across all five stanzas, the drama of his version is primarily rhythmic and durational. Melodically, Burton's rendition has no single climactic highpoint. The uppermost note of the melody—C4—is heard repeatedly and regularly in the first and third lines of each stanza. The drama therefore occurs not in some long-term ascent to a heroic climax, but in the rhythmic proportions and tempo of his delivery. Rhythmically, Burton presents fluctuating durations within and between each individual line. Befitting Roland Hayes's characterization of this work as a song sermon, Burton's rhythmic fluidity renders any attempt to locate stable tempi neither useful nor possible. In place of pulsing metric regularity, Burton's singing presents narrative irregularity. Taking the stanza as the largest structural unit, Example 2.11 illustrates the comparative length of each verse. The duration of each stanza is represented by the size of its square and noted numerically, in milliseconds, within that square. Burton's control of the pacing creates a natural curve. The narration accelerates from stanza 1 (*feeling*) through stanza 2 (*nailing*), finding

---

[14] For further historical context for the composition and meaning of "He Never Said a Mumberlin' Word," see Robert Darden (2014, 41–42) and Richard Beaudoin (2022).

Example 2.12 Transcription of the pitches, lyrics, and thirty-five inhales in Dashon Burton's 2015 recording of "He Never Said a Mumberlin' Word." See ⏵ Audio Example 2.9.

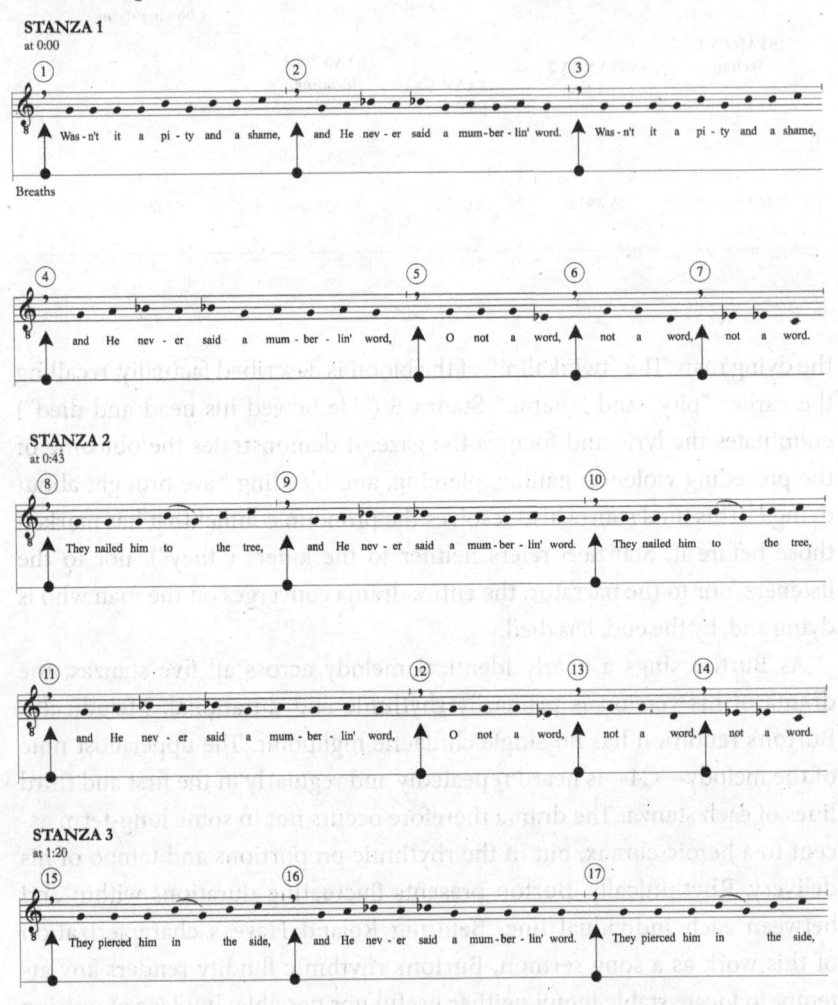

its apex in the relatively brief stanza 3 (*piercing*). From there, a deceleration begins in stanza 4 (*bleeding*) and finds a final calm in stanza 5 (*bowing/dying*), the longest stanza of all. Burton's pacing tells the story. The most violent verb—*piercing*—is associated with the fastest delivery of the melody in stanza 3, while the most expansive declaration—*died*—is saved for the final stanza's implication of eternity.

Moving from stanzas to individual lines, Example 2.12 presents a specialized transcription of the lyrics, pitches, and breath sounds across the entirety

Example 2.12 Continued

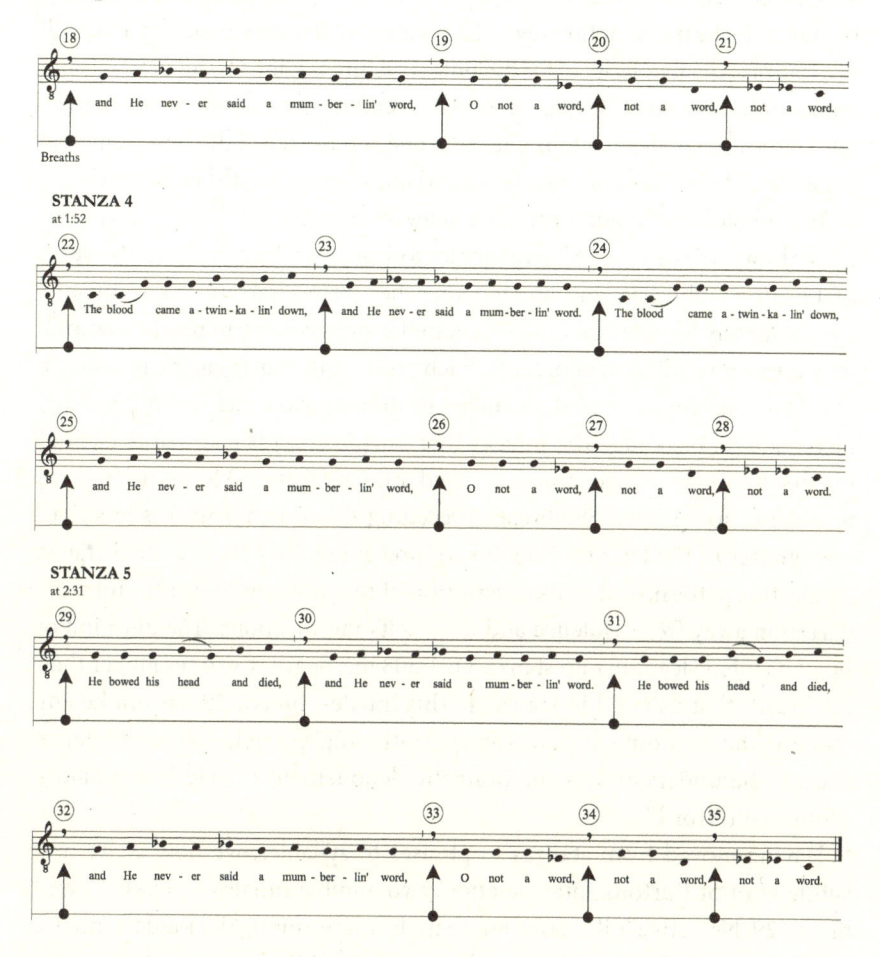

of Burton's recording.[15] The melodies in each stanza are nearly identical and allow Burton's song sermon to gain narrative and dramatic momentum atop a repeating melodic structure. Each breath sound is notated and numbered. I count thirty-five audible inhalations during the track. Some are more vivid than others, but each one can be identified by ear. Admittedly unorthodox within music studies, the act of counting breaths both respects and celebrates Burton's sounds *as they are*. I have no interest in raising the expressive level of these thirty-five inhalations above those of his sung melodies; however, I am

[15] Audio Example 2.9 presents the opening of Burton's recording. Readers are invited to audit the complete track on *Songs of Struggle and Redemption: We Shall Overcome* (Burton 2015).

also not content to ignore them. They are part of his recording and deserve to be counted. The transcription reveals the pattern of Burton's breathing across all five stanzas. The regularity of his melodic structure is joined by an exacting and regular inhale pattern. Burton takes seven audible inhales within each stanza, one before each of the first four lines, and one before each of the three cadential iterations: "[breath] O not a word, [breath] not a word, [breath] not a word."

The inhales that inaugurate each stanza—breaths 1, 8, 15, 22, and 29—track the arc of the lyric. All five inhales foreshadow the content of the verse that Burton is about to sing, and together they form a narrative. Such breaths are not merely ways for the singer to gain the air necessary to produce sound, they create an audible corporeality. Each pre-breath stanza can be measured. The first four verses record an intensification of violence: feeling, nailing, piercing, and bleeding. The inhales that Burton sounds just before each of the first four stanzas become more rapid, moving from 1,320 ms, to 978 ms, to 712 ms, to 305 ms. The breath preceding the fourth stanza is less than one quarter of the length of the breath preceding the first. The final stanza breaks this pattern, and in its description of the moment of death, shifts the narration away from violence and toward its ramifications. The duration of Burton's inhale leading into stanza 5 is 1,508 ms, nearly six times longer than the breath that ushered in stanza 4. This inhale—breath 29—is unlike any other on the recording. It stands as a narrative highpoint in the performance and can be understood as the dramatic denouement of "He Never Said a Mumberlin' Word."

Having moved from stanzas to phrases to syllables, we now arrive at a subtle level of Burton's interpretation: two audible inhales—breath 15 and breath 29. Narrative foils of one another, these are among the loudest inhales on the track. In their own way, each embeds itself in the poetic diction and narrative unfolding. I will call breath 15, which immediately precedes the violence of stanza 3, the *ujjayi* breath, and breath 29, which precedes the final stanza, the solemnizing breath. Both moments are the expressive highpoints not only of Burton's breathing sounds, but of his entire recording. These two breaths—like two contrasting chords in a piece of piano music—have *functional* differences related to their spectral content. Likewise, each inaugurates a contrasting aspect of Burton's narrative pacing. The first initiates a rapid acceleration, the second signals the death scene.

Breath 15 is the amongst the loudest and most sonically complex on the track. Occurring at 1:20 and inaugurating stanza three ("They pierced him in the side"), it represents a continued escalation of violence and forms the

Example 2.13 Annotated spectrogram of 1:18–1:23 of Dashon Burton's 2015 recording of "He Never Said a Mumberlin' Word," highlighting breath 15 in the oval. See ⏵ Audio Example 2.10.

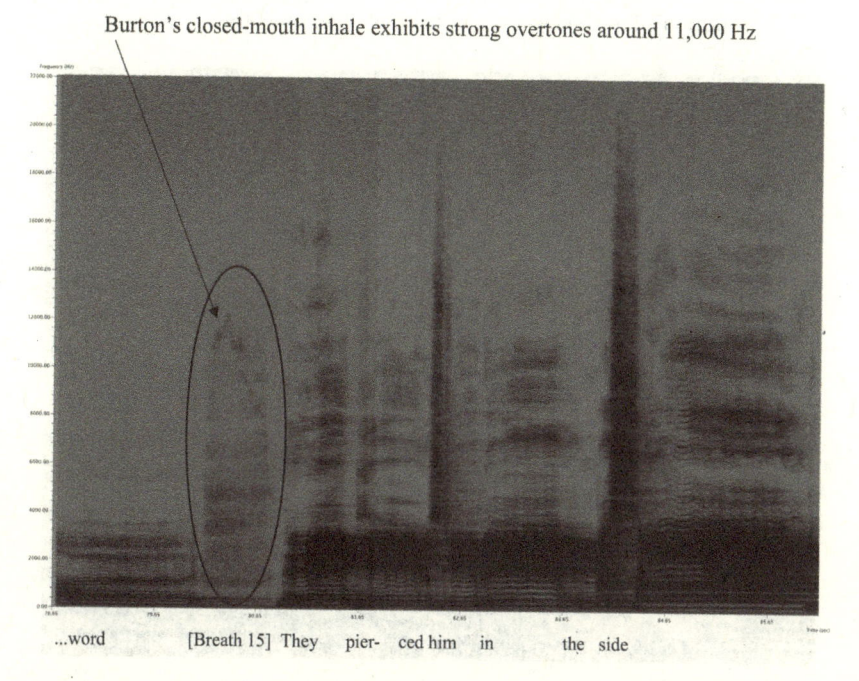

Burton's closed-mouth inhale exhibits strong overtones around 11,000 Hz

...word   [Breath 15] They   pier-   ced him   in   the side

centerpiece of the feeling-nailing-piercing-bleeding-bowing/dying trajectory. Example 2.13 displays this breath's spectrographic trace, showing time (in seconds, on the x-axis) and frequency (in hertz, on the y-axis). For those unaccustomed to reading spectrograms, lyrics are provided for orientation. Unlike all other breaths on the track, breath 15 exhibits higher energy in its upper register, which can be seen in the darker, curving line around 11,000 Hz. Burton's breath here is quicker than any of the other pre-stanza breaths, and a single listen reveals its signature feature: the glottis is tightened as Burton takes this breath through his nose. The resulting sound is related to the *ujjayi* breath (Saraswati 1994, 167). Colloquially called "the ocean breath," this term can refer to an inhalation taken through the nose whose distinctive sound results from a narrowing of the glottis. Recalling Kimberly Bain's description of Rashida Bumbray, Burton's fifteenth breath makes audible the "heavy emotional toll required to perform" a work with such violent content. This breath contains the shock and unease portrayed in the subsequent lyric: "They pierced

Example 2.14 Annotated spectrogram of 2:29–2:41 of Dashon Burton's 2015 recording of "He Never Said a Mumberlin' Word," highlighting breath 29 in the oval. See ⊙ Audio Example 2.11.

Burton's long inhale includes delicate mouth sounds

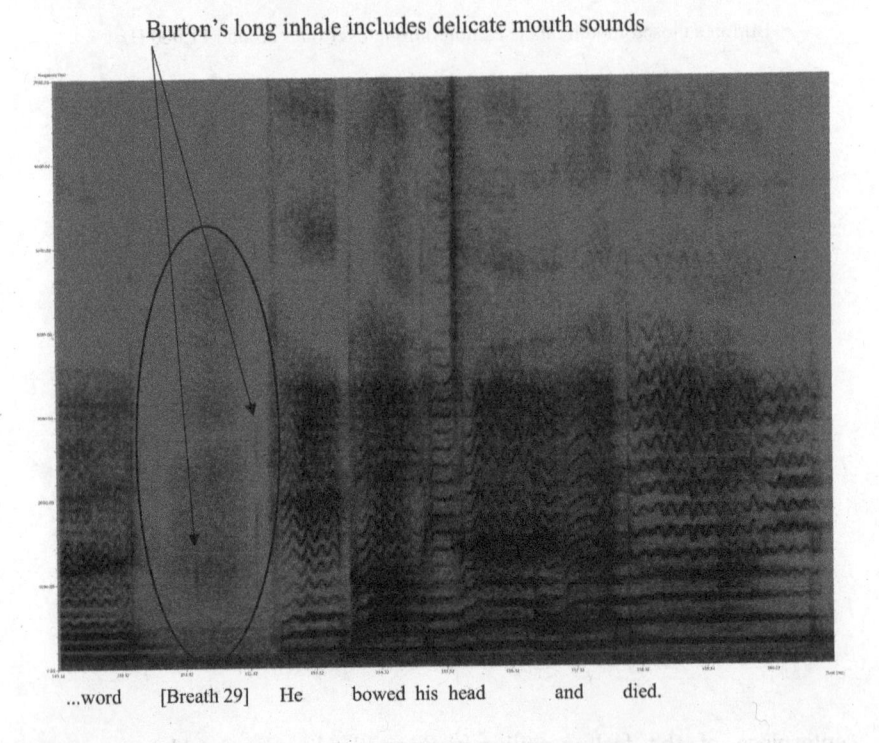

...word   [Breath 29]   He   bowed his head   and   died.

him in the side." Listening to breath 15, we anticipate the pain of what Burton is about to sing, and this breath reveals an anguish all its own.

Breath 29 is the dramatic foil to the rich spectral fingerprint and quick pacing of breath 15. Occurring at 2:31 and inaugurating stanza 5 ("He bowed his head and died"), breath 29 acts as a narrative highpoint in the recording. Example 2.14 provides a spectrographic picture of this breath in context. Burton's inhale sets a seal over the entire song sermon. It is a knowing, solemnizing breath.[16] The act of solemnizing confers dignity. It marks an earnest sobriety—a kind of wise awareness—and a sublime, awe-inspiring nobility. This lengthy inhalation becomes a signal event in the recording.

---

[16] "Solemnizing breath" appears in Felicia Hemans's nineteenth-century poem "The Ruin," where it is used to describe the sound of wind passing through a ruined architectural structure: "Thou bindest me with mighty spells!— / A solemnizing breath, / A presence all around thee dwells, / Of human life and death" (1836, 287).

Unlike the effortful breath 15, breath 29 turns the narrative away from the violent world of the killers ("they") and toward the intimate, interior death scene of the dying man ("he"). Though not loud, breath 29 is vividly audible, and when it is acknowledged as an integral part of the music—when it is counted—it acts as a pivotal moment of audition and understanding.

The expressive quality of breath 29 is enhanced by the fact that Burton inhales, and then audibly *stops* inhaling, before singing his next note. The hesitation creates a small but meaningful gap between the breath and the "He" that opens stanza 5. Burton's pause recalls a pointed sentence from Li Ang's novella *The Butcher's Wife*: "Many a pair of curious ears had been lured by that well-timed pause" (1986, 37). Burton's cessation of breath is indeed suspenseful and marked by subtle, intimate mouth sounds. These small but expressive sounds provide traces of his corporeality. Indeed, this is a cinematic moment in Burton's recording. *If the recording were stopped after breath 29, the listener would still have a sense of the content of the final stanza.* In the small interstitial moment between the completion of this breath and the beginning of stanza 5, even a first-time listener knows that Burton's song sermon has reached its moment of reckoning.

Although both breath 15 and breath 29 can be classified physiologically as inhales, their spectral content sets them apart as entirely different sound objects. Comparing the respective ovals in Examples 2.13 and 2.14, the rapid air flow and narrowed glottis of breath 15 generates sonic activity as high as 12,000 Hz, whereas the slower air flow and more relaxed glottis of breath 29 generates activity only up to 5,000 Hz. The intense inhale that marks the impending violence of breath 15 ("They pierced him in the side") is pure air sound, whereas the solemnizing breath 29 ("He bowed his head and died") is infused with the delicate sounds of Burton's mouth, specifically his tongue releasing from the teeth and his lips parting. An inclusive analysis of Burton's recording—one which traces the interaction between his sung melodies, his interstitial breaths, and his subtle mouth sounds—allows the narrative totality of the track to speak. Failing to acknowledge the presence of Burton's breath is to miss a significant portion of his singing.

The preceding survey categorized the function of breath sounds within varied musical contexts. Inhales and exhales were codified as disruptors of rhetorical "blank places" in Goode's lesson on Beethoven, as anacruses to the four movements of Balestracci's recording of Barrière, as signals of clever non-closure in the Quatuor Mosaïques reading of Haydn, as integral elements of motive in recordings of Debussy's String Quartet by the Debussy, Harlem, Keller, and Alban Berg Quartets, as demonstrations of effortful climax in Bassingthwaighte's performance of Varèse, as phrase-altering ornaments in Kashkashian's recording of Bach, and finally as markers of narrative arc in Burton's unaccompanied song sermon. As this chapter concludes, I invite the reader to revisit their own beloved recordings with an ear toward the existence, rhythmic placement, and expressive capabilities of audible breath sounds. Examples will appear; they will likely abound.

3

Sounds of Touch

Touch sounds as music

I encourage the reader, if they are able, to tap their middle finger on a table. That is one example of a touch sound. There are countless others, including the squeak made by a guitarist's shifting hand or a pianist's foot engaging the damper pedal. Ears and microphones are adept at capturing these often-subtle sounds, preserving their music alongside that of the instruments. Classical performance practice and its related recording industry have normalized the exclusion of touch sounds while valorizing the precious-ness of tone. Heinrich Neuhaus closes a chapter in *The Art of Piano Playing* with a telling metaphor: "And I should like to end these pages on tone with the words I sometimes say to my pupils: tone must be clothed in silence; it must be enshrined in silence like a jewel in a velvet case" (Neuhaus 1983, 81, translated by K. A. Leibovitch). Neuhaus likens piano tone to a cushioned jewel, one that requires protection in the form of a metaphorical velvet case of silence. The implication is that tone might be harmed by touch sounds or other sonic debris.

Touch sounds seemingly soil tone's clothing. They are the dust that mars tone's luster. The connection between clothing and sound is provocative. The sartorial metaphor is that sound can *get dressed* and that its ideal garment is *silence*. The silent-save-for-the-notes approach to classical recording regards non-notated events as undesirable because they spoil the requisite quie-tude that surrounds tone. In this chapter, I study recordings in which tone is not enrobed in silence but is metaphorically *disrobed* via audible touch sounds. The resulting tracks are, in a manner of speaking, unclothed: they preserve not only the notes, rhythms, and timbres denoted in the score, but all the sounds made by the musician's body and that body's interaction with an instrument. My argument is not that touch sounds automatically make recordings more desirable, only that recordings that include them are not, by definition, compromised. Some tracks are clothed and are beautiful; some are unclothed and are likewise beautiful.

Sounds as They Are. Richard Beaudoin, Oxford University Press. © Oxford University Press 2024.
DOI: 10.1093/oso/9780197659281.003.0004

A musician's touch can leave a sonic trace. Recordings of notated music document one or more performers manipulating their instruments to produce sound. It is the traces of this manipulation—of the musician interfacing with their instrument—that I explore here. As with breaths, touch sounds are interwoven into what one might call the "sanctioned" sounds that are commonly understood to comprise the "music" on a track. It does not take much energy or movement to make touch sounds, but their impact and presence can be significant. Physicist Eric J. Heller reminds us that the "energy needed to make audible sound is very small. You can shout for a year, and the energy produced *that winds up as sound* would not be enough to boil a cup of water" (2013, 5, italics in original). Just because touch sounds are often quiet does not mean that they lie outside the bounds of music theory. They are audible and comprise an integral part of the track. Categorizing touch sounds requires an approach different from that devoted to breath sounds, largely due to the diversity of instruments used to play classical music. Every instrument has its own way of interacting with the body of its player.

My survey is designed as a small tour of the body, from fingertips to hands to hips to toes. The traversal begins with the motivic fingernail clicks of pianists William Chapman Nyaho and Claudio Arrau. From the nails, I move to the foreshadowing fingertips of the Guarneri Quartet with Bernard Greenhouse. Then it is on to the percussive fingerfalls of cellist Zara Nelsova. The hand in motion is studied via audible squeaks in classical guitar recordings by Ana Archilés, Valerie Hartzell, and Julian Bream, and the sounded movement of clacking tuba valves is heard in a recording by Velvet Brown. Moving away from the hands, I investigate the sounded movements of Glenn Gould's body—in particular, his posterior—via his creaking piano chair. Finally, I arrive at the feet, whose touch is investigated in two contrasting modes: one loud (Bruno Walter's podium stamps while conducting the Columbia Symphony Orchestra) and the other soft (the damper pedal in tracks by pianists Lucille Chung, Sheila Arnold, and Anthony Hewitt). This anatomical journey foregrounds the sonic traces of bodies touching instruments.

Fingernails and motive

William Chapman Nyaho's 2020 recording of R. Nathaniel Dett's "Honey: Humoresque" from his 1913 piano suite *In the Bottoms* exemplifies a track in which unwritten sounds fuse with written ones within a specific motive. The recording was made in Seattle, Washington, engineered by Doug Haire and mastered by Richard Price. Example 3.1 transcribes the only phrases where fingernail clicks are audible. Dett's forty-eight-bar movement includes three iterations of its opening motive: in mm. 1–4 (in the F major tonic), mm. 9–12 (in the A minor mediant), and mm. 21–24 (again in the F major tonic). Chapman Nyaho's track includes few audible clicks, virtually all of them coming during the iterations of this main motive. Moreover, all

Example 3.1 R. Nathaniel Dett, "Honey: Humoresque" from *In the Bottoms*, annotating the fingernail clicks in three appearances of the opening theme in the 2020 recording by William Chapman Nyaho. See ▶ Audio Example 3.1.

the clicks occur in the same location within the melody, even as it migrates to other key areas. The one-to-one connection between motives and clicks produces a timbral signature within Chapman Nyaho's recording of Dett's humoresque.

The clicks in Chapman Nyaho's track align, in part, with Dett's accent marks when they occur in both hands simultaneously. These moments include the E diminished seventh to F major motions in mm. 3–4 and mm. 23–24, as well as the G♯ diminished seventh to A minor motion in mm. 11–12. A third click shared by all three phrases appears on the third sixteenth note of beat 1 in mm. 4, 12, and 24, just before the fermata in each bar. The fermati all coincide with a notated accent. However, in each case, Chapman Nyaho's finger click coincides with the note *before* the fermata. Hearing these three phrases side by side demonstrates that, in Chapman Nyaho's hands, the generative phrase of Dett's "Honey" is marked by a recurring fingernail rhythm.

Claudio Arrau kept his nails long and, like Chapman Nyaho, they clicked on the keys. One of numerous examples of this sound within Arrau's oeuvre occurs in his Philips recording of Beethoven's Sonata in C major, Op. 2, No. 3, made in Amsterdam's Bachzaal in April 1964. Hearing the clicks might awaken the detective in all of us. Their precise locations suggest that, with a little effort, we might deduce exactly which fingering Arrau is using. In the spirit of Jonathan De Souza's *Music at Hand*, we might even go so far as to prove *which nails on which hand* were longer than the others. Music theory has long encouraged a dissociation between so-called pure pitch material and the physical acts that generate sound. De Souza has perceptively reminded the field that "the 'dissociation' between pitch and movement might be better understood as a mobile, flexible *association* between action and instrument" (2017, 20, italics in original). While I see my approach as complementary to De Souza's, there is little overlap. The line between performance analysis and recording analysis is here fruitfully drawn. Whichever finger might be identified as generating the click on a given beat, the focus of this chapter is to register the sonic trace that appears on the recording, rather than using audible events as clues to construct a forensic re-enactment of what was happening in the studio, at the piano, in the hand, or on the key.

There are five iterations of the opening four-bar motive across the first movement of Op. 2, No. 3. The most active objects in these passages are the oscillating sixteenth-note thirds followed by descending eighth notes. These figures beget Arrau's fingernail clicks, which prompts the question: are differences in the clicking sounds related to variations in the motive? The answer is yes, and Example 3.2 illustrates the process. It transcribes Arrau's clicks during the five iterations of the opening bars across the first movement of Op. 2, No. 3: mm. 1a–4a, 1b–4b, 109–12, 139–42, and 233–36. The first two iterations are the opening of the piece and its return after the first ending, both in the C major tonic. The third iteration is the false arrival of the theme in D major. The fourth and fifth iterations occur, respectively, at the moment of recapitulation and at the conclusion of the notated cadenza, both in the tonic. The D major version is the outlier. Alongside the non-tonic key, it is missing the oscillating thirds in its third bar, it is marked *pianissimo* (as opposed to *piano* in all the other appearances), and the pattern of the fingernail clicks is different. The clicks during the four C major presentations are uniform. In each of these tonic appearances, the downbeats of the first and third measures are click-free and there is a timbral emphasis on the anacrustic eighth notes leading into the second and fourth measures. By contrast, the D major presentation has fewer clicks. They are softer and articulate a different pattern from the more assertive and click-rich tonic motives. Across Arrau's track, each tonic recapitulation of the first theme thereby recalls not only the opening material as notated in the score, but also the click pattern that accompanied its initial presentation.

Arrau's clicking sounds have not gone unnoticed by commentators. His recordings stand at the intersection between a musician's physical grooming preferences and the norms of classical recording. Such an intersection begets critical dialogue and produces vibrant disagreements. Two venues of critique can be addressed: industry publications (which tend toward the diplomatic) and online debates (which tend to be unvarnished and occasionally confrontational). It will benefit us to experience both arenas of debate. Critics writing for industry publications cordially disagree about the musical impact of Arrau's fingernail clicks. Christopher Headington, writing about Arrau's Philips recording of music by Mozart, has reservations about both the clicking and the playing:

> Arrau's way with Mozart, at least in his latter years, was serious and forceful, as the C major Sonata on the first disc reminds us. As a matter of fact, this comes from his last recording sessions in June 1988, when he was 85, and as SJ pointed out in his review, we can only find the playing impressive if we bear the artist's age in mind. It is too stiff and chunky in the outer movements to be enjoyable, particularly when we remember that Mozart asked pianists to make legato passages "flow like oil," while the

Example 3.2 Ludwig van Beethoven, Piano Sonata in C major, Op. 2, No. 3, first movement, annotating the fingernail clicks in five appearances of the opening theme in the 1964 recording by Claudio Arrau. See ▶ Audio Example 3.2.

slow movement is uneasy and jerky in both rhythm and sonority. Similar criticisms apply in some degree to the two following sonatas recorded during the same sessions, and like SJ I notice an occasional clicking sound which may be the pianist's fingernails—detracting from Philips's very natural recording—and there's some loud breathing, as at 3'07" on track 8 of this first disc and in the A minor Sonata on the third. (1992, 80)

One would not be faulted for challenging Headington's logic, in which sounds made by the pianist are counted *against* the "naturalness" of a recording. Likewise, the reader would also not be faulted for wincing when Headington tells us that the only reason to find this music-making impressive is if one bears in mind the pianist was eighty-five years old. John M. Eargle's ears heard things differently. Writing about Arrau's Philips recording of Chopin's waltzes, Eargle accepts the clicking, even as he is lukewarm about the interpretation:

Arrau's piano is somewhat bright, but of excellent timbre and regulation. The uncanny clarity inherent in CDs seems to elucidate piano recordings more than almost any other kind. One hears all the trappings of live performance, including the performer's often agitated breathing and the minute clicks of fingernails on the keys. These are details which are perfectly natural, but which are so often lost through traditional LP processing. For my tastes, the playing is too monochromatic, with not enough exploration of contrasts. (Eargle 1983, 34)

Headington states that the clicks detract from the "naturalness" of the recording, while Eargle calls these same details "perfectly natural."

While Headington and Eargle disagree about the merits of fingernail clicks, both communicate their ideas in measured terms. By contrast, online dialogues on the merits of non-notated touch sound in classical recordings often proceed with less decorum. While lively and unedited, web-based audiophile forums exemplify the sort of dialogue that is prompted by touch sounds. Such forums permit evocative eavesdropping. With all the attendant caveats about the veracity and utility of online discussion groups, the tone of the thread "FA: Arrau Beethoven Box Set" from October 19, 2006, on the online Google Group Rec Music Classical Recordings forum provides refreshing insight. Below is the transcript of a comment made by forum member Tony Overington and two replies from Todd Schurk and Gabriel Parra, respectively. The recording being debated is Arrau's 1998 fourteen-CD set of Beethoven Sonatas and Concertos, released as Philips 462 358-2. The set includes the same 1964 recording of Op. 2, No. 3, analyzed in Example 3.2. The topic of debate is Arrau's fingernail clicks, addressed in three consecutive comments:

> *TO*: Your disproportionate defense of Arrau—which is often quite belligerent—becomes very tiring after a while. Whatever one's opinion of Arrau, the fingernail clicks are very annoying, not least because they are intermittent (had they been constant, like a background noise such as tape hiss, then they wouldn't be such a nuisance). But I'm not sure if that registers with you, as you seem bent on attacking anyone who combines a negative comment with Arrau's name, whether the negative comment directly refers to him or his playing (which in the case above it doesn't). (4:31 p.m.)
>
> *TS*: Why bother to read what I write then? Guess I get under your skin . . . or is it nails? I just suggested that a lot could be missed if one thought the extra "sounds," whatever they may be kept anyone from the more important aspect of the recording—which is the music being made. The "clicking" (what little of it there is) does not bother me in the least bit. Guess it's you it bothers. (5:39 p.m.)
>
> *GP*: I don't find them very annoying. I even once read a critic fancifully referring to them as evocative of the sound of castanets. (6:45 p.m.)

The equation of clicks with castanets is intriguing, as it characterizes fingernails as percussion instruments. Equally intriguing is the suggestion that Arrau's clicks "wouldn't be such a nuisance" if they were "constant." While the constancy of so-called background noises—and specifically the hissing of wax cylinders—will be taken up in Chapter 5, the *intermittentness* of Arrau's fingernail clicks is precisely what makes them interesting. They are tied to specific motives within specific keys.

There is one more significant development of the clicks in Arrau's 1964 recording of Op 2, No. 3. The apotheosis of his fingernail sounds arrives during Beethoven's notated cadenza. This elongated, unbarred measure—bar 232—is itself the apotheosis of the opening motive. The clicks in the cadenza complete an arc that extends back to the beginning of the piece.

Example 3.3 Ludwig van Beethoven, Piano Sonata in C major, Op. 2, No. 3, first movement, m. 232, annotating the fingernail clicks in the 1964 recording by Claudio Arrau. See ▶ Audio Example 3.3.

The figure on the third and fourth beats of bar 1 is now ramified up and down the keyboard in bar 232. Example 3.3 includes a transcription of this measure as heard in Arrau's 1964 recording. Arrau's recording of Beethoven's flourish—an ornamented cadential 6/4 in the home key—includes the most intense flurry of fingernail clicks heard on the track, solidifying a timbral link with the movement's opening motive, its tonality, and its associated touch sounds.

Taken together, the Chapman Nyaho and Arrau examples fuse fingernail clicks with specific motives as they appear under the hand. Key-specific handshapes reveal that clicking and key relations are intertwined. Fingernail sounds act as timbral markers and participate in motivic and harmonic development.

Foreshadowing fingertips

Moving below the fingernails, we come to the flesh of the fingertip. When playing bowed string instruments, it is normal to depress the desired pitch with the left hand before inaugurating the sound with the bow. When fingertip placements are audible, the ear is given evocative foreshadowing of the pitches that follow. Compared to pre-downbeat breath sounds, pre-downbeat touch sounds are comparatively rare. Spotting one sparks curiosity.

The opening of Franz Schubert's String Quintet in C, D. 956, operates like the first sentence of an epic: "124 was spiteful" from Toni Morrison's *Beloved* (1987, 1) or "Call me Ishmael" from Herman Melville's *Moby-Dick; or, The Whale* (1979, 2). Microphones offer the ear the possibility of hearing what goes on just *before* the notated chord, when the hands of the musicians ready themselves not only for the root-position C major triad but for the hour of music that follows it. In June 1990, at the American Academy of Arts and Letters in New York, the Guarneri Quartet—violinists Arnold Steinhardt and John Dally, violist Michael Tree, and cellist David Soyer—were joined by cellist Bernard Greenhouse to record D. 956. During the session, recording engineer John Newton and tape editors Hein Dekker and Jean Van Vugt captured just such a collection of sounds immediately preceding the opening chord. Example 3.4 transcribes the combination of unpitched taps and light hammer-ons that make up this faint preparatory gesture. The transcription asserts one possible way of denoting the intricate and unexpectedly groovy nature of these collective, pre-downbeat touch sounds.

Analyses of the first movement of D. 956 tend to idealize the opening of the piece as though it emerges from a sanctified and transcendent void.

Example 3.4 Franz Schubert, String Quintet in C major, D. 956, first movement, mm. 1–2, transcribing the pre-downbeat fingertip placement sounds in the 1990 recording by the Guarneri String Quartet with Bernard Greenhouse. See ⏵ Audio Example 3.4.

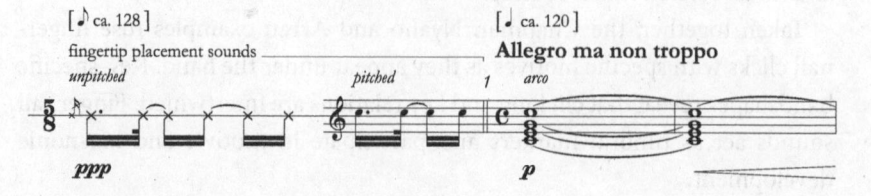

Martin and Vande Moortele write: "The Quintet begins with a pregnant stasis: a closed-position C major triad held for two full bars in the upper quartet before giving way to a common-tone diminished-seventh chord in bar 3. No first-time listener is likely to discern the tempo immediately, not at least until the crescendo starts to swell or the first violinist cues the change in harmony" (2015, 132). The Guarneri/Greenhouse recording fails to fit their description. The track begins *not* with a closed-position C major triad but with a series of touch sounds—some pitched, some unpitched—that fall into a rhythm and suggest a tempo. Leaving aside what Martin and Vande Moortele mean by "pregnant," the Guarneri/ Greenhouse recording punctures any implied "stasis" that is meant to precede the opening triad. On this recording, there is music prior to Schubert's first measure.

The inclusion of touch sounds just before an opening downbeat is relatively rare, since the silence that precedes the first sound on a track is normally simple to preserve, or produce, in the editing phase. Sounds engineers Caroline Haigh, John Dunkerley, and Mark Rogers recommend that "All tracks on an album have to start and finish cleanly with no noises before the start or during the final reverb die-away, and with appropriate gap lengths between movements and works" (2021, 337). They go on to make an unexpected distinction between preparatory breaths and preparatory touch sounds: "Immediately before the start of a take, there might be a variety of noises. An intake of breath before the downbeat can be left in the mastered compilation as it can feel very natural, especially in chamber music where there are wind/brass instruments or singers. Noises that are knocks and bumps should be removed; care should be taken to make sure that any reverb from the removed noise is no longer present under the start of the piece; if it is, either another take or noise-removal software will be needed" (2021, 338). Coming as it does from three experts, this advice nicely ties together findings from the preceding chapter (on the commonness of pre-downbeat, anacrustic breaths) and the current chapter (on the rarity of pre-downbeat touch sounds). The fingertip placement sounds in the Guarneri/Greenhouse recording of Schubert's quintet are intimate. They do not carry with them the kind of musical weight that one might ascribe to a theme or a referential sonority. This will change in the analyses that follow, where sounds of touch interact more profoundly, and prominently, with the overall form of the work being recorded.

Dancing fingerfalls

Studio 7 of the RIAS Funkhaus in Berlin was the site of a spirited dance on April 30, 1959, when Zara Nelsova recorded the Courante from Bach's Cello Suite in D minor, BWV 1008. To be specific, the dance took place across the fingerboard of Nelsova's 1726 Stradivarius, the "Marquis de Corberon." The microphones positioned by recording engineer Heinz Opitz and producer Hermann Reuschel captured both the sound of her cello and the sound of her hands contacting it. The 2015 remastering and re-release of Nelsova's original tapes by Ludger Böckenhoff on Audite 21.433 carries the following disclaimer: "The historical publications at Audite are based, without exception, on the original tapes from broadcasting archives. In general, these are the original analogue tapes, which attain an astonishingly high quality, even measured by today's standards, with their tape speed of up to 76 cm/sec. The remastering—professionally competent and sensitively applied—also uncovers previously hidden details of the interpretations" (2015, 2). Audite's promise of "previously hidden details" is kept. This record preserves the sound of Nelsova's fingerfalls.

I am using the term *fingerfall* to mean the sound of fingers as they alight on the string and fingerboard; this is an analogue of the more common word *footfall*, meaning the sound of footsteps. While fingers are not commonly thought of as "stepping," a cellist's fingers do just that. The impact of fingers on the fingerboard are often vividly audible and merit the term, as they momentarily monopolize the frequency space.[1] Many of Nelsova's left-hand placements add a prominent, metallic click. Others contribute a more subtle, fleshy sound of the finger tapping the fingerboard. Such click-less fingerfalls are still audible. Taken together, these varied tap types create a lively landscape of touch sounds across Nelsova's track.

Ledbetter (2009) emphasizes the momentum of Bach's compositional strategy in this particular Courante, writing that "the objective seems to have been to blur the boundaries by an almost total lack of full cadences within strains" (2009, 191). While Nelsova's tempo accentuates the Courante's *phrasal blur*, one aspect of the recording cuts against the forward-tumbling flow. A series of percussive fingerfalls generates a kind of meta-dance atop

---

[1] A vivid example of audible fingerfalls can be found in the Quatuor Végh 1973 recording of the Finale of Beethoven's String Quartet in E-flat major, Op. 127. In bars 5–7 and 13–15, first violinist Sandor Végh produces a prominent click each time his finger alights on G4, A♭4, and A4.

(and within) the Courante rhythm. The effect is not of two competing musics, but of a single music with embedded, note-specific timbral triggers that go off as certain fingering patterns are engaged.

Example 3.5 presents the complete score of the Courante and indicates the location of each of Nelsova's fingerfalls.[2] The form of Nelsova's recording is AAB, as she takes the first repeat but not the second. The example is a full transcription neither of Bach's score (slurs have been removed) nor of Nelsova's interpretation (as it does not represent her bowings). Instead, the example demonstrates which pitches are accompanied by touch sounds. By my count, Nelsova's track includes ninety-eight fingerfalls. The majority occur, as one might expect, on pitches that are unavailable as open strings: nineteen on G3, sixteen on E3, twelve on F3. The more surprising discovery is the subtle rhythm formed by these taps. Given the global key of D minor, the preponderance of rhythmically highlighted non-tonic tones (G and E) on weak parts of the measure (and weaker parts of the beat) enliven the metric flow considerably. At times, Nelsova seems to be performing in magical lockstep with a mridangam player who is underscoring a small collection of mostly non-tonic pitches.

Nelsova's percussive fingerfalls contribute propulsive energy to the Courante's harmonic unfolding. The opening ten measures illustrate the interplay of taps and phrasing. The jerky, offbeat rhythm of the falls accentuates the opening chromatic bass descent from D in m. 1 to the emphatic A on the downbeat of m. 6. Nelsova's fingerfalls present a series of syncopated hammers that delay any coincidence of accent between pitches and finger sounds until the arrival of m. 5, the beginning of the second four-bar group. The tapping sounds on the fourth sixteenth note of mm. 3.1, 3.2, and 4.3 (both times through the form) energize and freshen the downbeat of bar 5, which gets a tap on both passes.

It is rare for Nelsova's fingerfalls to coincide with downbeats. All the audible taps in the A sections (mm. 1a–16a and mm. 1b–16b) occur on offbeats, save for the F3 that begins m. 5, the A3 that begins m. 9, and the C♯3 that begins m. 10. All the remaining A section taps are on relatively weaker beats, the majority sounding as syncopations. In the B section (mm. 17–32), the only downbeat fingerfall is the C♯3 in m. 25, a structural leading tone that is

---

[2] Audio Example 3.5 presents the opening of Nelsova's recording. Readers are invited to audit the complete track on *Zara Nelsova: Cello Concertos, Sonatas & Suites* (Nelsova 1959/2015).

Example 3.5 J. S. Bach, Courante from Cello Suite in D minor, BWV 1008, slurs removed, annotating the fingerfalls in the 1959 recording by Zara Nelsova. See ⏵ Audio Example 3.5.

itself foreshadowed by the enormous G3 *thwack* on beat 2 of bar 24. The latter is one of Nelsova's most emphatic touch sounds. The rhythmically propulsive nature of these syncopated finger-on-fingerboard sounds are inextricable from the pitch material. They regularly emphasize non-tonic pitches—mainly G, E, and C♯ in the key of D minor—and are embedded within the signal captured by the microphones in the RIAS Funkhaus. The spectrogram demonstrates that these sounds are not separate from the cello pitches. They do not lie in the bandwidth apart from the notes and, as a result, they are all but impossible to remove.[3]

One final, expressive, non-notated sound in Nelsova's track deserves attention. It is the final audible pitch—C2—a sound that occurs *outside* the bounds of Bach's score but *inside* the bounds of Nelsova's recording. It thereby highlights the kind of sonic inclusion on display across this chapter, and indeed this book. As seen in Example 3.6, after reaching the concluding D2 at the end of bar 32, Nelsova holds the final note, *arco*. She then releases her bow and allows the D2 to resonate under her depressed fingertip. Such a strategy is common. What happens next is uncommon. At 1:34.5, Nelsova *releases* her finger from the D2. When she does, the tonic note disappears and the pitch falls to the open-string C2, sounding the subtonic pitch in D minor.

Nelsova's concluding C2 sets up a pleasing contradiction, one that points up the difference between scores and tracks. On one hand, the concluding C gently undermines the Courante's D minor tonality. The very definition of the subtonic is as "the crucial first step in a falling line that leads toward the dominant" (Laitz 2016, 21). The C inaugurates an implied descent that never materializes. On the other hand, anyone who has handled a cello knows that the sound of the vibrating low C is commonplace when taking the instrument into one's hands or setting it down. As such, the sound is associated with the instrument at rest. From this perspective, the open C functions as a resolution, not of Bach's Courante, but of Nelsova's track. Taking both identities into account, the *score* concludes with a resolved, tonicized D while the *track* concludes with a reassuring, open-string C that signals Nelsova's cello returning to its resonant, unfingered state.

Squeaking shifts

Traveling from the fingertips down to the fingers themselves, we alight upon classical guitar music. In the robustly populated world of guitarists, the topic of squeaks has been the focus of much interpretive, pedagogic, and technological effort. Classical guitarists and their sound engineers go to great lengths to remove squeaks from their recordings, teaching manuals regularly

---

[3] At the moment of transition between the two A sections (between m. 17a and m. 1b), Nelsova assertively places her finger on the fingerboard, creating a prominent hammer-on D3 at 0:29.6 just before the *arco* D3 that forms the pickup to bar 1b. Nelsova's rhythmic touch sound generates an energetic coupling between the paired A sections.

Example 3.6 J. S. Bach, Courante from Cello Suite in D minor, BWV 1008, m. 32, annotating the audible open C string at the end of the 1959 recording by Zara Nelsova. See ⏵ Audio Example 3.6.

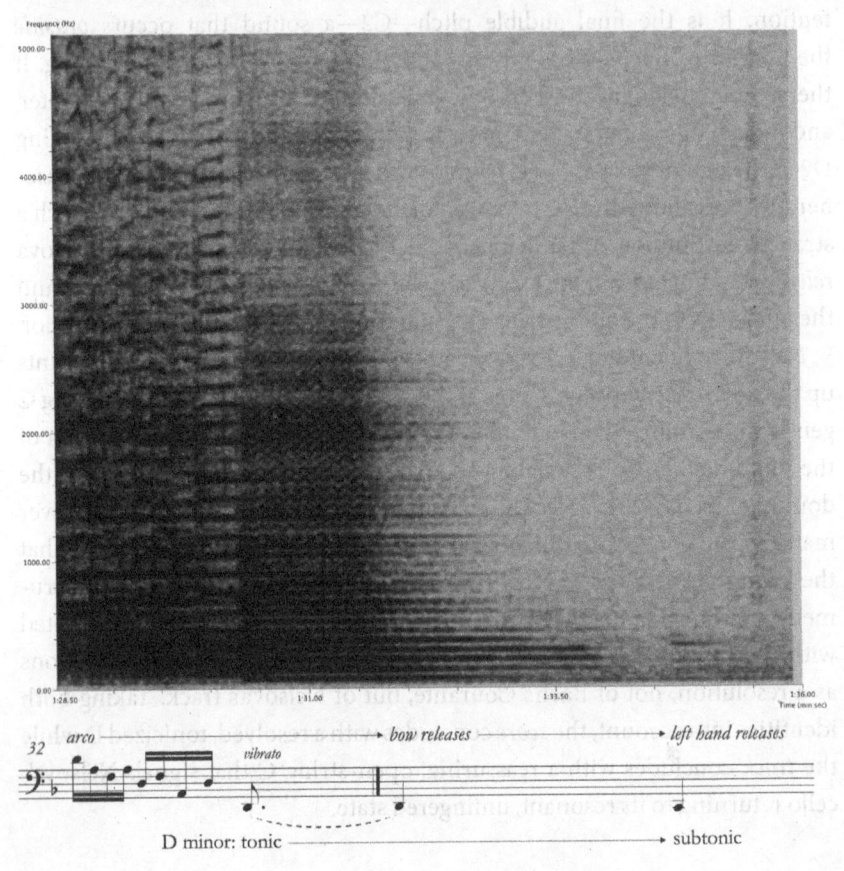

address methods of avoiding these sounds, and string manufacturers (in consultation with virtuosos) devote themselves to developing products that reduce their likelihood. Neither pro- nor anti-squeak, I recommend that these sounds simply be recognized, and that their function be addressed. It is possible to inquire as to whether guitar squeaks, like other touch sounds, have the potential to become expressively tied to harmonic, rhythmic, and formal developments.

In general, classical guitarists regard squeaks as non-musical annoyances, and a great deal of inherited technique is designed around their eradication. Sharon Isbin counsels aspiring guitarists: "You can avoid left-hand squeaks by preventing your calluses from scraping against the coils. There are three basic ways to do this: lift the finger, slide on the flat part of the fingerpad, or slide at an angle on either side of the fingertip" (1999, 26). Christopher Parkening offers a rare firsthand account of a guitarist working through the issue of squeaks. His testimony, coauthored with Kathy Tyers, is revealing, as one rarely encounters written documentation of a musician talking in detail about their fingertips:

> It was then, too, that I understood something about the squeaks that often happen when a guitarist's left hand slides up and down the fingerboard. Guitarists tend not to notice them since we get used to hearing them when we play. But the public notices.
>
> My dad suggested spreading olive oil or talcum powder on the strings and the fingerboard. Oiling the strings made them even squeakier, and applying talcum powder made them sound dead. Nothing seemed to work until my dad had the brilliant idea, which remained more or less our secret for years, of sanding the metal-wound lower strings. First we tried heavy-grit sandpaper on strings that had been taken off the guitar. When we put them back on, they sounded thuddy and dead. I almost abandoned the idea, but then I got to thinking: Why couldn't I try the refined sandpaper that I used to smooth the unevenness off my right-hand fingernails? I tried that, and the strings sounded a little better, although they still didn't have the lively sound we wanted. I put brand new strings on and tried sanding only the top portion of the bass strings, just on the top side. Again, it was better, but it still sounded slightly dead.
>
> Each time I sanded the strings and started to play, my fingertips picked up a black line of grit from the metal filings I'd sanded off the string. *Well,* I thought, *that's what's making the string dead!* So the next time I sanded the top section, I took several tissues and wiped the tops of the strings. The tissue ended up crisscrossed with black lines, but the sound was perfect—no squeaks, but still nice and bright. (2006, 61–62, italics in original)

If guitarists go to such lengths to quell squeaks, it would seem that these sounds are, by definition, undesirable. The truth, however, is more nuanced. In some instances—and in some genres—the squeaks can be understood as part of the music.

John Williams has a more nuanced philosophy on squeaking sounds. In an interview with fellow guitarist Michael O'Toole on October 21, 2017, Williams was exceedingly specific about when squeaks have value:

> I don't think squeaks are musical. The shift along a string between notes and chords—and indeed any sound which occurs during that movement—often forms part of the musical sound on a musical instrument such as the violin or cello: it's the connection between the notes. However, the squeak that comes from a guitar—for example when you shift from one barré chord to another—is different. In this instance, the sound of the squeak itself is not connected to the music and comes a fraction of a second after the shift. It's basically an interfering noise—it is not musical or nice. (O'Toole 2020, 83)

Williams's testimony provides a wealth of insight. First, he acknowledges that position-shift squeaks on instruments in the violin family form part of the musical sound. By contrast, on the guitar, the sound that can accompany the shift between barré chords is an interfering noise which is not connected to the music. He then makes a distinction between genres, claiming that, in styles that utilize acoustic steel-string guitar, squeaks are accepted "as part of the culture. The steel string sound has a much brighter resonance so that the squeaks probably don't register as being so different or undesirable when set against that . . . or maybe it's just a cultural acceptance" (O'Toole 2020, 83, ellipsis in original). His comment echoes sentiments found in Chapter 1, where the point was made that non-notated sounds have been accepted (and even developed) in genres other than classical music. Finally, Williams draws a subtle distinction between types of shifts: "If you're converting that squeak into the sound of movement like a 'mini-mini-glissando' which you get on violin all the time, then the squeak is converted into a shift and is just part of the movement from one note to the next. You then avoid position shifts which might seem practical but might not relate directly to the rhythm of the music as it is happening" (O'Toole 2020, 85). This last clause is central to my investigation of the musicality of guitar squeaks. While seemingly closing the door on such sounds, Williams leaves it ajar when he connects the relationship of a given squeak to the rhythm of the music "as it is happening."

There exist recordings where the melody, rhythm, harmony, and squeaks all contribute to the creation of expressive musical meaning, a point demonstrated by a comparative analysis of three recordings of Francisco

Tárrega's ¡Adelita! mazurka para guitarra. Before turning to the squeak-inclusive analysis, it will be useful to describe the general harmonic form of the piece. The music on the five-line staff in Example 3.7 transcribes only the pitches, rhythms, and expressive markings of the score, and is based on the 1902 Antich y Tena edition. Tárrega's sixteen-bar mazurka is in binary form, with the first part in E minor and the second in the parallel major. Bars 1–8 comprise two self-enclosed four-bar phrases, each presenting a harmonic progression that moves from tonic to first-inversion supertonic seventh to augmented dominant ninth to tonic. Tárrega's melodic game in these two opening phrases is to decorate nearly all the downbeats with appoggiaturas: the 4-3 resolutions in mm. 2 and 6 and the 9-8 resolutions in mm. 3, 4, and 7. Aside from the cadence in bar 8, the only exceptions are the downbeats of the initiating tonic phrases (m. 1 and m. 5) whose 8-7 motions reverse the prevailing consonance/dissonance pattern.

The second part of the binary form—the E major phrases in mm. 9–16—contrasts with the A section. Likewise cast in two four-bar halves, the B section is designed as an antecedent-consequent, with mm. 9–12 moving from tonic to a half cadence and mm. 13–16 moving from tonic to tonic. Subtle connections between the A and B sections abound, as when the melodic ascent of bar 4 becomes a descent in bar 12, or when the dissonant, weak-beat melodic Gs that complete the augmented dominant in the A section are transformed into the reiterated, stable downbeat G♯s that occur on five of the eight bars in the B section. Bar 14 marks Tárrega's point of furthest remove. The fermata delays the forward flow and coincides with a French augmented sixth chord: C–E–F♯–A♯. Complying with centuries of tonal expectation, the augmented sixth C–A♯ resolves out to the octave Bs on the downbeat of m. 15. While not a case of extreme chromaticism, in the context of this short work the dissonance at the end of m. 14 is the moment of highest harmonic and rhythmic intensity. The gravity of the augmented sixth plays out not only harmonically and rhythmically in Tárrega's score, but instrumentally and sonically in the recordings, another nod to Tárrega's embedding of his knowledge of the instrument within the design of his composition. This is not to say that every guitarist fingers ¡Adelita! identically. Different shifting strategies generate different sonic traces.

Example 3.7 annotates the squeaking sounds in three recordings: Ana Archilés (2019), Valerie Hartzell (2011), and Julian Bream (1970).[4] The sound engineer for Archilés's track is uncredited, for Hartzell it was Todd

---

[4] Audio Example 3.7 presents three passes through mm. 12a–16a: first Archilés, then Hartzell, then Bream.

Example 3.7 Francisco Tárrega, *¡Adelita! mazurka para guitarra*, mm. 1b–16a, annotating the squeaks in recordings by Ana Archilés (2019), Valerie Hartzell (2011), and Julian Bream (1970). See ⏵ Audio Example 3.7.

Hulslander; for Bream it was John W. Bower. In general, all three tracks exhibit few squeaks. When these sounds do appear, their location and rhythmic placement create expressively divergent music. The example leaves aside each guitarist's individual approach to the notated glissandi (such as in bar 11b) and focuses on the squeaking sounds. Each guitarist avoids squeaking throughout the A section. (Both Archilés and Hartzell create brief squeaks on the E minor cadence in m. 8a and 8b as they release the E minor triad.) During the B sections, all three guitarists are squeakless through the antecedent (mm. 9–12, including repeats). During the consequent (mm. 13a–16a), the recordings diverge, to dramatic effect. Archilés sounds a single shift-related squeak in m. 13a between the sounding B3–E4 dyad on beat 2 and the embedded melodic B3 on the anacrusis to beat 3. From there, she navigates the subsequent measures without any squeaks through the augmented sixth and its resolution in mm. 14–15. Hartzell, too, is squeak-free during the bulk of the final system, sounding only a small squeak of release after the fermata in m. 14a and a set of shifting squeaks after each of the last two beats of m. 15a. Bream's recording is the outlier. He shatters the otherwise squeakless soundworld with a decidedly squeak-rich approach to the closing measures. Bream's recording of mm. 13a–16a includes no fewer than ten squeaking sounds. These occur in every measure other than the cadential tonic in m. 16 and are concentrated around the augmented sixth in m. 14 and the arrival of the dominant in m. 15.

Compared to those of Archilés and Hartzell, Bream's recording of mm. 13a–15a is dense with touch sounds. Bream had several fingering options, and there are ways of playing this passage that would have preserved the squeaklessness of the rest of his track. A 1983 Deutsche Grammophon recording by Narciso Yepes, for example, almost grinds to a halt during m. 15a, so careful is Yepes to move into first position and avoid all squeaks whatsoever. By contrast, Bream's squeak-rich final system timbrally signals difference and drama. He opts for a fingering solution that dramatizes Tárrega's point of furthest remove—the augmented sixth and its resolution into the dominant in mm. 14–15. Archilés or Hartzell might have made similar sounds that were subsequently edited before their records were released, but the point here is that Bream's recording preserves them. His shifting *registers*.[5] The mazurka's most dissonant measures are marked in Bream's track by the

---

[5] For a producer's perspective on Bream's recording, see Mark Marrington, *Recording the Classical Guitar* (2021).

novel appearance of timbral squeaks. His fingering decisions cause sounds of touch to surround the moment of greatest harmonic dissonance.

Bream spoke about his relationship to squeaks, revealing himself to be more accepting of their existence than Williams:

> Another difficulty is the squeaks you make sometimes as your fingers travel up and down the fretboard, like the clatter of jacks on the harpsichord. It would be lovely if squeaks were not there, but they nearly always are. Some performers manage to eliminate a lot of the squeak; John Williams, for instance, doesn't squeak very much, partly because I know he takes especial care not to squeak, but also because his left-hand release action is meticulously correct. I squeak more than some, possibly because I tend to let myself go in concerts. If I worried about taking my fingers off the string, and then putting them down again on the same string, merely to avoid the squeak, I might lose the musical line. I know that if you keep your fingers on the string while you move to the next position, you risk a squeak. But at least the melodic line is unbroken, and there are ways of minimizing the squeak. That's what I'm working on at the moment. Christ, I sound like the Prime Minister and the problems of inner cities; you know, "I'm working on it at the moment." After a while, though, I don't think some of these sounds matter too much, provided they are not too distracting from the music or distressing for the listener. (Palmer 1982, 111)

Bream is as lively an orator as he is a musical interpreter. While his vivid and self-deprecating narration states that "It would be lovely if squeaks were not there," he is more pragmatic about their existence and, in a special nod to the relationship between studio recordings and live performances, makes plain that "I tend to let myself go in concerts." His 1970 recording of *¡Adelita!* is a prime example of such *letting go*. By no means a free-wheeling reading, his playing reflects a judicious desire to preserve an integral line—the A–G♯–F♯ inner voice in m. 15—on a warmer part of the instrument, using a fingering that generates shifting sounds. The resultant squeaks occur alongside the apex of harmonic dissonance within the work, allowing sounds of touch to fuse with concurrent linear, harmonic, rhythmic, and formal arcs. The result is no less expressive than Archilés's or Hartzell's recording of Tárrega's mazurka. Bream's reading is, however, one in which the unwritten sounds of touch appear during the greatest harmonic and registral drama in the score.

Percussive valve clacks

Tuba valves commonly come in two types—rotary or piston—and the modern instrument can be fashioned with three, four, or five of them.[6] When activated rapidly and forcefully, these valves make a sound resembling a classic twentieth-century typewriter. Like the key clicks made by larger woodwinds such as the bassoon, the sounds made by the valves of low brass instruments are a natural aspect of their manipulation. To differentiate from the fingernail *clicks* studied earlier, I will call valve sounds *clacks*.

Tuba valve clacks are sounds of touch that imbue a track with sonic evidence of rapid hand motions and can add levels of timbre and rhythmic activity that run parallel to melodic material. The tuba, Clifford Bevan reminds us, has been "a favourite with the avant-garde of every era" (1997, 154), and valve clacks have become part of its sonic palette. Claude Baker's *Omaggi e fantasie* for tuba and piano (1981, revised 1987) has passages of notated valve percussion. These sounds are so integral to tuba timbre that they appear in software suites that seek to mimic the sound of the instrument. The software company Native Instruments produces a package called Symphony Series–Brass that allows users to reproduce the sound of a brass ensemble, instrument by instrument. Native Instruments describes their product as "a 32-piece brass section and top soloists recorded in the prized acoustic space of St Paul's Church, San Francisco" (2022). The digitized "expressions" available in the tuba category include breath sounds and valve clacks.

Non-notated tuba valve clacks can be heard on Velvet Brown's 2001 recording of Alice Gomez's *Bonampak* for tuba and piano. Brown commissioned the work and recorded it with pianist Roberto Arosio in the Bryan Recital Hall of the College of Musical Arts at Bowling Green State University. The Tonmeisters for the session were David McCollum and Maria Cristina Fava. In the liner notes, Fava refers to the "obsessive rhythms" of Gomez's "virtuoso, driving, and powerful" composition (2003, 6). Fava's descriptions apply to both the written and unwritten music. Some passages on the track feature Brown's valve clacks, even as they do not appear in the score. Example 3.8 presents mm. 60–75 of *Bonampak* and transcribe Brown's

---

[6] For a discussion of the development of valved brass instruments, see Arnold Myers (1997, 120–30).

Example 3.8 Alice Gomez, *Bonampak* for tuba and piano, mm. 60–75, annotating the valve clacks in the 2001 recording by Velvet Brown and Roberto Arosio. See ▶ Audio Example 3.8.

clacks as a separate, percussive, timbral layer.[7] I count sixty clacks in the excerpt, forty-two of which occur on the pitches C♯ and G, with the remaining on E and B♭. Given that C♯ and G appear mainly on the first and third sixteenth of any given beat, these clacks reinforce the prevailing 2/4 meter. The synchronicity between Brown's valve clacks and the passage's notated meter contrasts with the audible fingerfalls in Zara Nelsova's Bach recording, which emphasized non-tonic notes and fell on offbeats. By contrast, the non-notated clacks in Brown's recording reinforce the prevailing meter and intensify a sense of groove.

The expressive nature of Brown's valve clacks has a deeper connection to the musical material. The title of Gomez's work refers to the name of a Mayan archaeological site in the Mexican state of Chiapas. The composer recalls the genesis of the work: "While looking at a picture of a Mayan procession, I felt a sense of actually being there. I could hear the rhythms of the marching footsteps and percussion instruments as musicians blew into large hollowed-out logs. The hypnotic effect of these paintings was realized in my work, *Bonampak*" (Fava 2003, 6). Gomez's inspiration seems to extend to Brown's recording. Just as Gomez imaginatively added the sound of marching footsteps and percussion instruments to her experience of looking at a picture of a Mayan procession, Brown's valve clacks add to Gomez's clack-less notation. The result is a track that augments the tuba and piano pitches with a third strand of sound-making: the rhythmic and "hypnotic" valve percussion that emanates from the movement of the tuba valves under Brown's fingers.

Chair creaks

While hands and feet are common sites for touch sounds, the posterior deserves recognition. Hip-based body movements are akin to the shifting hand of the classical guitarist; both generate sounds of touch as they interact with their instruments. In the case of piano music, that instrument (or piece

---

[7] Expanding the theme of unwritten music, Brown's recording differs significantly from Gomez's score. In the 2013 Potenza Music edition of *Bonampak*, the tuba part is tacet from mm. 60 to 75. In Brown's 2001 recording, the tuba plays these measures in unison with the right hand of the piano. This is by no means an error: Gomez recalls talking about the change with Brown around the time of composition (personal correspondence, June 30, 2022), and Brown recalls requesting the change from the composer (personal correspondence, July 7, 2022). Out of respect for Brown's interpretation, Example 3.8 matches the music as heard in her recording and not as it appears in the Potenza Music score.

of equipment) is whatever the pianist is sitting on. Commonly, this is a piano bench. For Glenn Gould, it was a folding chair, customized by his father, that he used throughout his recording career. Gould's recordings provide a nearly limitless corpus for the study of the expressive potential of unwritten music. Having earlier touched upon Gould's creaking piano chair and the critical response it continues to receive, it is now time to give that instrument its due.

Gould's piano chair was fashioned in 1953 by Gould's father, Bert Gould, who shortened each leg of a folding bridge chair made by the London, Ontario, firm Hourd & Company Limited. The alterations placed the seat height at about 14 inches above the floor (Bazzana 2004, 109). Each leg could be adjusted individually, allowing Gould to sit just as he pleased. Its years of constant use made the chair exceedingly loose-jointed and caused it to creak audibly when Gould swayed or shifted his weight. Bazzana reports that Gould sought "an unusually low chair, one that had the 'give' he needed, both front-to-back and diagonally, in order to accommodate his movements while he played" (2004, 109). The decades of use caused its seat cushion to wear away, ultimately leaving Gould to balance on its central wooden support. Gould's hip and torso movements were thereby transmitted directly into the structure of the chair, which—despite his practice of pre-performance oiling—responded by making considerable sound. Gould was keenly aware of the sound-making properties of his chair. Garreth Broesche reports that during an outtake of his recordings of the Brahms Ballades, Op. 10, Gould commented that "the chair is keeping up its own independent dialogue" (2015, 195). Far from being dismissive of the chair sounds, Gould's statement openly acknowledges that the creaks coexist with the sounds made by the piano.

Gould's 1965 recording of the first of Arnold Schoenberg's *Six Little Piano Pieces*, Op. 19, includes dozens of creaks. It sounds as though there are flashbulbs going off behind Gould as he plays; however, these are simply the creaking, cracking, and clicking sounds of the chair. Reading the creaks as sounded movements of Gould's body unearths remarkable correlations. My measurements of the chair creaks will be superimposed upon an earlier analysis of the work by Jonathan Kramer. Schoenberg's Op. 19, No. 1, exhibits a unique process that Kramer calls "the emergence of foregrounded meter" (1988, 181). The unfolding of this compositional process will be understood in relation to the creaking sounds made by the piano chair when Gould recorded the piece in 1965. I am not claiming a broad conclusion about Gould's general pianism, but rather identifying a non-trivial correlation between sounds made by Gould's body and a recognized formal trajectory within the work that he is playing. Overlaying Kramer's analytical findings with this new creak data reveals a correlation between the composition's trajectory of metric clarification and Gould's touch sounds. There is a marked decrease in the sounds made by Gould's chair that coincides with a gradual clarification of meter across Schoenberg's work.

Most commentators who engage with Gould's chair sounds are, either subtly or explicitly, dismissive of it. Bazzana characterizes the sounds as "the most enduring symbol of Gould's eccentricity" (2004, 108). Writing about the "cult of Glenn Gould," Bernard Holland lists the chair among Gould's "personal oddities," writing: "When [Gould] did attend functions, it was usually with his custom-made folding chair held under the arm like a baby blanket" (2007, B7). Paul Sanden is one of the few commentators to discuss the chair as part of Gould's instrument, devoting several paragraphs within his writings on corporeal liveness to the expressive content of the creaking sounds (2009 and 2013). Sanden does not provide visualization or quantification of these sounds, instead offering a prose description of the chair in action. In doing so, he opens the door for other scholars to make a more detailed case for the evocative soundworld created by its creaking.

Gould's recording of Schoenberg's Op. 19, No. 1, is one of the most creak-laden tracks in the pianist's discography. Beyond the acknowledgment that the chair sounds are music, there exists a deeper question: does the concentration of creaks relate to the musical material in Schoenberg's work, not simply to the relative speed or activity level of the music, but to its architecture? Since offering my own analysis of the score might appear self-serving in relation to my newly collected creak data, I turn to existing literature. Published analyses of Op. 19, No. 1, are plentiful. Schoenberg's *Six Little Piano Pieces* have generated a great deal of analytical commentary, and Gould himself was aware of the amount of ink spilled about this work, writing: "I wonder if any group of pieces of comparable total duration (five and a half minutes, give or take a *Luftpause*) has ever elicited as much analytical scrutiny as Schoenberg's Op. 19" (Gould and Page 1984, 124).

Kramer devotes half of a chapter in *The Time of Music* to Op. 19, No. 1. Kramer claims that Schoenberg's seventeen-measure work does not unfold a preexisting archetype (e.g., a miniature sonata form), but rather presents a unique formal trajectory related to a process whereby meter moves from vagueness toward clarity. He characterizes the work as exhibiting an emerging metric regularity, writing: "Foregrounded meter is a goal, not an assumption,

Example 3.9 The three formal sections of Arnold Schoenberg's Op. 19, No. 1, according to Kramer (1988), alongside their incipit, timing, and number of chair creaks in the 1965 recording by Glenn Gould.

SECTION in Kramer (1988)	INCIPIT in Schoenberg Op. 19, No. 1 (1911)	TIMING in Gould (1965)	CREAKS in Gould (1965)
I. mm. 1–6		0:00–0:29.3	55 creaks
II. mm. 7–12		0:29.3–0:51.5	19 creaks
III. mm. 13–17		0:51.5–1:26.0	11 creaks

of this music" (1988, 181). As seen in Example 3.9, Kramer divides the work into three parts: section I (mm. 1–6), section II (mm. 7–12), and section III (mm. 13–17). He outlines a trajectory from metric nebulousness to audible regularity, from an opening phrase that articulates no recognizable meter to a closing phrase where the written meter *becomes* the sounding meter. He writes of section I: "The opening is metrically nebulous. It is impossible to hear beats unequivocally as downbeats or upbeats in mm. 0–1" (1988, 181). The second section presents an emerging but still uncrystallized sense of meter: "The middle section is the middle stage in the evolution toward metric clarity: there are hyperbeats and hence hypermeasures, but shallower levels of organization are ambiguous" (1988, 182). Kramer highlights bar 13 as the focal point of the work: "Measure 13, which initiates the third section is also the movement's structural downbeat: it is the strongest metric accent, and it is also accented rhythmically" (1988, 182). He concludes: "Subsequent to the focal point of the movement in m. 13, the foreground meter remains unchallenged. The written meter becomes the sounding meter, whether it is 2/4 or 6/8. Not only foregrounded meter but also a metric hierarchy emerges unequivocally" (1988, 182). In Kramer's eyes (and ears), Op. 19, No. 1, is Schoenberg's innovative essay on the composing-out of an emerging metric clarity.

The point is not simply that there are so many creaks in Gould's recording, but where they are found, and where they are not. Along these lines, Example 3.9 also includes the number of chair creaks within each of Kramer's three formal sections. I count eighty-five creaks in this seventeen-measure work. There are fifty-five creaks in section I, nineteen creaks in section II, and eleven creaks in section III. There is a significant concentration of creaks during the first section (mm. 0–6), a reduction during the middle section (mm. 7–12), and finally a near but not complete cessation of creaking sounds during the third section (mm. 13–17). On average, the density of creaks is one creak per 0.51 seconds in section I, one creak per 1.29 seconds in section II, and one creak per 2.90 seconds in section III. Gould's chair sounds reinforce Kramer's conclusion regarding the emergence of metric clarity: "Whereas as a multi-level graph of metric hierarchy would be unthinkable in mm. 0–6, it could faithfully represent the metrical relationships in mm. 13–17" (Kramer 1988, 182). There is a marked decrease in Gould's physical motion, as evidenced by the sound of his chair, during this recording of Schoenberg's unique composition in which the meter becomes clarified. Within this specific recording of this specific work, the frequency of Gould's touch sounds correlates to the gradual emergence of a metrical hierarchy. As Schoenberg's written meter becomes the sounding meter, Gould's physical shifting largely abates.[8]

Podium stamps

On January 18, 1961, in the American Legion Hall in Hollywood, California, Bruno Walter led a rehearsal of Mahler's Ninth Symphony with the Columbia Symphony Orchestra. Both the original 1962 Columbia LP release and its

---

[8] The correlation between Gould's chair creaks and the emergence of metric clarity in Schoenberg's Op. 19, No. 1, is discussed at length in Richard Beaudoin (2021).

1994 Sony Classical compact disc reissue include a 21.5-minute track entitled "A Working Portrait: Recording the Mahler Ninth Symphony—Narrated by John McClure."[9] McClure was the producer on the session and his narration is interwoven with excerpts from Walter's rehearsals. Of particular interest is Walter's approach to Mahler's second movement Ländler. At 11:15 of "A Working Portrait," McClure comments on Walter's foot-stamping at a specific moment in the score:

> Incidentally, you will hear Doctor Walter stamp on the podium at the downbeat before the entrance of the main violin theme, seventeen seconds from the beginning of the movement. His years in Vienna had gotten the Ländler rhythm so firmly in his blood, he was unable to control this dance-derived impulse. And he did it each time the bar returned, even during the takes, despite my reminders. (Walter 1962/1994, 11:15)

"A Working Portrait" includes three separate versions of Walter's rehearsal of the opening of the second movement. Setting aside here McClure's comments about the Ländler being "so firmly" in Walter's "blood," it is the case that the dance on which the movement is based is marked by hopping and the stomping of feet. True to McClure's word, Walter's podium stamps are audible on all three rehearsal takes, as well as the final version released on the recording proper. Example 3.10 presents the full score of the opening thirteen measures of Mahler's movement and transcribes Walter's podium stamps during each iteration.[10] McClure is correct that Walter stamps "each time the bar returned" but incorrect when he says that this foot sound occurs "at the downbeat before the entrance of the main violin theme." The podium stamp occurs on, or near, the *second beat* of the bar.

Walter's foot-stamp in bar 9 is audible in all four versions. Takes 2, 3, and the final version all have Walter's stamp coincident with beat 2. His foot sound lines up with the G in the violas and bassoons. Take 1 is the outlier. It is marvelously idiosyncratic. Walter stamps fractionally *after* beat 2. The sound alerts the second violins that the rhythm, the tempo, and the character undergo a sudden change. Walter's stamp signals the heavy, fiddle-like texture requested by Mahler's marking: *Schwerfällig, wie Fiedeln*. The

---

[9] I am grateful to Steven Rings for drawing my attention to this example.

[10] Audio Example 3.9 presents four separate passes through mm. 1–13: Take 1, Take 2, and Take 3 (all from "A Working Portrait"), plus the final version as released on the recording proper.

subsequent takes, as well as the final version, have Walter stamping squarely on beat 2. There are other differences. In both Takes 1 and 2, Walter continues the stamping after bar 9. In Take 2, Walter marks the third beat of bar 10 with a foot stamp *and* a vocalization.

Walter did not reserve his stamping for these 1961 rehearsals in Hollywood. Decades earlier, on January 16, 1938, he recorded Mahler's Ninth Symphony with the Vienna Philharmonic in the Wien Musikvereinssaal and stamped

Example 3.10 Gustav Mahler, Ninth Symphony, second movement, mm. 1–13, annotating the podium stamps in four separate takes during Bruno Walter's 1961 rehearsal and recording session with the Columbia Symphony Orchestra. See ⊙ Audio Example 3.9.

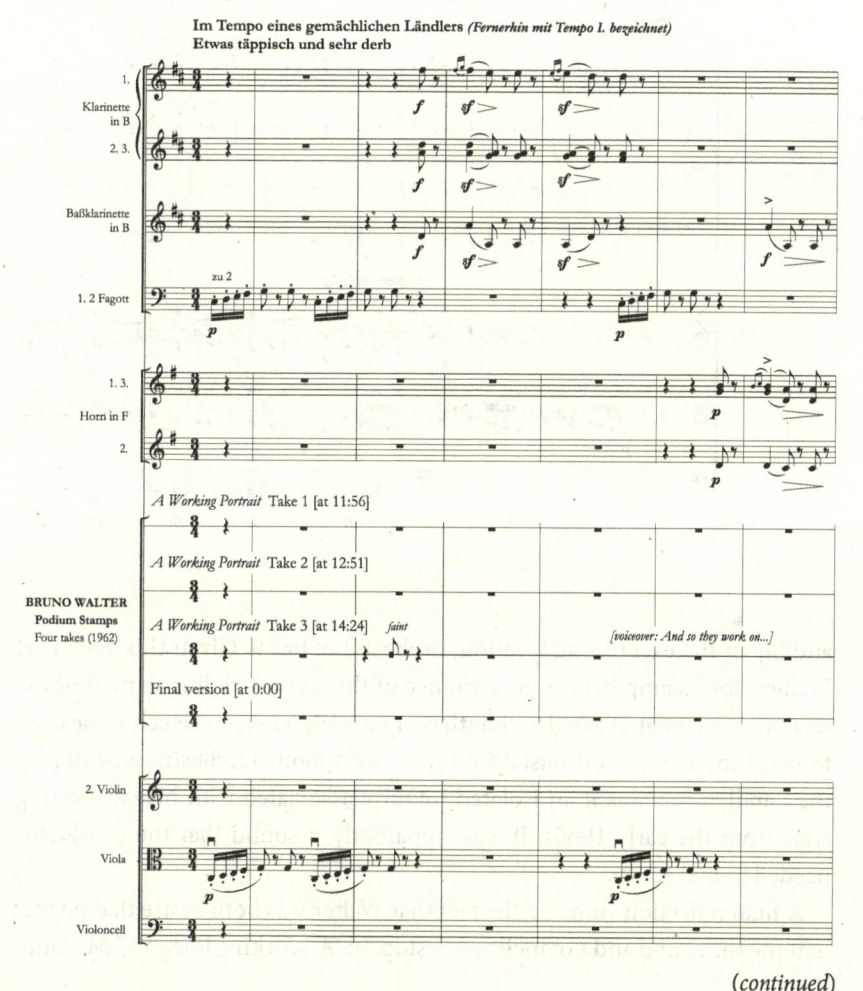

(continued)

Example 3.10 Continued

audibly in the exact same location, on beat 2 of bar 9. Given this evidence, Walter's foot stamp before the entrance of the second violins in m. 9 of the second movement of Mahler's Ninth is not merely a rehearsal technique used to teach the Hollywood-based Columbia Symphony Orchestra how to play the Ländler, nor was it an isolated impulse associated with his conducting style from the early 1960s. It was, apparently, a sound that the conductor needed to make.

A final reflection sums up the fact that Walter was both aware that he was making the sound and not inclined to stop. In "A Working Portrait," McClure describes Walter in the control room after the recording session, listening to playbacks with some of the orchestral musicians and sound engineers:

> Bruno Walter listens with his eyes shut, conducting again, occasionally making a remark to one of the musicians. Deep breaths explode from him at climaxes or crucial downbeats. And when the very audible foot-stamping is heard, he looks at me, smiling: "Guilty!" he says. "No doubt about it. Guilty with extenuating circumstances." And we all laugh. (Walter 1962/1994, 15:34)

Walter's podium stamp *in that particular bar of that particular symphony* is a gesture—and a sound—that he made when he rehearsed and performed the work, across decades, across continents, and across orchestras. That single podium stamp is integral to Walter's sounded interpretation of Mahler's notation.

Timbral damper pedals

At the opposite end of the volume spectrum from Walter's foot stamps are the subtle sounds produced by the feet of pianists. Those who play the instrument will know that even perfectly maintained pedals make sound as they engage the damper system within the instrument. Such sounds are generally rather quiet and vary from piano to piano. *From Afar*, a 2022 Deutsche Grammophon double-album by Víkingur Ólafsson, presents a cornucopia of pedal sounds. Each of the two discs includes the same repertoire—works by Thomas Adès, J. S. Bach, Béla Bartók, Snorri Sigfús Birgisson, Johannes Brahms, Sigvaldi Kaldalóns, György Kurtág, Wolfgang Amadeus Mozart, and Robert Schumann—performed on a grand piano (disc 1) and an upright piano (disc 2). The timbre of the upright is further altered by a layer of felt covering the strings. Describing disc 2, Ólafsson writes: "In this recording, the microphones are so close you can hear the keys depressed and released, the pedals creak, even the pianist breathing. I want the sound to reach the listener very much as if sitting on the piano bench with me—a very different experience from sitting in a spacious concert hall listening to a shiny, black Steinway D" (2022, 12). Whether playing an upright or a nine-foot grand, pedal sounds are a familiar sonic component of piano-playing.

While most non-notated sounds studied in this book were chosen for their perceptibility, there comes a point where decidedly quiet sounds require analytical attention. Such is the case with the sound that accompanies the engagement of the damper pedal. In the following comparative analysis of three recordings of Alexander Scriabin's Prelude in E-flat minor, Op. 16, No. 4, the auditor might not initially perceive the pedal sounds clearly. They are quiet and might require a pair of headphones. Visiting the quiet world of touch sounds is akin to looking through a microscope. There is a world of expressive meaning occurring near the floor (as the pianist's feet work the pedals) and captured at low levels of signal (by the microphones).

The fundamental sound of the damper pedal has two components: the depression of the pedal, which causes the dampers to release *en masse* inside the instrument, generating a sound that resembles whispering the word "see"; and the release of the pedal, which causes the dampers to re-engage and silence the resonance, generating a sound similar to whispering the word "sit." In practice, these two sounds are heard in reverse order, as when a pianist plays a chord and then quickly clears the resonance by releasing and then re-engaging the pedal. Such an act results in the signature sound of the damper pedal in action: *sit-see.* In her article "Listening to the Piano Pedal," Elfrieda Hiebert differentiates between rhythmic pedaling and syncopated pedaling. According to Hiebert, rhythmic pedaling was the prevailing method of engaging the pedal in the late eighteenth and early nineteenth centuries, describing that "the treading of the pedal was made to coincide with the tone or chord (often designated 'rhythmic pedaling'), so that the strings of the piano would begin to vibrate immediately with the sound" (2013, 234). By contrast, syncopated pedaling can be "defined as lowering the pedal (i.e., raising the dampers) after the sound of the tone and lifting it (i.e., lowering the dampers) with the sound of the following tone; this connects the tones" (2013, 234). While it is possible to hear examples of both rhythmic and syncopated pedaling in recordings of Scriabin's Prelude Op. 16, No. 4, the examples I have chosen mainly include rhythmic pedaling, as treading the pedal after the chord (or note) in slow tempos is particularly useful in this E-flat minor *lento.* The relationship between rhythmic pedaling and slow tempi extends back to the nineteenth century, as Hiebert relates: "It appears that Liszt was aware of the benefits of pedaling in this manner. In a letter dated 27 July 1875, he wrote to Louis Köhler, 'The entrance of the pedal after the striking of the chords . . . is very much to be recommended . . . especially in slow tempi' " (2013, 234, ellipses in original).

The brevity and texture of Scriabin's Prelude Op. 16, No. 4, makes it a useful subject for the analysis of pedal sounds. The complete score can be seen as part of Example 3.11. The work is structured as a set of four three-bar phrases each culminating in a series of chordal quarter notes. These cadential gestures turn out to be rich repositories of damper activity. Scriabin's score includes no designated pedal marks, meaning that the foot-related sounds heard on each track are the result of each pianist's decision-making and not differing interpretations of pedal notations, which are themselves notoriously vague. The rhythmic similarity of mm. 3, 6, 9, and 12 sets in relief an important harmonic change at the close of the third phrase. Bar 3 includes three root-position tonic chords, bar 6 three root-position dominant chords, and bar 12 three root-position tonic chords. The outlier is m. 9, which, instead of a stable root-position triad, includes three quarter-note chords that sound a chromatic progression that moves from the Neapolitan sixth (F-flat major on beat 1) to a German augmented sixth (on C♭ during beats 2 and 3) that resolves to a cadential 6/4 on the downbeat of m. 10. In recordings where the *sit-see* of the damper pedal is audible, the chromaticism of bar 9 is associated with increased pedal activity.

Example 3.11 provides a comparative transcription of damper pedal sounds in recordings of Scriabin's Prelude by Lucille Chung (2002), Sheila Arnold (2000), and Anthony Hewitt (2016).[11] While there are other unwritten sounds on these three recordings—including sounds of breath and, notably, on Hewitt's track, birdsong—the focus is here on sounds created by the movement of the feet.[12] The example uses one symbol to stand for all pedal sounds, be they *sit*, *see*, or the *sit-see* pair.[13] The tracks by Chung, Arnold, and Hewitt offer a Goldilocks-like comparison of the formal and rhetorical role played by pedal sounds. Arnold's measured and motivic pedaling is positioned between Chung's near silence at one extreme and Hewitt's (hyper)active, pedal-forward approach at the other.

Chung made her recording on September 14–15, 2002, at Dynamic Studio in Genoa, Italy, and the track was recorded and edited by Rino Trasi.

---

[11] Audio Example 3.10 presents three separate passes through mm. 10–12: first Chung, then Arnold, then Hewitt.

[12] The birdsong heard in Hewitt's recording of Scriabin's Prelude Op. 16, No. 4, is that of the European robin. I am grateful to Frank Lehman for this identification.

[13] Each *sit-see* sound has its own internal rhythm and pacing. While most occur rapidly, some have a suspenseful, hesitating quality wherein the *sit* and the *see* are separated by a gap. An exemplar of a hesitating *sit-see* can be heard in Sheila Arnold's 2000 recording, just after the downbeat of m. 7 (at 0:36.3).

Example 3.11 Alexander Scriabin, Prelude in E-flat minor, Op. 16, No. 4, annotating the damper pedal sounds in recordings by Lucille Chung (2002), Sheila Arnold (2000), and Anthony Hewitt (2016). See ▶ Audio Example 3.10.

From the perspective of pedal sounds, Chung's recording is straightforward: there are nearly none. To be sure, Chung is engaging the pedals. The resulting resonances are audible, but the *sit-see* sounds are not. There are four exceptions: two faint damper pedal sounds are heard at analogous moments in bars 2 and 11 (after the dotted sixteenth-note B♭4), and two clearing pedal sounds are faintly evident after the downbeats of bars 7 and 10. These four aside, Chung's track places its pedal activity outside the bounds of audibility. The track demonstrates her decision to engage the damper pedal discreetly, a microphone placement that minimizes pedal sounds, a careful post-production editing, or a combination of all three. The resulting track recalls Neuhaus's sonic ideal, as the tones of Chung's piano are, by and large, "clothed in silence."

Sheila Arnold's 2000 recording of Op. 16, No. 4, includes a greater number of pedal sounds than Chung's, and their placement demonstrates a thoroughgoing logic across its twelve bars. Arnold made her recording between February 2 and 5, 1999, in the Klaus von Bismarck Saal of the WDR Funkhaus. The track was produced by Bernard Wallerius alongside Tonmeister Andreas Beutner and Toningenieur Christoph Gronarz and released on the Edition Zeitklang label. I count nineteen pedal sounds in Arnold's 1:23 track. Her pedaling epitomizes a thoughtful, patterned approach. The chordal arrivals that punctuate each phrase are met with an identical sequence of pedal sounds. There is a damper sound after the anacrustic dotted eighth in mm. 2, 5, 8, and 11, followed by another after the downbeat in mm. 3, 6, 9, and 12. The only divergence from this pattern is Arnold's additional damper release in the middle of bar 9, which corresponds to the novel chord change on beat 2. A concurrent pattern is created by Arnold's treading on the pedal just *after* the downbeat; she produces a post-downbeat pedal sound nine times in this twelve-bar work, in bars 3, 4, 5, 6, 7, 8, 9, 10 and 12. The regularity of her touch sounds creates expectation. Arnold's pedaling contributes to a track wherein the motivic logic of Scriabin's score is fused with the *sit-see* of the damper pedal.

When compared to the sonic reticence of Chung's track and the logical pedal patterns of Arnold's, Anthony Hewitt's 2016 recording of Op. 16, No. 4, for Champs Hill Records—recorded in the Music Room, Champs Hill, West Sussex, UK, in 2014 and produced, engineered, and edited by Patrick Allen—displays a flamboyant approach to pedaling. This is not to say that his track disregards the melancholy mood of Scriabin's *lento*. However, the otherwise placid surface of the track is teeming with the life of unwritten touch sounds. Taking up the sartorial metaphor that began this chapter, Hewitt's recording is less *clothed* than most others. It is not enrobed in silence. Instead, the silence is pulled back, allowing the activity of the feet to be perceptible. I count twenty-six pedal sounds in Hewitt's recording. Two aspects of their location are notable; one is cumulative, the other rhetorical. Hewitt's pedaling increases steadily across the work. There are three sounds in mm. 1–3, six in mm. 4–6, seven in mm. 7–9, and ten in mm. 10–12. The rhetorical design of Hewitt's pedaling is evident when appraised alongside Arnold's. For Arnold, the self-similar chordal arrivals of bars 3, 6, 9, and 12 are pedaled in the same fashion. Each has a single *sit-see* sound just after the first chord (the exception being m. 9, where the sound also occurs after beat 2). In Hewitt's recording, bars 3, 6, 9, and 12 include a pedal sound *after nearly every chord*. The pattern is broken only in the final measure, where beat 2 is not followed by a pedal sound. This "missing" *sit-see* contradicts the thrice-heard pattern and plays with an attentive listener's expectation. Hewitt's change of pattern signals that the drama is over. When Hewitt arrives at the final cadence of Scriabin's prelude, one might say that the damper pedal cadences as well.[14]

The deeper analytical point about Hewitt's recording concerns the difference between the first and last phrases. In the score, bars 1–3 are nearly identical to bars 10–12. A theorist analyzing Scriabin's piece could rightly make the claim that the last three bars essentially recapitulate the first three. Analysts of Hewitt's track can make no such claim. Hewitt flutters his damper pedal throughout the final system, producing three pedal sounds in bar 10 and five in bar 11. The latter tells a vivid story. In the score, bar 11 seems to repeat bar 2. In the recordings by Chung and Arnold, the number and type of audible events in these two bars are the same, differing only in terms of timing. In Hewitt's track, bar 2 and bar 11 are wildly different. Bar 2 is entirely devoid of pedal sounds; indeed, Hewitt is holding the damper during the first two bars. The effect is of a lightly drawn blur. Bar 11, by contrast, is animated by the flickering damper sounds after nearly every note. Any sense of recapitulation is replaced by a sense of newness. The listener first encounters the melody in a state of repose (bar 2), and later it is surrounded by a lively entourage of pedal sounds (bar 11). Hewitt's recording exemplifies the role of

---

14 The birdsong in Hewitt's track comes to the fore on the downbeat of m. 12, at the final resolution to the E-flat minor tonic. As the bar progresses, the birds quiet and become fully silent during the closing resonance. It is unknown whether their conclusive silence is the result of post-production editing or evidence of avian harmonic sensitivity. Whatever the cause, the end of the track exhibits concurrent cadences in Scriabin's prelude, Hewitt's piano pedals, and the singing European robins of Champs Hill.

touch sounds in providing an accurate experiential description of the music *as heard on the track*. Attentiveness to the score alone becomes inadequate since it ignores the activity that is taking place at Hewitt's feet.

A conclusion to the study of damper pedals requires returning to Sheila Arnold's recording. The final twenty-three seconds of her track include a compendium of pedal sounds, each with different rhetorical and sonic implications. Example 3.12 presents mm. 11–12 of Scriabin's prelude

Example 3.12 Alexander Scriabin, Prelude in E-flat minor, Op. 16, No. 4, mm. 11–12, with an annotated spectrogram illustrating five *sit-see* pedal sounds in the 2000 recording by Sheila Arnold. See ▶ Audio Example 3.11.

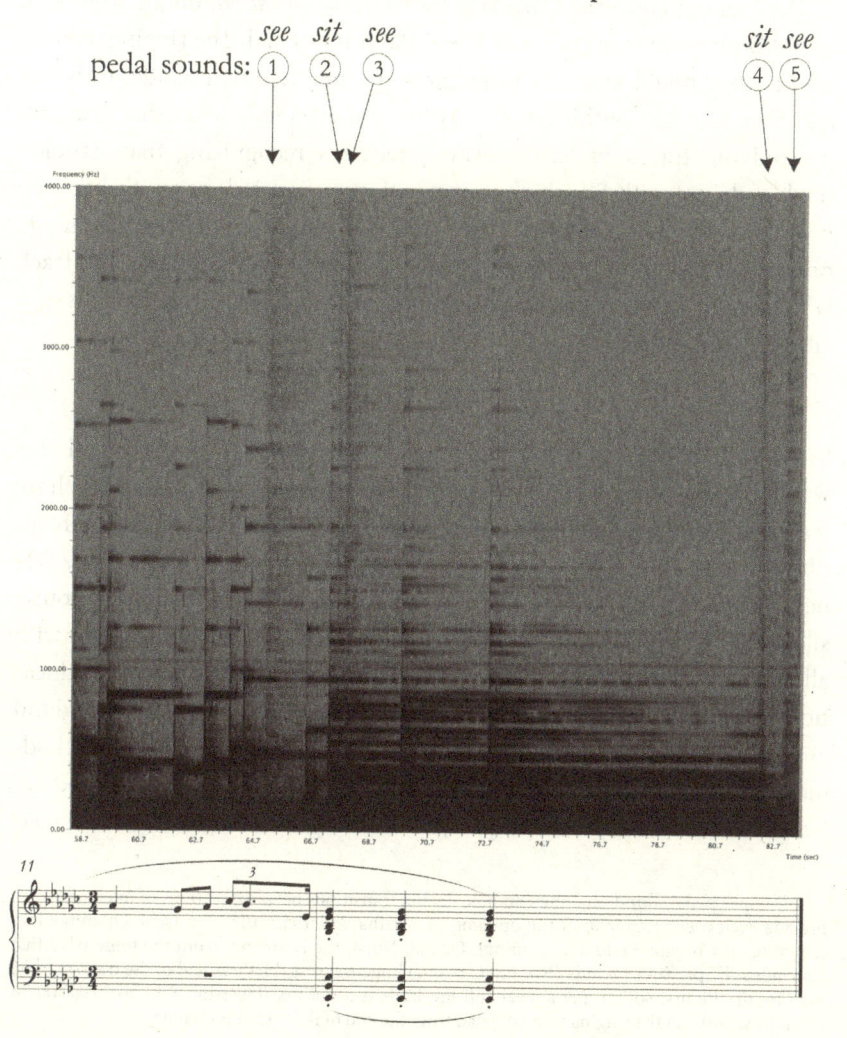

alongside a spectrogram of Arnold's recording. Five pedal sounds are audible. The first is a *see* sound—a depression of the damper—between the two final notes of m. 11. The second and third sounds are a rapid *sit-see* pair just after the arrival of the tonic chord on the downbeat of m. 12. The fourth occurs after Scriabin's notation has concluded, when Arnold releases the pedal and ends the resonance of the E-flat minor tonic after the conclusion of m. 12. The fifth pedal sound (the *see* at 1:22.8) is plainly visible on the spectrogram and vibrantly audible on the recording. This final event of the track is triggered by Arnold's depression of the damper pedal as she *prepares to begin the next piece in the set*, the buoyant *Allegretto* in F-sharp major, Op. 16, No. 5.

The theorist concerned primarily with Scriabin's score might argue that Arnold's performance ends with the E-flat minor triad. The ringing damper sound, they might argue, is in preparation for the next prelude in the set and therefore has nothing to do with the melancholy *lento* that precedes it. Studying tracks *in toto*, however, requires recognizing that Arnold's track ends not with Scriabin's root-position tonic triad, nor with her own resonance-silencing damper pedal release. It ends with the chromatic rainbow of a damper pedal activation. The last thing audible on the track is the sound of dozens of strings simultaneously freed from the felts and vibrating together.[15]

Sensitizing oneself to unwritten music takes time. Having worked this way for many years, it is only recently that my patience and openness have reached a point where the full sonic life of a given track is constantly perceptible. Akin to a yoga practice or a meditation that emphasizes sensory awareness, I now listen to recordings of notated music without (sub)consciously silencing non-scored sounds. I perceive touch sounds in counterpoint with all other musical material. This effort is often in conflict with music education, which regularly foregrounds notated events above all others. Sound engineers are experts at hearing the totality, and I admire them. My methodology hearkens back to the census metaphor from Chapter 1. Tracks need not be studied exclusively for their passport-holding *citizens* (the notes and rests

---

[15] Damper pedal sounds are often audible during transitions between sections of interconnected prelude cycles. For example, in the opening of Martha Argerich's 1975 Deutsche Grammophon recording of Chopin's Prelude in E minor, Op. 28, No. 4, the resonance from the tonic triad that concluded the previous prelude (No. 3 in G major) lingers across the threshold of the track marker. As a result, the first sound that appears on the track is not a first-inversion E minor triad (as in Chopin's score), but the ringing G major triad from the end of the previous prelude.

whose lineage can be traced to markings in the score), but for the full complement of *persons* (sounds of all kinds) that are present to the ear.

The analyses of fingernails, fingertips, fingerfalls, hands, hips, and feet now complete, I extend an invitation to the reader to listen again to recordings that they love with newfound sensitivity to sounding bodies, be they made of brass, bronze, copper, felt, gold, ivory, nylon, plastic, platinum, silver, skin, steel, or wood. Heinrich Neuhaus recommended that tone be "enshrined in silence like a jewel in a velvet case." Each of the musicians studied in this chapter—William Chapman Nyaho, Claudio Arrau, the Guarneri Quartet, Bernard Greenhouse, Zara Nelsova, Ana Archilés, Valerie Hartzell, Julian Bream, Velvet Brown, Glenn Gould, Bruno Walter, Lucille Chung, Sheila Arnold, and Anthony Hewitt—created tracks that spoil Neuhaus's desired enshrinement, sometimes spectacularly. Accepting sonic totalities is a purposeful act of intellectual enlargement. I do not hear touch sounds as blemishes upon the work being recorded. My mode of analysis does not enshrine tone as much as open the doors to let tone interact with the world outside of the metaphorical velvet case. I like to imagine that tone is happy to be outdoors and to reconnect with touch sounds. They are, after all, close relatives.

4

Sounds of Effort

Sounded effort as music

Within classical music, paradigms of effortlessness hold sway. The archetypical virtuoso blends extraordinary skill with intense self-discipline to produce captivating interpretations. Their poise in the face of technical complexity can seem unreal. In colloquial terms, they *make it look easy*, a phrase seemingly incompatible with something as revealing as a grunt. But grunts appear on classical recordings, and when they do, they turn out to be vividly expressive objects. The virtuoso performs flawlessly, be it onstage, in the recording studio, even on the subway platform. In *Loving Music Till It Hurts*, William Cheng unpacks a "social experiment" in which violinist Joshua Bell busked, incognito, in Washington, DC's L'Enfant Plaza metro station, playing the Chaconne from J. S. Bach's Partita in D minor, BWV 1004. Cheng uses the scenario to investigate both the unreasonable expectations of perfection that surround classical musicians as well as the rapt naïveté of the cognoscenti who adore them, at one point quoting one of Bell's admirers as saying that the violinist "plays like a god."[1]

Delineating an array of unhealthy stereotypes, Cheng writes, "In the experiment, the superhuman musician and music represented the definitive controls, the unerring centers around which variables came and went in the form of capricious passersby" (2020, 35). The problem is made plain: classical musicians are often advertised as "unerring," "superhuman," and god-like. The music of genius composers (like Bach) flows through the skillful intellect

---

[1] In his April 8, 2007, article for the *Washington Post*, columnist Gene Weingarten—the mastermind of the Washington, DC, metro station stunt—touted Bell's virtuosity across numerous professions: "He's soloed with the finest orchestras here and abroad, but he's also appeared on 'Sesame Street,' done late-night talk TV and performed in feature films. That was Bell playing the soundtrack on the 1998 movie 'The Red Violin.' (He body-doubled, too, playing to a naked Greta Scacchi.) As composer John Corigliano accepted the Oscar for Best Original Dramatic Score, he credited Bell, who, he said, 'plays like a god'" (Weingarten 2007).

Sounds as They Are. Richard Beaudoin, Oxford University Press. © Oxford University Press 2024.
DOI: 10.1093/oso/9780197659281.003.0005

of genius interpreters (like Bell) and into the priceless instruments crafted by genius luthiers (like Stradivari). Surrounded by such a surfeit of perfection, it is no wonder that when listening to a classical musician perform, we do not expect them to sweat and strain like the rest of us. Classical artists are not the sort of musicians who (need to) utter sounds of exertion. Virtuosos do not pant and moan. We do not expect "gods" to grunt.

Within the classical recording industry, it is undesirable, even strange, for a performer to signal that they are at the limits of their physical abilities. Stranger still would be to acknowledge that some musicians *need* to produce sounds of effort to play well. Of all the unwritten music in classical recordings, sounded effort—grunts, groans, moans, growls, and the like—is the most transgressive. Performing classical works requires effort and, while all musicians breathe when they play, not all cross the threshold into vocalizing. Whether voluntary or involuntary, certain compositions elicit certain performers to make sounds of effort, and sometimes these are preserved on tracks. Classical music's unspoken distaste for sounded effort is reflected sartorially. This music was (and, to some degree, is still) performed in tuxedos and dresses, garments associated not with hard work but with luxurious socializing. Sweat is contained inside formal wear. Engineers "dress up" their tracks to hide sounded effort. With few exceptions, classical record labels seem satisfied when they have successfully projected a sonic image of instrumentalists who are poised, non-sweaty, and (aside from their instruments) silent.

Whether it be cellists moaning in the recording studio or conductors yelping on the podium, sounded effort has historically been greeted with derision. The hyphenated adjective often used to describe audible exertions is "extra-musical." Critic Michael Jameson invokes the term while reviewing cellist Pieter Wispelwey's recordings of music by Benjamin Britten, writing that "the excessive resonance and very close focus of the sound conveys a distracting array of extra-musical sounds, though Wispelwey himself is not completely innocent here, with occasional intrusive grunts and intakes of breath" (1992, 54). Jameson's verdict is that Wispelwey is "guilty" of intruding on Britten's music. Critic David Vickers reveals the impact of grunts on his estimation of conductor René Jacobs: "However, the 2008 Aix-en-Provence performance of *Belshazzar* is infuriating because René Jacobs's decisions—unhistorical, unstylish, and profoundly unmusical—cause a cornucopia of horrible aberrations. His conducting technique is astonishingly bad; he frequently grunts loudly and gestures bizarrely as if he is hanging up the washing to dry, regardless of the musical metre and mood" (2011, 104). Reception of sounded effort can also veer toward the comic, as when Lindsay Kemp, reviewing a recording of music by Henry Purcell, admits that grunting can make the listener feel as though they have company:

> The well-known *Round-O* (taken from *Abdelazer*), played on solo gamba, really comes in for the treatment, with the strenuous effort thus caused to its executant (presumably Jay Bernfeld) being emphasized by sniffing and grunting so immediate that it may well have nervous listeners glancing over their shoulders to check that they are alone. (1992, 151)

The implication is revealing. According to Kemp's logic, a person auditing a classical recording is meant to feel "alone" with the composer's music, even as they listen to a hard-working performer playing it. A sniff or grunt creates nervousness. An unsettled desire to look "over their shoulders to check that they are alone" arises the moment that the body of the performer becomes audible. Kemp's quip signals that many classical recordings are engineered to establish a private, quasi-sacred commune between auditor and composer, with the performer acting as a corporeally silent medium.

One might keep score. Composers are free to notate whatever sounds they wish. Listeners are likewise free to make sound while they listen. Performers and sound engineers, however, are hemmed in from both sides, as neither composers nor listeners seem especially interested in hearing traces of performative effort. While there are exceptions, the norms of the industry require the transmission of the composer's notation to the ear of the listener with nary an inhale, to say nothing of a moan.

Sounds of effort in classical music are nothing new. Johannes Brahms grunted, hummed, and snorted when he played the piano. Even as present-day critics regularly call for grunt-free recordings, I can imagine the rapturous reviews that would welcome the discovery of high-fidelity recordings of Brahms playing his complete works, even if he uttered small moans during the proceedings. As these recordings do not exist, evidence of Brahms's sound-making can be found in Roger Moseley's summary of commentaries by those who heard the composer play live:

> One means by which Brahms compensated for his failing dexterity was his voice. His playing had been accompanied by a "gentle humming" since the 1850s, but in later years this noise transformed into what Ethel Smyth

described as "a sort of muffled roar, as of Titans stirred to sympathy in the bowels of the earth." Ferdinand Schumann was less poetic in registering "a sort of gasping, grumbling or snoring," which was "audible as far back as the tenth row," and Brahms's biographer Max Kalbeck once heard such extraordinary sounds accompanying Brahms's solitary piano-playing ("a growling, whining, and moaning, which at the height of the musical climax changed into a loud howling") that he thought the composer must have surreptitiously acquired a dog. (2009, 144)

As one of the earliest documented performers to groan, it is intriguing to wonder why Brahms did so. Along these lines, I am bemused by Moseley's assertion that the grunts were Brahms's compensations for his own "failing dexterity." Effortful sounds emerge just as often from youthful, fully dexterous musicians, and I see no reason to assume that Brahms groaned in an effort to distract his listeners from wrong or missing notes. Moseley continues his conjecture by claiming that "Brahms's grunting may have been designed to emphasize his masculinity: as a young man he was embarrassed by his high-pitched voice, and he tried to lower it, to somewhat unpleasant effect" (2009, 144). While Brahms's feeling about the pitch of his voice might be verifiable, to claim that his grunting was a strategy to signal masculinity is not. There are myriad reasons why a musician might hum, growl, or moan. To suggest that Brahms was grunting to seem more "masculine" seems a bridge too far. I see no reason to conclude that Brahms's vocal elaborations were a way of "compensating" for pianistic shortcomings or that they were "designed" to project masculinity. To repurpose Glenn Gould's self-assessment quoted in Chapter 1, Brahms might have played "very much less well" if he didn't "indulge in a few vocal elaborations."

It is necessary to distinguish between written and unwritten sounds of effort. Notated grunts are common in scores composed after 1945. Toru Takemitsu's solo flute work *Voice* (1971) requires the player to growl into the headjoint. Grunts and moans alike appear in Julius Eastman's *Femenine* (1974). Olga Neuwirth includes a grunt-heavy aria in her opera *Lost Highway* (2002–2003). Donal Henehan summarized a 1986 New York Philharmonic performance of György Ligeti's choral works *Aventures* (1962) and *Nouvelle aventures* (1966) as "Three singers (Karen Beardsley, Joyce Castle and John Brandstetter) engaged in a wordless but eloquent erotic triangle, making their points with hisses, gulps, gurgles, snarls, moans, barks, grunts and other subverbal devices" (*New York Times*, May 22, 1986, Section C, 28).

Ligeti's reliance on "subverbal devices" to sonify eros is no outlier. Notated grunts and moans often arise when composers wish to evoke sexual activity. Sounds of effort are not unique to scores by Takemitsu, Eastman, Neuwirth, or Ligeti. I recall listening for the first time to Janine Jansen's 2002 recording of Chiel Meijering's 1999 solo violin work *La vengeance d'une femme*. At 4:59, Jansen utters an expressive moan that evokes a sound one might hear, or make, during sex. Her moan is not improvised; it is called for in the score. The passage is reproduced in Example 4.1. Meijering's notation denotes the sound using a trio of markings: the word "moan" appears above the staff, housed in a rectangle; the onomatopoetic "ahhh! . . . ." appears below the staff, as a quasi-lyric; the "x" notehead itself is followed by a dipping curved line, suggesting that the moan should descend (as many moans do).

Jansen performs the written notation, prominently sounding the moan in bar 121. Lest the reader be concerned that I am projecting a sexual implication onto a potentially non-sexual sound, Meijering's score continues with the following character markings: "Feel it coming!" (m. 130), "There you go: the juice is squirting in!" (m. 133), "Keep it coming baby!" (m. 138), "fountain of love!" (m. 139), and "Almost a rigor mortis" (m. 144). Jansen's moan accurately and effectively corresponds to the notation in Meijering's score. It is a proper sonification of written music. While both written and unwritten sounds of exertion are expressive, non-notated effort belongs to a different category, as it transgresses both the norms of score-centric recording practices and the expectation of bodily silence among classical recording artists.

Whether good or bad, alluring or distracting, integral or extraneous, sounded exertions raise questions. How can one properly analyze a track that includes non-notated sounds of effort? What is their formal, rhythmic, and expressive implication within the work being recorded? How should

Example 4.1 Chiel Meijering, *La vengeance d'une femme*, mm. 120–22, corresponding to 4:56–5:03 in the 2002 recording by Janine Jansen. See ⊙ Audio Example 4.1.

theorists differentiate between vocalizations; are differences between moans and grunts akin to differences between, say, a dominant ninth chord and a half-diminished seventh? Most important, where do these sounds occur on a given track, and where might they never (or rarely) occur? The answers to these questions provide insight into the personality of performers in the act of recording. Categorization is complex. Does one group these sounds according to shared timbres or according to the identity of the musicians from which they originate? The former would allow for testable accuracy—moan x originates at point y and lasts for z milliseconds—while the latter operates along more ambiguous lines—a grunt from a teenage virtuoso might be read differently than one uttered by a nonagenarian.

I organize audible exertion into two main categories based on the character of the sounds themselves: climactic and intimate. The former is more common and occurs when an emphatic vocalization is heard at (or near) a moment of musical and formal climax. Climactic effort will be illustrated by analyses of tracks by Yannick Nézet-Séguin, Pablo Casals, and Fazıl Say. The second category appears during less climactic passages whose musical rhetoric suggests an ongoing process. Intimate effort will be studied in recordings by Claire Chase, Hélène Grimaud, and Evgeny Kissin. These two broad classes are following by an investigation of three specialized categories. In the first, a recording by cellist Giambattista Valdettaro moves beyond grunts to full-voiced growling that becomes a thoroughgoing, rumbling counterpoint. In the second, conductor Georg Solti's moans act as phrase dividers. I conclude with a discussion of "unheard" grunts, relating them to two "archives of absence." In one, grunts are silenced by teachers and mentors long before the musician arrives in the recording studio. In another, the erased and obscured grunts in late recordings by pianist Joyce Hatto allow for a speculative analysis of grunts unheard.

Sound, sex, and somaesthetics

When discussing unwritten sounds of effort *as music*, it is necessary to address their (potential) similarity with sounds that can occur during sex. I will explore grunts, groans, and moans in musical contexts. Since similar sounds are sometimes associated with sex, it will be useful to identify sonic intersections between these two environments. I will not claim that musical moans are dissimilar from sexual ones, and I do not intend to fully disambiguate them. While most (if not all) performers who moan are not doing so in an explicitly sexual context, it would be naïve to assume that all listeners receive the sounds without recognizing a similarity.[2] Evidence of the connection can be found in record reviews. Fazıl Say's 2001 moan-rich recording of Franz Liszt's Piano Sonata in B minor inspired the following assessment from critic Jed Distler, likening the interpretation to a pornographic film: "I can't say I care for the Liszt Sonata's hollow, bloodless miking, nor the pianist's callow, finicky conception. He impatiently plows through the tender D major theme as if its overt lyricism were a source of embarrassment and drops a beat each time before he launches into the exposition's infamous octave section. What's more, his characteristic moans and groans now exceed the official porno movie limit" (2001). Richard Osborne's February 2000 review of Hélène Grimaud's interpretation of two late Beethoven sonatas, which appear on the recording immediately after the composer's Fourth Piano Concerto, likewise makes an analogy between effortful music-making and effortful sex:

> It is a measure of Grimaud's force of personality that the sonatas do not sound small-scale after the concerto: if anything they sound bigger. Two sequences in particular stay in the mind: the exultant end of Op. 110, a coronary-defying race to the summit, and the theme and variations, *Gesangvoll, mit innigster Empfindung*, in Op. 109, which Grimaud realises with terrific intensity, the playing accompanied by a good deal of audible breathing and gentle moaning, like some slow-drawn act of sexual congress.
>
> The recordings of the two sonatas present the playing pretty much as it is: powerful, aggressive, sweeping all before it even at the cost of moments that are ungracious and unkempt. (2000, 48)

I am intrigued by Osborne's use of the phrase "as it is" to describe Grimaud's recordings, especially as they support his feeling that her music-making is, at times, "ungracious and unkempt." The very tracks that inspired Distler

---

[2] John Corbett and Terri Kapsalis report that "A short list of songs that contain female orgasm sounds includes Marvin Gaye's 'You Sure Love To Ball' (1973), the Time's 'If The Kid Can't Make You Come' (1984), Duran Duran's 'Hungry Like A Wolf' (1982), Prince's 'Orgasm' (1995) and 'Lady Cab Driver' (1982), Chakachas's 'Jungle Fever' (1973), Major Harris's 'Love Won't Let Me Wait' (1975), The League of Gentlemen's 'HG Wells' (1981), Little Annie's 'Give It To Me' (1992), Lee 'Scratch' Perry's 'Sexy Boss' (1990), Aphrodite's Child's '666' (1972), P. J. Harvey's 'The Dancer' (1995), and Lil Louis's 'French Kiss' (1989)" (1996, 105). In a footnote, Corbett and Kapsalis add that "there are a few converse examples of male sex sounds, including the Buzzcocks's 'Orgasm Addict' (1977) and works by audio artist Rune Lindblad and Japanese extremist Gerogerigegege" (1996, 110).

to compare Say's vocalizations to a "porno movie" and Osborne to liken Grimaud's to "sexual congress" will be analyzed below. For now, it will suffice to say that there exists some overlap between audible exertions that can take place during music-making and sex, and that such sounds have not historically been welcome in recordings of classical music.

If a critique of sex sounds as "intrusions" into ostensibly non-sexual spaces sounds familiar, it is perhaps because the reader follows professional tennis. The sport features an ongoing and public debate about effortful vocalizations made by its players as they strike the ball. While tennis players of all genders grunt loudly while playing, professional women's players have received the lion's share of criticism (and increased scrutiny by the Women's Tennis Association). Journalist Katy Waldman summarizes the situation vividly:

> If female players sounding their barbaric yawps on the Wimbledon green prove *sooo* distracting, perhaps the better question is: Why? Because of sex. A woman grunting on the tennis court sounds like she's having a baby or having sex. And not very ladylike sex—primal, bestial, no-holds-barred sex, the kind that stodgy Wimbledon-goers are loathe to imagine in their country club." (2012)

The tennis court and the classical concert hall are, in many ways, of a piece with one another. Historically, all were spaces where white, elite, well-dressed folks went to watch (sweating) performers entertain and edify them. In the domain of classical music, prohibitions against sounds of effort bleed from the concert hall into the recording studio, where grunts and moans—especially those by women—are considered inappropriate. Sex-related sounds can seem even more egregious on records which unlike concerts, are audited (repeatedly) via headphones and high-end, ultra-clear speakers.

Whether made by a tennis pro lunging for a backhand or a double bassist executing a two-octave shift, grunts meld the sonic and the physical. In both cases, the grunter is creating a sonic self. To study grunts in music is to practice somaesthetics, a field Richard Schusterman provisionally defined as "the critical, meliorative study of the experience and use of one's body as a locus of sensory aesthetic appreciation (*aisthesis*) and creative self-fashioning" (1999, 302). Recordings artists like Say and Grimaud—alongside musicians working in track-centric genres like pop—fashion themselves through their recorded oeuvre. It makes sense for theorists to pay close attention to the totality of evidence provided by these records of musical identity.

Grunting in tennis has similarities with classical music recordings. Both are generally decried. When exceptions are granted, they are given to men. In "The Somaesthetics of the Grunt: Policing Femininity in the Soundscapes of Women's Professional Tennis," Anita Stahl writes perceptively about efforts to silence women on the court. She takes up the example of nine-time Grand Slam winner Monica Seles, whose dominance of the sport in the 1990s ran alongside criticism of her grunting. Via a combination of on-court penalties and intense media attention, Seles was shamed into quelling her vocality. In the 1992 Wimbledon final against Steffi Graf, Seles bowed to pressure, quieted herself, and was defeated. Stahl writes: "On the hyper-surveilled center court, she [Seles] followed instructions to please the many individuals and institutions behind the surveillance, self-disciplining herself into defeat. The desire to please others at the expense of her own success is an essential quality of conventional, white, Western femininity and is at odds with the conventions of competitive sports" (2021, 148). An analogous statement might be made about the collective silencing of vocality in classical music, whose conventions are at odds with (at least some) performer's needs.[3]

Music, of course, is not tennis. Classical recordings are a sonic art form, making grunts potentially more disruptive to the fundamental activity than they are on the tennis court. The sentiment is made plain by Maria Sharapova, reported in a dispatch from the 2005 Australian Open tennis tournament: "Li said she was not put off by Sharapova's constant loud grunting during points, grunts which prompted one spectator to yell 'shut up.' Sharapova also brushed aside concern about the noise she makes during points. 'What do I think? I don't think, that's my whole opinion. I don't think about . . . what my mouth does when I play out there,' she said").[4] Tennis is not based on the sounds made by the player, but on the exact location of a ball within a set of marked lines. Recordings, on the other hand, are judged chiefly on their sonic content. Even so, should pianists think—or be made to think—about what their mouths do when they play? The comparison has bearing in the realm of performance science. Physiology research has connected grunting in tennis with increased stroke velocity and force. In "The Effects of 'Grunting' on Serve and Forehand Velocities in Collegiate Tennis Players," O'Connell et al.

---

[3] The connection between grunting in tennis and music predates the Seles era. Geoffrey Horn's April 1985 *Gramophone* review of a Deutsche Grammophon recording by Leonard Bernstein and the Vienna Philharmonic concludes that Beethoven's *Egmont Overture* has been "rather spoilt by occasional grunts (from Bernstein?) more appropriate to the Centre Court at Wimbledon" (1985, 1206).

[4] "Ruthless Sharapova Cruises Through," CNN.com, January 21, 2005, ellipsis in original.

(2004) used a measurement called *repeated measures multivariate analysis of variance*—which they abbreviate as "RM-MANOVA"—to analyze dynamic and static tennis strokes. They conclude:

> The RM-MANOVA indicated dynamic velocity and isometric force of both serves and forehand strokes were significantly greater when the subjects grunted ($F = 46.572$, $p < 0.001$, power = 1.00). Peak muscle activity in the external oblique and pectoralis major muscles was also greater when grunting during both types of strokes ($F = 3.867$, $p = 0.05$, power = 0.950). Grunt history, gender, perceived advantages, and disadvantages of grunting, years of experience, highest level of competition, and order of testing did not significantly alter any of these results. The velocity, force, and peak muscle activity during tennis serves and forehand strokes are significantly enhanced when athletes are allowed to grunt. (O'Connell et al. 2014, 3469)

Some musicians need to vocalize to play well. Seles evidently felt similarly. If vocalizing allows a musician to play with the maximum amount of expressive force, it might make sense for listeners (and theorists) to be more accommodating. There would be repercussions. The classical recording industry is, after all, an industry, and some consumers might refuse to purchase or stream grunt-heavy tracks. Even so, the historical trajectory of on-court grunts during the post-Seles era—the sounds are now a routine and largely undiscussed aspect the game—makes me wonder if a similar wave of acceptance awaits classical musicians.[5]

———

When might sounded effort be expected? A plausible guess would be during moments when high levels of virtuosity combine with climactic formal arrivals. Indeed, a common type of sounded effort occurs at moments of structural, harmonic, registral, and dynamic climax. Whether consciously or not, some musicians embellish a culminating musical process with a triumphant or effortful vocalization. Not all climactic exertions are alike. The category can be refined into three subcategories, each of which will be demonstrated

———

[5] Music and sex are not the only activities where grunts can signal pleasure. There is also food. Sophie Elkan's review of the Oxford restaurant the Ivy Brasserie provides an apt example: "Dedicated viewing of *Bake Off: The Professionals* has left me with the firm conviction that a good pud should cause two audible reactions: first, an intake of breath on being presented with your dish and second an involuntary grunt of desire on tasting it. My cheesecake ticked both boxes" (*Ox Magazine*, May 2, 2022).

via an accompanying example. First, the exultant holler that accompanies formal apotheosis will be studied on a track by conductor Yannick Nézet-Séguin leading a performance of music by Pyotr Ilyich Tchaikovsky. Second, Pablo Casals provides a classic example of tense moaning during a climactic cadence in music by Robert Schumann. Third, a recording by Fazıl Say of music by Franz Liszt requires a brief detour into performance science to explore a phenomenon that I will call "grunt lead." All three subcategories connect non-notated climactic vocalizations with moments of culmination. It is vanishingly rare to hear powerful and emphatic utterances used to signal softer, subtler moments in the work being recorded. Loud, elated, and emphatic vocalizations coincide with (score-based) events such as structural arrivals, registral highpoints, and harmonic resolutions. These climactic vocalizations will later be contrasted with intimate exertions, a category of shorter and more muted utterances that are generated in response to ongoing (as opposed to culminative) physical and mental effort. There is a substantial experiential chasm between a conductor's shout from the podium and a pianist's secreted moan.

Climactic exertions 1: The exultant holler

The basic form of climactic exertion—the exultant holler—is common in sport. The player scores and lets out a celebratory howl, the goalkeeper shouts after making a save, the runner makes an effortful moan as they cross the finish line. For obvious reasons, such sounds are less common in music, especially in classical recordings. This does not mean that they are entirely absent. A 2010 film recording of Yannick Nézet-Séguin conducting Tchaikovsky's *The Nutcracker* with the Rotterdam Philharmonic Orchestra includes an archetypical exultant holler.[6] Nézet-Séguin's vocalization occurs during the peak of Tchaikovsky's grand orchestral arc, in the culminating Act II *Pas de deux* between the Sugar Plum Fairy and the Cavalier.[7] Example 4.2 includes Tchaikovsky's own piano reduction of mm. 47–57 of the *Pas de deux*, corresponding to 1.18:39–1.19:54 of Nézet-Séguin's recording, and

[6] I am grateful to Alexander Rehding for drawing my attention to this example.

[7] Alongside the Rotterdam Philharmonic Orchestra, the film features the Jongenskoor Rijnmond, Jongenskoor Rivierenland, and Jongenskoor Waterland, conducted by Arie Hoek. The performance was recorded live on December 23, 2010, at De Doelen, Rotterdam, the Netherlands, and published online on the AVROTROS Klassiek channel on January 18, 2011.

Example 4.2 Pyotr Ilyich Tchaikovsky, *The Nutcracker*, Act II, *Pas de deux*, mm. 47–57 of the composer's piano reduction, corresponding to 1.18:39–1.19:54 of Yannick Nézet-Séguin's 2010 performance of the complete ballet with the Rotterdam Philharmonic Orchestra, annotating his vocalization leading into bar 55. See ▶ Audio Example 4.2.

includes a transcription of the conductor's elated vocal sound. The example illustrates how isolated Nézet-Séguin's holler is, while demonstrating the repetitive phrases—replete with chromatically rising bass motion—that culminate in (and elicit) his vocal burst just before bar 55.

Robin Holloway, who considers *The Nutcracker* to be "the summa of Tchaikovsky in his true genre," highlighted "the sheer hugeness of the emotion released" in the *Pas de deux* (1993, 623). Seen in this light, the climax of the *Pas de deux* is *the climax of the climax* of the entire ballet. Nézet-Séguin was leading a performance of the complete score, rather than the shorter suite, a fact that helps to contextualize the cumulative effort that preceded his massive, ebullient vocalization. Nézet-Séguin's utterance is heard 79 minutes and 37 seconds into the Rotterdam Philharmonic's performance. Holloway's characterization of the *Pas de deux* as a "release" means that the *fortissimo* arrival at bar 55 might be classified as *the release atop the release*. This would, in turn, allow Nézet-Séguin's shout to be *a release atop the release atop the release*.

Within the norms of orchestral conducting, Nézet-Séguin's climactic shout is transgressive. While conductors occasionally make sounds of their own, in general they project silence toward both the audience and the microphone. Artur Rodzinski's poetic and self-referential description of the art of conducting is telling: "I never for a second am conscious of Mr. Rodzinski conducting the work. I like to think that the music goes from the orchestra to the audience without going through myself" (1947, 74).[8] Nézet-Séguin's climactic vocalization breaks Rodzinski's paradigm. Tchaikovsky's music does not go from orchestra to audience. At 1.19:37, the written music is augmented by an unscripted holler. The conductor's sound fuses with the orchestra's, forming a sonic entity that bears the fingerprint of Nézet-Séguin, not as a balletic orchestral leader but as a momentarily prominent sound source. His elated shout arrives considerably earlier that the downbeat of bar 55, allowing it to be plainly and vividly audible before being drowned out by the swell of the orchestral downbeat. The sounds that envelop his lone holler include piccolo, two flutes, oboe, cor anglais, two clarinets, bass clarinet, two bassoons, four horns, two trumpets, three trombones, tuba, timpani, cymbal, and strings.

---

[8] Rodzinski critiqued fellow conductor Leopold Stokowski, who he claimed "plays music sexually" (1947, 74). His implication is that whenever a conductor makes the audience aware of anything other than the orchestral sound, the result is too corporeal, too sexual, and therefore in bad taste.

While the visual aspect of music-making has remained outside my study, I will make an exception in this case. In the film of this passage, the editors cut away from the conductor just before his vocalization. For the previous four-teen seconds (1.19:20–1.19:34) the viewer sees a single shot of Nézet-Séguin facing the camera, without any other musicians in the frame. At 1.19:34, the view suddenly shifts to encompass the full stage, a panoramic shot of the orchestra. While the wide angle reinforces the score's grand *tutti*, it also mitigates recognition of the shout. The holler shot places Nézet-Séguin's back to the camera and blurs his corporeal presence within the sea of orchestral musicians that partially surround him. While the viewer is still able to see the conductor from behind as he executes an emphatic left-twisting body gesture coincident with his shout of release, it is obvious that the directors decided not to maintain the conductor's close-up during his holler.[9]

Climactic exertions 2: The tense moan

Pablo Casals's recording of the Schumann Cello Concerto, made with the Prades Festival Orchestra on May 29–30, 1953, is the *locus classicus* of re-corded grunts. Across all three movements, Casals's voice is heard along-side his cello. His first entrance, on the downbeat of bar 5, is preceded by a moaning sound that sets the tone for the rest of the recording. Some of his vocalizations fall under the category of climactic exertions, perhaps none more so than the five utterances that decorate the cadence just before the first *tutti* of the opening movement. Example 4.3 provides a condensed orchestral score of mm. 30–33 alongside a transcription of Casals's five vocal sounds. The harmonies in this section are cadential. They move from tonic (A minor, m. 30), through the submediant (F major, m. 31), the cadential 6/4 (m. 32), to a dominant ninth (m. 33). Bar 34 (not seen in the example) resolves the dom-inant to its A minor tonic and ushers in the rest of the orchestra for a *fortis-simo tutti*. Over this harmonic scansion, Schumann composes two ascending

---

[9] Conductor vocalizations can have a programmatic connection to the work being recorded. Leonard Bernstein produced them so often that David Gutman, in a November 1992 *Gramophone* review, coined the phrase "Bernsteinian grunt" to identify (and roundly disapprove of) a sound uttered by conductor Giuseppe Sinopoli in his 1992 Deutsche Grammophon recording, with the Staatskapelle Dresden, of music by Richard Strauss: "In *Ein Heldenleben*, the music is persuaded to collapse into carefully characterized but disparate episodes at the expense of overall sweep. The in-exorable drive of a conductor like Fritz Reiner is sorely missed and, to cap it all, the conductor (or possibly the timpanist?) emits the odd Bernsteinian grunt, most intrusively as tonic and opening material are reached (6′17″ into track 5)" (1992, 100).

Example 4.3 Robert Schumann, Cello Concerto in A minor, Op. 129, first movement, mm. 30–33, annotating five climactic vocalizations in the 1953 recording by Pablo Casals and the Prades Festival Orchestra. See ▶ Audio Example 4.3.

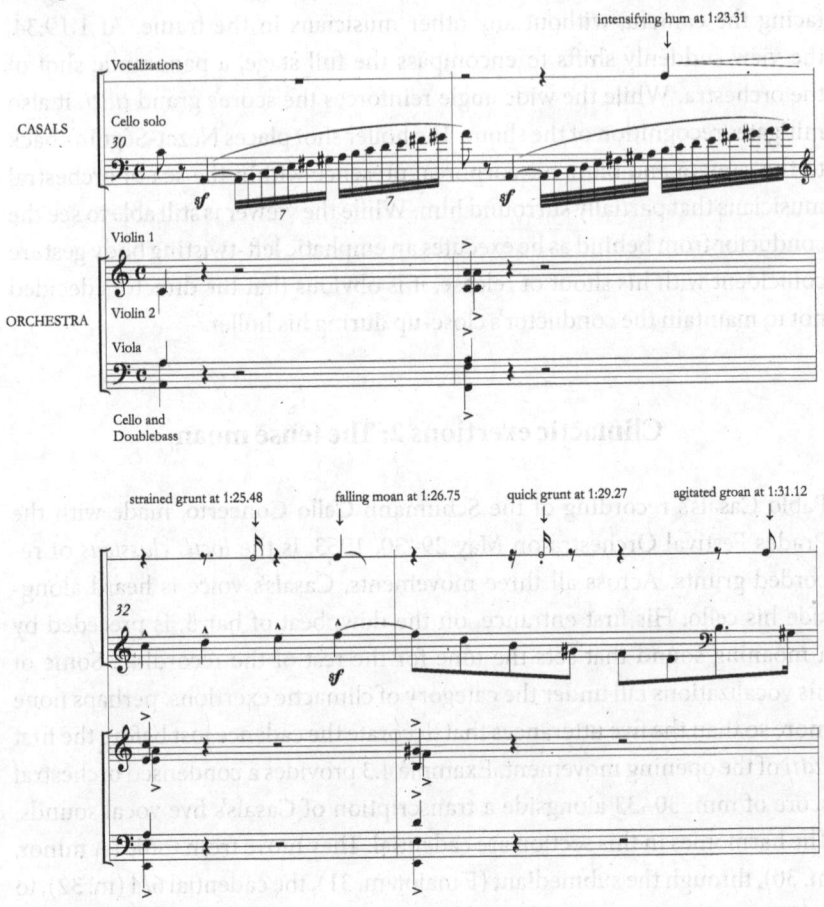

roulades (mm. 30–31) that prepare a climactic four-note scalar ascent in bar 32. The last note is emphasized further with a *sforzando* after which the cello line falls precipitously in bar 33.

Register is a key aspect in Schumann's cadential construction; it also seems to inspire Casals's vocalizations. Writing about the concerto, Peter H. Smith highlights "Schumann's recourse to the traditional compositional technique of registral coupling as a means of creating a contrapuntal framework to house soloistic figuration linking one register to another" and goes on to emphasize that "coupling eventually becomes a means of creating dramatic emphasis for the cello's climactic approach to closure in mm. 30–34" (2016, 61). In his 1953 Prades recording of these bars, Casals makes five unwritten sounds. The first is an intensifying hum at 1:23.31 whose *crescendo* embellishes the thirty-second-note scalar passage over the F major predominant. The second is a rapid, strained grunt at 1:25.48 that acts as a pickup to beat 3, arriving just before the cello reaches E over the cadential 6/4. Casals's third vocalization functions as a release. His falling moan precisely coincides with the *sforzando* F5 at 1:26.75 and signals the peak of the cello's ascent. Casals lets the listener know that this is the apex of cadential intensity, his falling moan suggesting the direction the melody will soon follow. Bar 33 includes vocalizations that decorate the cello's fall through a dominant ninth arpeggio. Casals's fourth vocal sound is a quick, clipped grunt between the B4 and G♯4 in m. 33. The fifth is an agitated groan that comes before the final note of the same bar. Casals vocally annotates Schumann's dramatic "approach to closure." The cellist's laborious, gasping sounds during the registral ascent reinforce the feeling of tension inherent in the cadential 6/4, while his falling moan has the quality of a vivid denouement. Blending Casals's audible exertion with Smith's reading of Schumann's registral architecture engenders a more complete analytical perspective. Within the form of the opening movement of Schumann's concerto, Casals's quintet of vocal sounds reinforces mm. 30–34 as a site of climax in both the harmonic form (via the cello and orchestra) and in the domain of sounded effort (via the cellist's vocality).

Casals has been accused of histrionics. Robert Cowan's *Gramophone* review of this recording of the concerto directs criticism at the cellist and composer alike: "Maximum contrast is afforded by Casals's 1953 recording of Schumann's Cello Concerto, a startlingly demonstrative affair with heavily thrashed accents, savage entries and a general proneness to exaggeration that makes a meal out of Schumann's already heightened psycho-musical pathology" (1994, 68).[10] Whatever the reader's opinion of Casals or Schumann, the reviewer's use of the term "exaggerated" is, strictly speaking, correct, derived as it is from the Latin root *exaggerat-* (meaning "heaped up"). Casals

---

[10] David Blum recalls Casals teaching the Schumann Cello Concerto in an equally dramatic manner: "Casals then began to play, taking the student through the piece phrase by phrase. As he did so, he became increasingly immersed in the emotional atmosphere of the work. 'Pain, pain . . .' he called out. 'All is pain—the poor man!' In one passage Casals's bow slashed upon the string and then forged a hair-raising crescendo, culminating in a sforzando that had the intensity of a shriek" (1980, 3, ellipsis in original).

indeed *heaps* five unwritten vocal sounds onto Schumann's notation in mm. 30–33.

Not all listeners dismiss Casals's unwritten sounds as exaggerations. Some find in them evidence of his humanity; others hear something to admire and emulate. Reviewing Casals's Prades recordings, Elaine Fine offers a personal and unvarnished appraisal of the grunting sounds preserved there, which includes a detour into the topic of disability:

> There is a wonderful documentary film by Laurel Chiten called "Twitch and Shout" made at a convention of people with Tourette Syndrome. The film shows people with Tourette Syndrome letting down the guard they must always have up in their daily lives and expressing themselves without restraint in a supportive environment filled with people who have the same condition. The musicians who participated in the Casals Prades festivals might have had a comparable musical experience. (2003)

Fine uses Chiten's film about the welcoming environment of the Tourette Syndrome convention to make an analogy with the feeling generated by Casals's sounded effort. She concludes that his recordings encourage a similar type of empathy:

> Columbia Masterworks released recordings of some of the concerts from the Festival. There are many reasons why most of the recorded performances here were not made into records. There are missed notes, a few slips in intonation, gruff sounds here and there, and a lot of expressive grunting and groaning by Casals as well as some of the other musicians. I actually enjoy the grunts. After listening to so much of Casals's playing I even get the distinct desire to grunt while playing myself (I restrain myself). (2003)

For some musicians, grunting sounds on audio tracks remove inhibitions in their own performance practice. Casals's recordings inspired Fine to consider grunting while playing. Her parenthetical admission of restraint is further evidence that even when musicians enjoy grunting, they self-silence. No doubt that some listeners are repelled by grunting, but that is precisely the point. In appraising sounds as they are—rather than what normative classical recording practices expect them to be—scholars can approach audio tracks as musical documents. Notated sounds will connect directly to symbols in the score, and non-notated sounds will emerge from the body and equipment of the musician in the act of interpreting that score. To some, sounds of effort will be transgressive; to others, they will be encouraging. Still others might feel transgression and encouragement simultaneously.

Climactic exertions 3: Grunt lead

Franz Liszt was somewhat of a specialist in composing climactic highpoints. One such moment arrives in the 700th measure of his Sonata in B minor, S. 178. In the context of this thirty-minute solo piano work, bar 700 concludes the sonata's final *Presto*. This measure is a locus of significant pianistic and rhetorical effort.[11] Bar 700 opens a pulsating *fortississimo* texture spanning the lower half of the keyboard and ushers in the final iteration of the *Grandioso* theme first introduced some 595 measures earlier. In his 1949 *édition du travail* of Liszt's sonata published by Éditions Salabert, Alfred Cortot includes a commentary about this measure that, while bordering on the hyperbolic, makes clear its exultant position within the sonata's architecture:

> We regret not to find, on this ultimate affirmation of the theme of faith, the indication "glorioso" which alone would have suited its character of apotheosis. But the triple *forte* with which Liszt accompanies it already allows the performer to hear under what exterior of solemn majesty it must impose itself, as the symbolic conclusion of a gigantic musical work and a sound poem whose last image is thus dedicated to the glorious evocation of the celestial omnipotence in its absolute plenitude. Hammer all the chords powerfully, with the maximum sound that the instrument at your disposal can produce, but avoid any violently struck attack. (Liszt 1949, 46)[12]

[11] According to Kenneth Hamilton, the music following m. 700 was a late addition by Liszt: "Of the greatest importance of all was the rewriting of the coda. Until the very last compositional stage, the Sonata ended soon after the apotheosis of theme 4 (bars 700–10) with a forceful presentation of theme 1 prefacing a loud, extrovert cadence in B major" (1996, 56).

[12] « On regrette de ne pas trouver, sur cette ultime affirmation du thème de la foi, l'indication "glorioso" qui eut, seule, convenu à son caractère d'apothéose. Mais le triple forte dont Liszt l'accompagne permet déjà à l'interprète d'entendre sous quels dehors de majesté solennelle elle se doit de s'imposer, comme conclusion symbolique d'une œuvre musicale gigantesque et d'un poème sonore dont la dernière image se voit ainsi consacrée à l'évocation glorieuse de la toute puissance céleste, dans sa plénitude absolue. Marteler puissamment tous les accords, avec le maximum de sonorité dont peut faire preuve l'instrument dont on dispose, mais en évitant toute attaque violemment heurtée. » (Liszt 1949, 46)

Alongside advising the pianist to hammer the chords powerfully, Cortot opines that Liszt should have written "glorioso" at this moment in the score. The compositional design sets up bar 700 as a moment of dramatic rhetorical impact. As seen in Example 4.4, bar 700 is prepared by an undulating chromatic scale in four octaves descending to a pounding, low-register dominant seventh chord in bar 699. As the harmony resolves to B major, the time signature changes from 4/4 to 3/2, allowing metric expansiveness to accompany the arrival of the major tonic. The modulation between the two meters is elegantly (if straightforwardly) achieved via a notated triplet in the last half of bar 699, foreshadowing the shift from duple to triple meter.

Example 4.4 also transcribes Fazıl Say's grunted, quasi-singing vocalizations that precede many of the chordal attacks. Released in 2001, Say's recording was made in 1999 at the Salle de l'Arsenal in Metz, France, engineered by Eberhard Sengpiel and produced by Friedemann Engelbrecht. Say's vocalizing requires a new classification within performance analysis. I will call it "grunt lead," after the existing category in music psychology called "melody lead." Caroline Palmer identified instances where musicians could be heard "leading with the tones of the melody" (1989, 334). Later work by Goebl (2001) investigated examples where melodic voices anticipate the arrival of accompanying ones, helping to solidify the analytical concept of "melody lead." Senn, Kilchenmann, and Camp conclude that Martha Argerich, in her 1975 Deutsche Grammophon recording of Chopin's Prelude in E minor, Op. 28, No. 4, sometimes "plays the solo voice's onsets earlier than the accompaniment's: in bars 1–4, the melody leads in seven of nine instances (78%), the average melody lead is 28 [milliseconds]" (2009, 110). Say's recording of Liszt's sonata goes a step further than "melody lead." One of Say's interpretive characteristics is to lead not with the melody, but with the grunt. Between mm. 700 and 707, Say produces at least nineteen vocalizations that precede melodic events. I say "at least" because the considerable volume of the piano music during this excerpt suggests that some of Say's vocality might have been covered by the resonance of his piano. Some of these grunts are a kind of low-pitched, effortful singing, though the tones are not identical to those in Liszt's melody.[13]

---

[13] For a traversal of this same passage *without* grunted vocalizations, see Zee Zee's 2021 recording. Bars 696–710 can be heard beginning at 24:01. Her recording was made at London's Maida Vale Studios on January 26, 2014, edited and mastered by Jennifer Howells, engineered by Andy Rushton, and produced by Emma Bloxham.

Example 4.4 Franz Liszt, Sonata in B minor, S. 178, mm. 696–710, annotating the "grunt lead" in the 2001 recording by Fazıl Say. See ▶ Audio Example 4.4.

The grunt at the end of bar 699 deserves special consideration. Say's vocalization begins at 6:30.74 and the dominant chord that appears as the final member of the triplet sounds at 6:30.90; the grunt lead is 16 milliseconds. This sound serves a defined rhetorical function within Liszt's passage. The transition from 4/4 to 3/2 includes a kind of metric modulation. The prevailing meter extending back to bar 616 is duple, the grand theme at bar 700—which Cortot refers to as *"thème de la foi"*—is triple. Liszt notates a quarter-note triplet on the last two beats of m. 699, thereby bridging the duple and triple realms. Without the score, a listener will be initially unaware that the triplet is a triplet. Its first two notes sound, for all intents and purposes, like quarter notes on beats 3 and 4 of m. 699. In Liszt's construction, the final note of the triplet—the chord that precedes the arrival into the tonic major—is set up to sound *at the location where one might expect the downbeat of m. 700*. The effect momentarily disorients the listener. Say adds a grunt at this moment, his vibrant vocal exertion occurring between the penultimate and antepenultimate notes of bar 699. The grunt masquerades, for a moment, as the downbeat of bar 700, taking the place of the expected tonic resolution.

Climactic exertions are not the only type of effortful utterance. At the opposite end of the spectrum are vocalizations made during quieter moments marked by ongoing, non-culminative musical processes. Intimate exertions lack the emphatic "we-have-arrived" quality inherent in the hollers, moans, and grunts by Nézet-Séguin, Casals, and Say. They are not celebratory sounds of achievement, but in-process sounds of grappling that provide narrativizing evidence of labor. Like climactic sounds, intimate exertions can sometimes find analogies in the erotic. While climactic vocalizations can be associated with caricatures of conclusive orgasm, intimate vocalizations inhabit a delicate landscape more associated with ongoing activity. The category maps onto Audre Lorde's notion of the erotic as a force associated with life itself:

> We tend to think of the erotic as an easy, tantalizing sexual arousal. I speak of the erotic as the deepest life force, a force which moves us toward living in a fundamental way. And when I say living I mean it as that force which moves us toward what will accomplish real positive change." (2004, 99)

I find intimate exertions to be reminders of the livingness of a performer. They are less markers of a "tantalizing sexual arousal" than of "the deepest life force." Three instances will develop the category of these sounds of ongoing effort. The first is a single moment of subtle vocalizing in Claire Chase's recording of *Sex Magic* by Liza Lim. The second demonstrates the threshold between panting and pitched vocalization in Hélène Grimaud's recording of Beethoven's Piano Sonata in E major, Op. 109. The third example allows a bird's-eye view of the formal position of stifled grunts in Evgeny Kissin's recording of the slow movement of Schubert's Piano Sonata in B-flat major, D. 960. Each case presents ongoing effort. The analogy would be to watching a marathon: listening to intimate exertions is akin to watching runners moving past, mid-race, rather than exultantly crossing the finish line.

Intimate exertions 1: Subtle vocalizing

Liza Lim's *Sex Magic* (2020) is a work for contrabass flute, alto ocarina, bell, Aztec death whistle, pedal bass drum, electronics, and installation of kinetic percussion instruments, all performed live by one musician. The piece was commissioned by Claire Chase as part of her twenty-four-year commissioning, performance, and recording project *Density 2036*. Lim's composition follows a notated score, mostly written on standard five-live staves. In the words of its composer, *Sex Magic* is "a work about the sacred erotic in women's history" and "a work about an alternative cultural logic of women's power as connected to cycles of the womb—the life-making powers of childbirth, the 'skin-changing,' world-synchronizing temporalities of the body, and the womb centre as a site of divinatory wisdom and utterance" (Lim 2020). Chase recorded *Sex Magic* at Studio 9 in North Adams, Massachusetts, in May 2022, with live-electronics and sound design by Senem Pirler. The recording consists of a single, unedited take captured using a Meyer Sound Constellation System. Matias Tarnopolsky produced the record, with Pirler as mixer and mastering engineer, Rick Jacobsohn as recording engineer and session producer, and David Dennison as technical supervisor and Constellation engineer. During one of the movements, Chase can be heard voicing an effortful, non-notated sound that replaces a pitch in Lim's score. Unlike the climactic, culminative sounds heard in the previous section, Chase's sound appears during a passage that, while virtuosic, is part of an ongoing musical process.

To situate Chase's sound of effort, it is necessary to contextualize its position within Lim's work. *Sex Magic* is divided into four main sections: "Pythoness," "Oracles," "Skin Changing," and "The Slow Moon Climbs." Chase's sound takes place during the "Oracles" section, which the composer defines as "Oracle, (Latin *oraculum* from *orare*, 'to pray,' or 'to speak'); divine communication delivered in response to a petitioner's request. Oracles were a branch of divination but differed from the casual pronouncements of augurs by being associated with a definite person or place" (2020). "Oracles" is itself divided into six parts: Salutations to the cowrie shells, Wombbell, Vermillion—on Rage, Throat Song, Moss—on the Sacred Erotic, and Telepathy. Chase's non-notated vocalization takes place during "Moss—on the Sacred Erotic," a movement for solo contrabass flute.

"Moss—on the Sacred Erotic" comprises mm. 103–145 of *Sex Magic*. The notation makes generous use of sweeping flute harmonics that Lim refers to as "warble." Chase's recording of "Moss—on the Sacred Erotic" lasts just under eight and a half minutes. The recording is intimate, with inhales and subtle mouth sounds audible throughout. Lim's notation is marked by a small collection of measures bounded by repeat signs, some asking the player to play a passage two, three, or as many as five times. One such moment occurs in m. 111, seen in Example 4.5. There is a great deal of activity in this measure. The time signature is 6/4 and the prevailing tempo at this bar is 75 quarter notes per minute. On the main staff, the accent mark noteheads denote tongue percussion within a flow of subdivided quarter-note triplets. Lim calls for a separate rhythmic pattern, notated above the staff, generating a texture of contrapuntal timbres all played by a single musician through a single wind instrument.

The virtuosity is extreme, even if the resultant soundworld is full of understated subtleties. The score asks that the first pass through m. 111 be played at a *mp* dynamic while the second pass should be played "*mf*, in upper register." The complex activity of this moment generates a dramatic, almost

Example 4.5 Liza Lim, *Sex Magic*, "Moss—On the Sacred Erotic," m. 111, annotating a vocalization in the 2023 recording by Claire Chase. See ⏵ Audio Example 4.5.

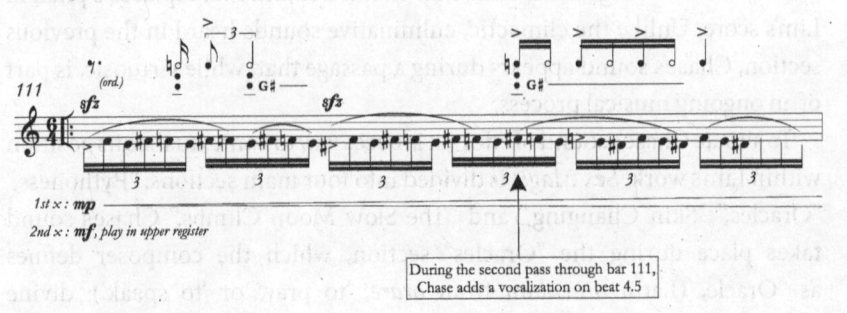

transcendental swirl, even at these relatively low dynamic levels. Example 4.5 pinpoints Chase's intimate exertion during her reading of Lim's passage. During the second pass through m. 111, midway through beat 4, Chase adds a subtle, intoned vocalization. Her sounded effort is small but expressive. It has characteristics that are unique among all the examples studied thus far, most notably as Chase's vocal sound momentarily eclipses (and essentially, replaces) the pitch material called for in the score of "Moss—on the Sacred Erotic."

Far from being a transgression or error, Chase's sound of exertion seems completely at home in the context of Lim's piece. The utterance appears in the "Oracle" section of the work, which is based on Lim's idea of "divine communication delivered in response to a petitioner's request." Chase's vocal sound is a form of (expressive) communication delivered in response to Lim's intricate, notated request. It embodies the dual (and dueling) perceptions of a score alongside a recording of it. Lim writes that "True intimacy involves an intertwining cross-modal sensory exchange" (2020). What could be more sensorially cross-modal than the performative effort becoming so extreme that a musician utters an expressive intonation of exertion?

Intimate exertions 2: Emphatic panting

Sounded effort need not be localized. There are tracks on which it is widespread, such as Hélène Grimaud's recording of Beethoven's Piano Sonata in E major, Op. 109, made at Purchase College in New York in 1999. The recording was produced by Larry Rock, and the recording engineer was Eberhard Sengpiel assisted by Dirk Sobotka and Jörg Mohr. Grimaud's recording of Op. 109 includes prominent inhales and exhales. As such, it might seem better suited for inclusion in the chapter on breath sounds. However, her recording extends the limits of breath sounds in two directions. First, the rapid nature of her breaths, at times an emphatic panting, places them in a category of vocalized effort. The term *panting* here is used simply to refer to quick breaths that suggest momentary breathlessness. Second, her breaths sometimes spill over into intimate, pitched sounds that cross the threshold into singing.

Grimaud's recording of Op. 109 reminded Richard Osborne of "a slow-drawn act of sexual congress." Whether the reader agrees with his analogy, there is no doubt a great deal of vocal exertion on these tracks. While most of these sounds are breathy, some have fleeting moments of pitch. All of them portray a musician exerting herself as she interprets Beethoven's score. Two examples of the intimate, breathy, and effortful sounds that characterize Grimaud's recordings occur in her reading of the sonata's last movement, Beethoven's winding set of variations marked *Gesangvoll, mit innigster Empfindung*. Grimaud's exertions cross the threshold between quick exhales and a kind of quiet singing. These are the moments that Osborne refers to as "gentle moaning." Purposefully setting aside Osborne's sexualized reading, I am interested in Grimaud's crossing of the threshold between breathing and vocalizing. The line between exhaling and intoning is a mysterious place in the physiognomy of the human vocal apparatus. The threshold will be well known to singers, making it all the more fascinating when it is explored by a pianist.

This far into our study, it is time to invoke multiple categories of unwritten sounds within a single transcription and watch them work together. Example 4.6 depicts the interaction of Grimaud's intoned vocalization, intense inhale-exhale pairs, and the *sit-see* sound of the damper pedal in mm. 25a–32. The passage opens with a trio of breaths (inhale-exhale-inhale) that cross the bar line from m. 24b to 25a. These breaths dramatize Beethoven's lingering on the B4 as the final sixteenth of m. 24b, then as the grace note and, one octave higher, the proper downbeat of m. 25. The melodic B♯ on beat 3 of m. 25 is accompanied by either a Grimaud inhale or perhaps a partially edited-out moment of her singing/moaning. The analogous note in the following bar—the A♯ on beat 3 of m. 26—is a moment of true, pitched vocality. Just before Grimaud strikes A♯4, she can be heard producing the same pitch with her voice. A threshold has been crossed. Breathiness has given way to singing. Her A♯ is followed by another, even subtler moment of singing on beat 3 of m. 27. The piano's notated melodic rise from A4 to E5 is gently reinforced by Grimaud's voice.

After her pitched vocalizations in mm. 26–27, Grimaud returns to relatively loud breathing. There follows an intensified doubling back, as Beethoven's *sforzando* on the downbeat of bar 29 inaugurates a recursion to the supertonic F-sharp minor from bar 26, now supporting a stratospheric A6 in the melody. All these sounds—written and unwritten—are directed at bar 30, when the arrival of a first-inversion B dominant seventh chord brings forth from Grimaud a series of inhales that are the closest thing to gasping, or panting, on the entire track. These gasps punctuate and interlace with the dotted rhythms across mm. 29–30 in the manner of a hocket. The

Example 4.6 Ludwig van Beethoven, Piano Sonata in E major, Op. 109, third movement, mm. 25a–32, including a spectrogram of 3:21–3:59 in the 1999 recording by Hélène Grimaud, alongside a transcription of her audible breaths, pitched vocalizations, and pedal sounds. See ▶ Audio Example 4.6.

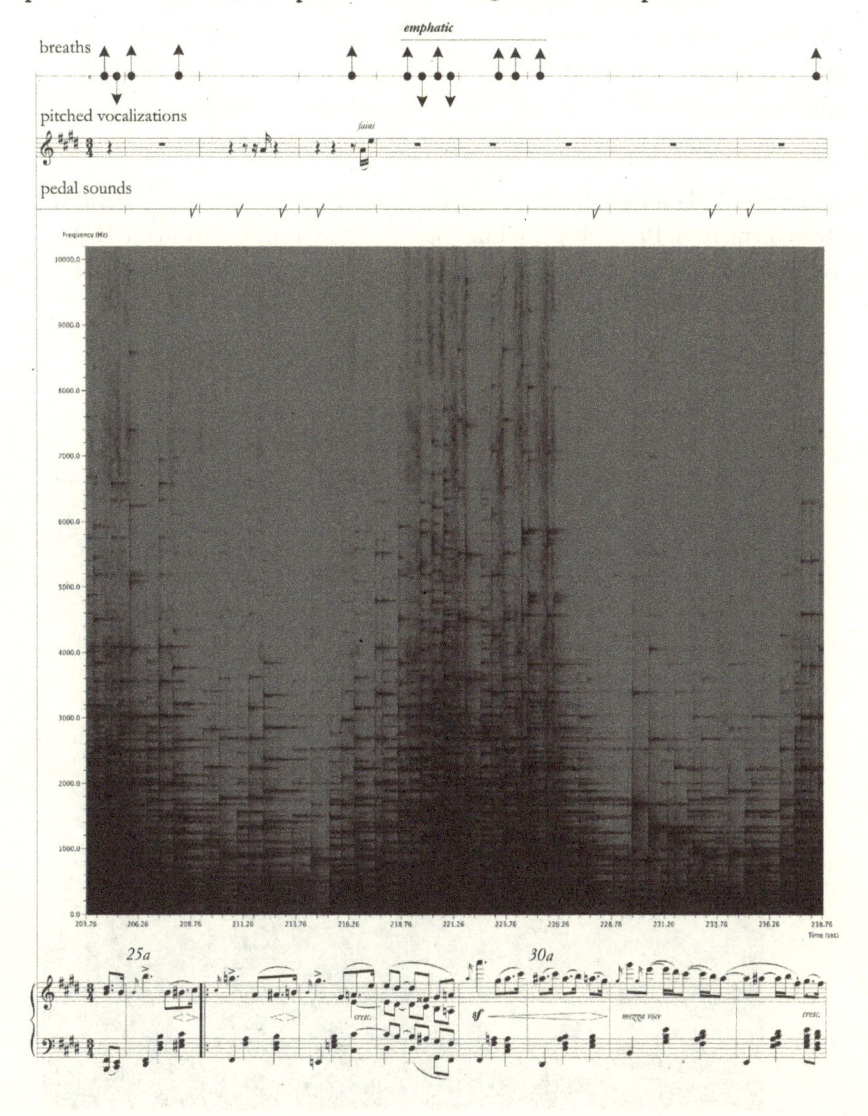

intensity of these beats is followed by a moment of sudden restraint. In bar 31, as if to create the starkest possible contrast—and to match Beethoven's notation of *mezza voce*—Grimaud is vocally silent. As both the pitched voice and unpitched breath sounds recede, the flicker of *sit-see* pedaling sounds are heard across the final tonic resolution, sounding almost like the flicker of a photographic camera shutter.

A second example also comes from Grimaud's recording of the last movement of Op. 109. In Variation 4, a trio of Grimaud's inhale-exhale pairs parallels the dynamic markings in Beethoven's score. Example 4.7 presents a spectrogram and score excerpt of Grimaud's second pass through mm. 106–9. What interests me here is not only where her breaths are heard, but

Example 4.7 Ludwig van Beethoven, Piano Sonata in E major, Op. 109, third movement, mm. 106b–9b, including a spectrogram of 8:27–8:51 in the 1999 recording by Hélène Grimaud, alongside a transcription of her three inhale-exhale pairs. See ⊙ Audio Example 4.7.

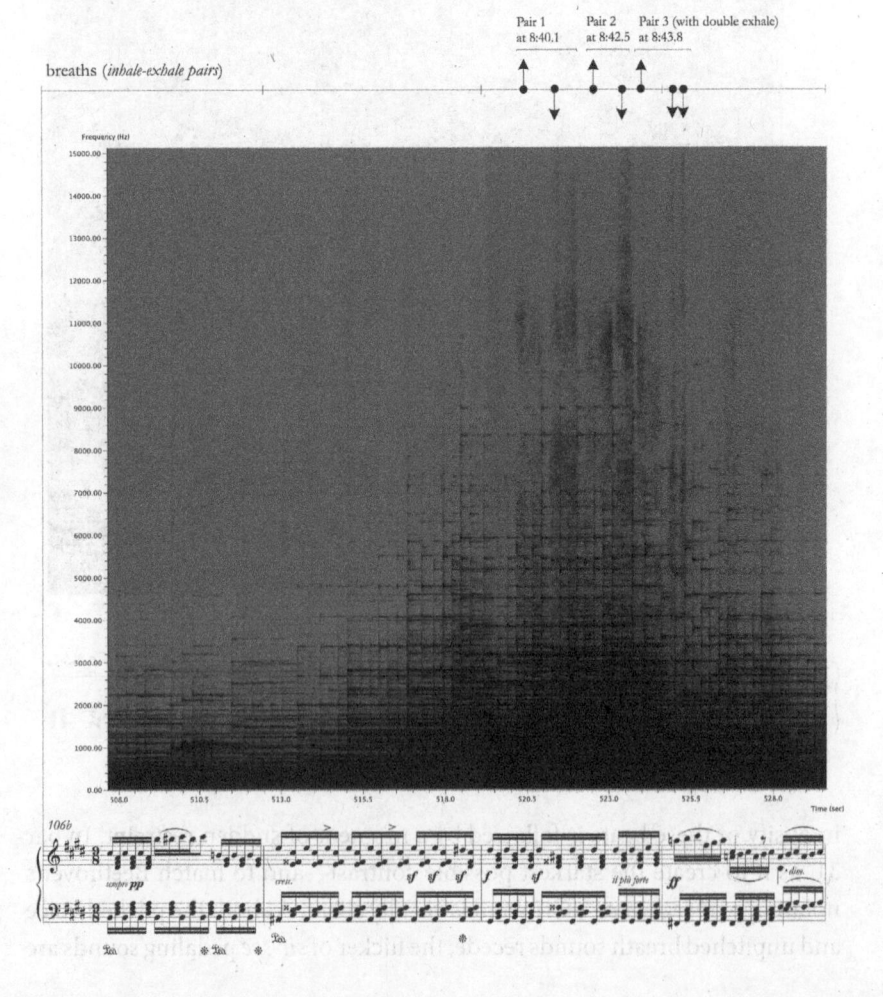

where they are not. On its own, the spectrogram looks like a small mountain whose peaks are Grimaud's inhales and exhales. There are no audible breaths in m. 106 where Beethoven marks *sempre p*. Likewise in m. 107, where the marking is *crescendo*, save for a faint mouth sound that can be heard between the first and second *sforzandi* in the last beat of the bar. Everything changes in bar 108. Beethoven places an intensifying dynamic marking on four consecutive beats: *forte* on beat 1, *sforzando* on beat 2, *il più forte* on beat 3, and *fortissimo* on the following downbeat. These sudden changes call forth more volume from Grimaud's piano, as well as a series of rapid inhale-exhale pairs. All three breath cycles are marked in the spectrogram. They begin with an inhale within the root-position G-sharp minor chord on beat 1 followed by an exhale during the D-sharp dominant seventh over its tonic pedal on beat 2. As a pair, these breaths flow in time with the changing harmony. The second inhale-exhale pair is more unpredictable. Grimaud inhales in the middle of beat 2 and then releases her breath in the middle of beat 3, when the harmony returns to G-sharp minor. The second pair of breaths is closer together than the first.

Grimaud's third breath pair is quicker and more insistent. The inhale arrives near the final sixteenth note of m. 108, where the harmony moves from G-sharp minor directly to a first-inversion E major. The latter is invoked as a passing chord, and the downbeat of m. 109 has the bass falling from G♯ to F♯ in support of a supertonic seventh chord. Grimaud's vocality surges here. She accompanies the arrival of m. 109 with two *exhales*. The effect is visceral. For the previous two measures, the texture had been stuck, both hands seeming to play an accompaniment for an unheard melody, bereft of the third-related cascading gestures that mark this fourth variation. The cascades reappear on the downbeat of m. 109, coincident with Beethoven's *fortissimo* marking, and Grimaud embellishes their arrival with her hitched double-exhale. Bar 109 of Beethoven's variations is not a moment of climax akin to bar 55 of Tchaikovsky's *Pas de deux*, bar 32 of Schumann's Cello Concerto, or bar 700 of Liszt's Piano Sonata. It is mid-phrase music, part of an ongoing process. It is not surprising, then, that Grimaud's exertion is meaningfully different from Nézet-Séguin's, Casals's, or Say's. During her three concentrated, effortful breaths, I do not hear Grimaud *celebrating an achievement*, but *making an ongoing attempt to achieve*.[14] While theorists of

---

[14] Those who wish to continue the analysis of Grimaud's exertions in her 1999 recording of the third movement of Op. 109 might investigate bar 59 (beginning at 5:40) where she executes a series of fluttering inhale-exhale pairs—each with a slightly different duration—that dramatize a bass descent.

motive, harmony, rhythm, and timbre will find great richness in Beethoven's notation, theorists who study Grimaud's track—and who take the time to account for all its audible events—will find much more music than appears in the score.

Intimate exertions 3: Stifled grunting

Having studied a single intimate vocal exertion (Chase) as well as two passages of multiple exertions (Grimaud), it is time to chart sounded effort across a complete, large-scale form. Evgeny Kissin's 2004 recording of the slow movement of Schubert's Piano Sonata in B-flat, D. 960, includes moments of stifled, strained grunting. Like the fingernail clicks by William Nyaho Chapman and Claudio Arrau, groans can fuse with specific motivic and harmonic events that reappear across a composition. In these instances, the return of specific motives can bring about the reappearance of unwritten music. A vivid example of such "timbral marking" occurs in Kissin's traversal of Schubert's *Andante sostenuto*. The track was produced by Jay David Saks, recorded by Mike Hatch at SWR-Studio, Freiburg, Germany on June 10–11, 2003, and released the following year on RCA Red Seal. Charting the unwritten music across the complete track, a narrative emerges. The vocalizations on Kissin's recording of the *Andante sostenuto* from D. 960 turn out to be structural.

Schubert's 138-measure, C-sharp minor slow movement has a tripartite architecture. Calling it "Schubert's Weigenlied," Eric Wen characterizes the movement as "the emotional core" of D. 960 (2016, 134). Example 4.8 presents the complete form of the movement, which divides into A (mm. 1–42), B (mm. 43–89), and A^1 (mm. 90–138). This reduction is designed specifically to demonstrate a correlation between Schubert's form and Kissin's stifled vocalizations. The example includes all notated dynamics in the A and A^1 sections, as well as the complete bass motion. Schubert notates *forte* only five times in the entire movement: four times during the A and A^1 outer sections (in mm. 12, 18, 101, and 117) and once during the interior B section (m. 72). The four iterations that occur in the outer sections all share a similar harmonic function: they appear during prolonged dominants within the local tonality. Charles Fisk summarizes the tonal motion of the A section as "Two great, nearly identical melodic arches: the first beginning in $C_\sharp$ minor and emerging into E, the second taking up this E major but then

Example 4.8 Franz Schubert, Piano Sonata in B-flat major, D. 960, second movement, the A and A^1 sections reduced to their bass motion and notated dynamics, with rectangles highlighting the four "frozen" dominants and their related *forte* markings.

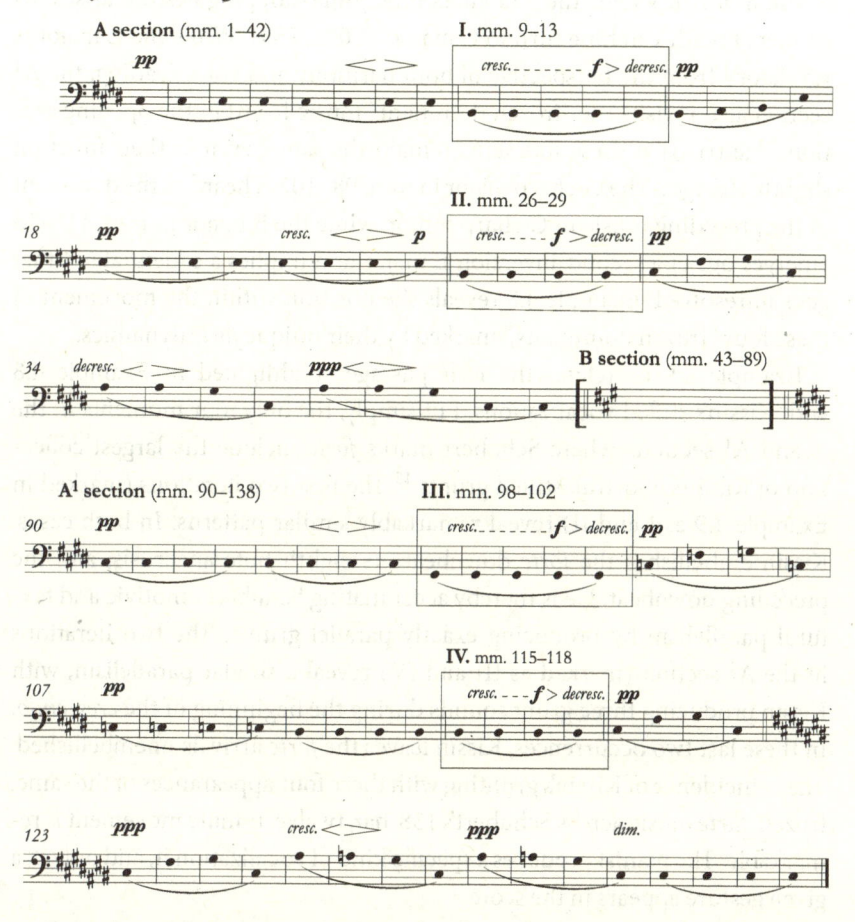

falling, finally, back to C♯ minor" (2001, 256). Both key areas are marked by stark, tonally "frozen" prolongations of their respective dominants: the G-sharp major in mm. 9–13 as the dominant of the preceding music in C-sharp minor, and the B major in mm. 26–29 as the dominant of the preceding music in E major. Schubert marks both passages with a *crescendo* that leads to a *forte*, followed by a *decrescendo*. These dominant prolongations have a character that is both frozen (the harmony is static) and intensifying (the dynamic increases). The same can be said of the two iterations that occur in the

A^1 section at mm. 101 and 117. An unexpected turn occurs in m. 103, when the music moves to C major, enharmonically understood as B-sharp major. Fisk rightly emphasizes this imaginative harmonic shift, referring to m. 103 as the moment when "the Andante's most time-stopping gesture arises, its sudden, breath-catching turn to C major" (2001, 259). While the C major is revelatory from the perspective of both harmony and voice-leading, the A^1 section also revisits the "frozen dominant" music heard in the opening section. The triads at these moments remain the same, even as their function slightly changes. The G-sharp major in mm. 98–102 is heard as the dominant of the preceding music in C-sharp minor, while the B major in mm. 115–18 emerges out of a second-inversion E major and implies a cadential 6/4 that goes unresolved. Example 4.8 reveals the position within the movement of these four "frozen dominants," marked by their unique *forte* dynamics.

Example 4.9 correlates the four passages highlighted in Example 4.8 with Kissin's stifled vocalizations. Put simply, the only four moments in the A and A^1 sections where Schubert marks *forte* include the largest collection of Kissin's effortful, stifled grunts.[15] The first two iterations (marked in Example 4.9 as I and II) reveal remarkably similar patterns. In both cases, Kissin embellishes the *forte* downbeat, its eighth-note anacrusis, and the preceding downbeat. He is thereby accentuating Schubert's motivic and textural parallelism by producing exactly parallel grunts. The two iterations in the A^1 section (marked as III and IV) reveal a similar parallelism, with Kissin producing three grunt sounds during the beginning of the *crescendo*. In these last two occurrences, Kissin leaves the *forte* arrivals unembellished. The coincidence of Kissin's grunting with these four appearances of the same, frozen, *forte* music across Schubert's 138-bar, twelve-minute movement is remarkable. The pianist produces a specific kind of vocalization if, and only if, a given gesture appears in the score.

Artur Rubenstein said of Schubert's *Andante sostenuto*: "there is nothing else as close as this music that shows us what death feels like" (Sachs 1995, 336). I do not hear Kissin portraying or impersonating the sounds of dying, though his vocalizations could be said to express strain. In a July 2004 review of the recording entitled "Kissin at His Mercurial Best and Laboured Worst," critic Jeremy Nicholas frames the vocalizations negatively: "In the *Adagio*, Kissin works hard to make sure we know how much he is suffering

---

[15] These stifled grunts are not the only non-notated sounds in Kissin's 2004 recording. He produces prominent breath sounds (e.g., at 0:11.52) and utters short, pinched vocalizations (e.g., at 2:01.93).

Example 4.9 Franz Schubert, Piano Sonata in B-flat major, D. 960, second movement, detailing the four "frozen" dominants seen in Example 4.8 and annotating the stifled grunts in the 2004 recording by Evgeny Kissin. See ▶ Audio Example 4.8.

on behalf of Schubert (there's even a weary grunt at 2′15″)" (2004, 69).[16] The labored grunts that mark these four passages give an impression of a musician who is having difficulty *not* because the music is virtuosic, but because of the rhetorical weight exerted by relatively simple, static harmony in a slow tempo. It is not technically extreme to execute these passages and, as a result, Kissin's sounded exertions suggest an exteriorizing of an interior narrative struggle. His intimate, stifled grunts call attention to four iterations of the static-yet-striving passage. Since grunts are relatively rare across the rest of the track, Kissin's recording of the *Andante sostenuto* exemplifies the interrelation between sounds of effort and large-scale harmonic, motivic, and narrative form.[17]

A thoroughgoing growl

Nothing quite prepared me to hear Giambattista Valdettaro's 2014 recording of Zoltán Kodály's Sonata for Solo Cello, Op. 8.[18] No recording of notated classical music that I have encountered includes more audible exertions than this one, and none includes unwritten sounds that so thoroughgoingly intertwine themselves with notated ones. Valdettaro makes Glenn Gould's voluminous vocalizing seem sedate. The packaging for Valdettaro's disc on the Velut Luna label—which was produced by Valdettaro himself and which includes the Kodály Sonata alongside solo works by Luigi Dallapiccola and Bernhard Cossmann—features a white rectangle on the back cover enclosing the capitalized words: "RECORDING STRICTLY LIVE-IN-STUDIO / NO EDITING." The theme is developed in the liner notes: "96kHz / 24bit original stereo recording made strictly live-in-studio at a little church near Casalserugo, Italy on February 19th, 2014" (2014). The phrase "strictly live-in-studio" suggests that there has been no post-production splicing or sound editing.

---

[16] *Pace* Nicholas, Kissin does not grunt at 2:15 in his 2004 recording of the second movement of Schubert D. 960. He does, however, grunt prominently at 2:24.3 and then again at 2:28.6.

[17] For another example of labored vocalizations that coincide with non-virtuosic formal arrivals, see Radu Lupu's 1971 recording of Brahms's Intermezzo in C-sharp minor, Op. 117, No. 3. The track was engineered by Tryggvi Tryggvasson and released on compact disc in 1987 as Decca 417 599-2. Lupu's moaned singing is prominent during both the *poco più lento* that concludes the opening section (mm. 41–44, beginning at 1:29) and the return of this music during the *più lento* that closes the piece (mm. 103–6, beginning at 5:29).

[18] I am grateful to Neil Heyde for drawing my attention to this recording.

Some might argue that Valdettaro's recording of Kodály's sonata is not worthy of study. It is not an interpretation that one might laud for its intonation (for sterling intonation, I recommend Emmanuelle Bertrand's 2011 Harmonia Mundi recording), nor does Valdettaro's interpretation include every bar of Kodály's score.[19] What these tracks do preserve is a professional cellist reading an iconic work while producing, with his voice, a near-constant growling rumble. By "near-constant," I do not mean to suggest that his vocal sounds appear unbroken or that they accompany every measure. That said, his growl is heard in nearly every system and runs alongside the cello sounds for several measures at a time. Valdettaro's vocalizations are as present as any motive in Kodály's three-movement score. They create the impression that the cellist is creating the music of the sonata with considerable difficulty and, at certain moments, perhaps even against his will. My attempts to describe and distinguish Valdettaro's growls are not meant to be pejorative. Coming upon this disc was, for me, akin to a Neo-Riemannian theorist first opening a late Schubert score.

The thoroughgoingness of Valdettaro's growl is impossible to portray without providing a spectrogram of his entire 27.5-minute recording, but representative examples offer insight into how these growls operate alongside and within Kodály's score. Their placement is not random. Valdettaro's growling is used extensively, though not exclusively, to embellish Kodály's notated *crescendi* and *sforzandi*. The cellist has a way of making his growl surge through hairpins, sometimes rising in pitch along the way. Encountering *sforzando* markings, Valdettaro often responds with his cello and his voice together, modulating his growl into a punctuating grunt. The cellist's voice impresses itself so profoundly and repeatedly that the listener is hearing almost as much unwritten music as written. Three excerpts—one from each movement—allow a varied analysis of Valdettaro's extraordinary sound-making as he records Kodály's sonata. The first example demonstrates the thoroughgoingness of his growling on the opening page of the first movement. The second studies a set of gestures from the middle movement, where Valdettaro's unwritten growls become as active and independent as the notated music itself. A third excerpt isolates a passage from

---

[19] Valdettaro's recording omits mm. 272–322 of the third movement of Kodály's sonata. As these bars correspond almost exactly to page 15 of the Universal Edition score, this might be a case of a missing leaf or a memory slip. It is unlikely to have been a splicing error, since the materials accompanying the disc emphasize that the recording is unedited.

the final movement to explore the correlation between Valdettaro's growls and Kodály's notated *crescendi* and *sforzandi*.

Example 4.10 transcribes the opening twenty-five measures of the first movement, corresponding to the first sixty seconds of the track and appearing at sounding pitch rather than Kodály's notated *scordatura*. The example also notates the fifteen growls, which vary in length from short bursts to rumbling counterpoints. Growls 1–4 are short and comparatively discreet. They decorate and extend the growl of the cello's open-string triads (B1–F♯2–D3) in mm. 1, 2, and 5. With growl 5, Valdettaro crosses the proverbial Rubicon. His unwritten vocal decoration extends from bar 6 to the downbeat of bar 10. When I play this track for friends, it is at this moment that eyes begin to widen. Growl 5 is an extended, morphing, churning vocal sound, during which the listener becomes aware that the following twenty-seven minutes might be unlike other recordings of this sonata. Growl 5 has a distinct relationship to Kodály's notation. It coincides almost exactly with the lengthy *crescendo* marking that culminates in the *sforzando*, *fortissimo* C♯6 in bar 10. This growl plants the seed for what becomes a lengthy and developmental relationship between the cellist's growling and the score's *crescendi*. Another emergent correlation born during the opening minute is motivic. Compare the music at the outset of growls 4, 6, 8, 10, 12, and 13. The melodic material in all six cases is a falling dotted quarter to eighth note figure initiated on beat 2. This motive saturates the opening of Kodály's sonata, and Valdettaro's growl accompanies nearly every iteration. The written and the unwritten music form a bond. The extended growl 13—the last of this group—sets itself apart and becomes a kind of culmination. Whereas the preceding dotted quarter + eighth + growl motives (growls 8, 10, and 12) all terminate before the following downbeat, growl 13 extends through the downbeat—through a notated rest—to conclude on beat 2 of bar 20. Growl 13 thereby marks the local culmination of the gesture. After this moment, the line will migrate into a lower register, the dynamic will change to *piano*, and the texture to *pizzicato*. At the threshold of change, Valdettaro marks the final appearance of the motive with an extended growl, one that supersedes the bar line and makes way for the new music to come.

The connection between growls, *crescendi*, and *sforzandi* deepens in Valdettaro's recording of the second movement *Adagio*. Surging growls abound across the movement, exemplified by the passage from 8:01 to 8:13, corresponding to mm. 133–35. Francesco Mastromatteo identifies two possible formal renderings of the movement, one of which he calls "a traditional

Example 4.10 Zoltán Kodály, Sonata for Solo Cello, Op. 8, first movement, mm. 1–25.1, notated at sounding pitch, annotating the fifteen growls in the 2014 recording by Giambattista Valdettaro. See ▶ Audio Example 4.9.

sonata-like ternary design" (2015, 113). Within that design, mm. 133–35 represent a pivotal transition. Bars 133–34 are the final two measures of the recapitulation, and bar 135 is the first measure of the coda. Example 4.11 provides the spectrogram and score of this formal threshold. Valdettaro is

vocally silent in bar 133, during the *piano* F♯3–D4–A4 *pizzicati* and the two
arco A4s that follow. Things change the moment Kodály notates *crescendo*
in bar 134. Marked in the spectrogram with a rising arrow, Kodály's hairpin
runs alongside Valdettaro's growl, the latter rising notably in pitch. This is
visible in the lowest part of the spectrogram, corresponding to the low pitch
of Valdettaro's voice, which shows an upward slant. The sound is not dissimilar to the engine of an accelerating car. Upon reaching its apex, the growl

Example 4.11 Zoltán Kodály, Sonata for Solo Cello, Op. 8, second movement,
mm. 133–35.2, notated at sounding pitch, including a spectrogram of 8:00–8:13
in the 2014 recording by Giambattista Valdettaro, annotating his ascending
growl leading into bar 135. See ⏵ Audio Example 4.10.

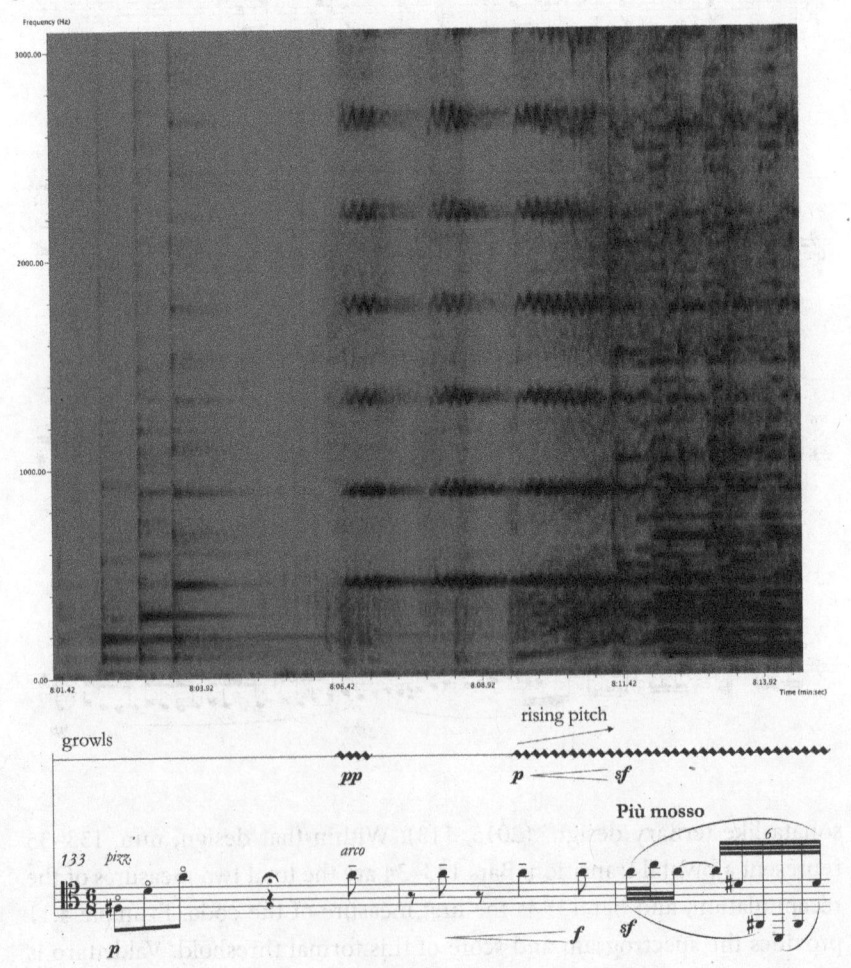

wavers slightly as Kodály marks a tempo change and a *sforzando* within the new, *forte* dynamic. Much about the interpretation of bar 134 might be expected: the cello gets louder, the vibrato becomes more intense, the duration of the final A4 is elongated. What is unexpected is the new sound source—Valdettaro's growl—and its attendant expansion of both pitch and timbre. His vocal surge entangles the written and the unwritten.

The third movement of Kodály's sonata is the longest in both notated measures and performed duration and includes dozens of growls. Many of Valdettaro's emphatic vocalizations coincide with notated *crescendi* and *sforzandi*. The correlation is made plain in a relatively quiet passage in mm. 568–78, during the movement's recapitulation. Perhaps no place within the entire 27.5-minute recording more vividly (and surprisingly) demonstrates the function of Valdettaro's growl as an embellishment of Kodály's notated *crescendi* and *sforzandi*. The passage includes both markings, twice: the hairpin from mm. 568–70 is capped off by the *sforzando* in m. 571, and the hairpins in mm. 573–76 lead similarly to the *arco* harmonic in m. 577. Each hairpin is accompanied by a surging growl, and each *sforzando* is met with an accented vocalization that quickly rises and falls. Example 4.12 includes both the notated transcription and the spectrogram.

The most vivid vocalizations in Example 4.12 are the two *sforzandi* at 8:22.61 and 8:31.25, respectively. The squiggly lines of the spectrogram capture Valdettaro's effortful grunt-moans. These vocalizations coincide with the *sforzandi*, *arco*, harmonics in m. 571 and m. 577. Of all the sounds called for in Kodály's score, natural harmonics have the potential to remain quite stable in terms of pitch. Natural harmonics in cello music often stand apart from fingered pitches, in that they imply *senza vibrato*. Valdettaro's two vocalizations stand out precisely because they superimpose wildly undulating vocal material atop *senza vibrato* natural harmonics. In most recordings of the work, the *fermati* in m. 571 and m. 577 capture ringing stasis. In Valdettaro's track, the harmonics arrive alongside vocally inflected gestures rich in improvisatory, chromatic energy.

The second of the two vocalizations in Example 4.12, which embellishes the sounding A5 harmonic on the second beat of bar 577, adds another layer of texture. Valdettaro's utterance includes *vocal fry*. Cornelius Reid defines vocal fry as a "rough, squeezed, vocalized sound," adding that it has "a tonal quality resembling a death rattle that is heard only in the lowest range of the voice" (1983, 404). Victoria Malawey provides evidence of this technique in popular music, demonstrating it spectrographically in Leonard Cohen's

Example 4.12 Zoltán Kodály, Sonata for Solo Cello, Op. 8, third movement, mm. 568–78, notated at sounding pitch, including a spectrogram of 8:17–8:34 of the 2014 recording by Giambattista Valdettaro, annotating his growled *sforzandi* and vocal fry. See ⓹ Audio Example 4.11.

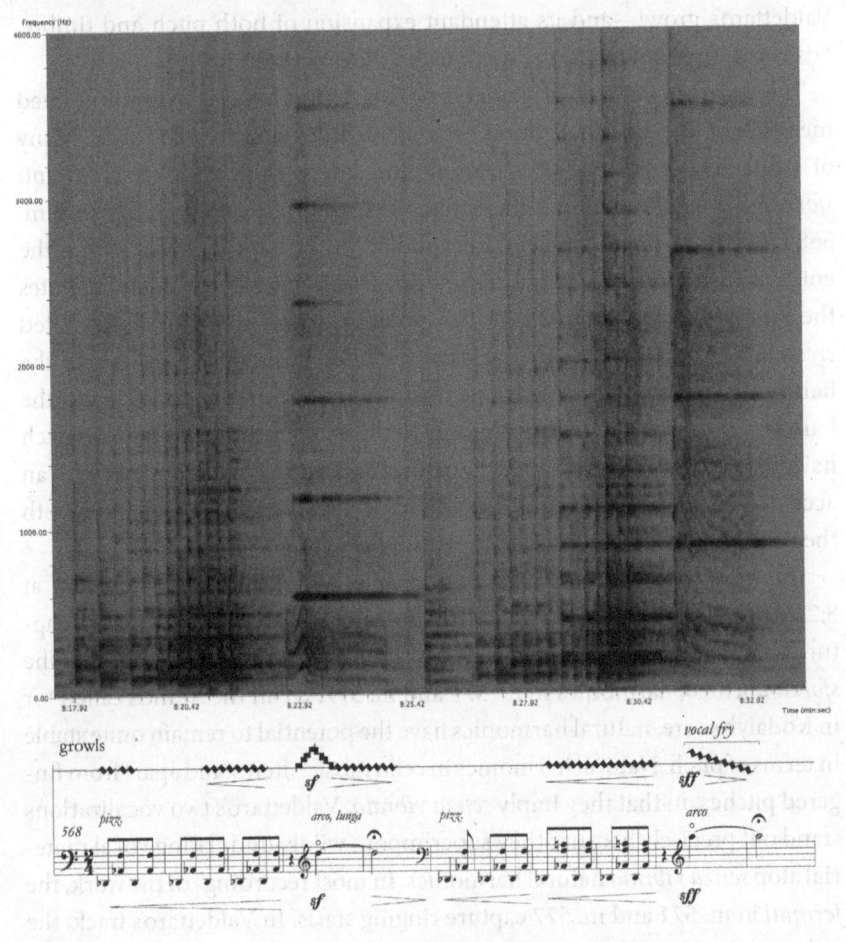

rendition of his oft-covered song "Hallelujah" (2020, 53). How unexpected it is, then, to find vocal fry playing an expressive role in a recording of Kodály's Sonata for Solo Cello, with Valdettaro's "rough, squeezed" vocalization turning Kodály's written A5 harmonic into a kaleidoscopic rumble, complete with implied "death rattle."

In a startlingly prescient (if entirely coincidental) commentary published in Italian in the July 1921 edition of *Il Pianoforte*, Béla Bartók praised Kodály's Cello Sonata *for its surprising vocal effects:*

Here Kodály expresses new musical ideas by new and at the same time the simplest possible means for the solo violoncello. And it is precisely the solution of this problem which has given the composer the opportunity to create a technique of an unusual and original style; it is by means of this that he arrives at the production of surprising vocal effects, beyond which or rather above which shines the intrinsic value of the work from the musical aspect." (Bartók 1976, 478)[20]

To be sure, Bartók was not imagining, nor would he likely have sanctioned, the vocal effects with which Valdettaro ornaments Kodály's score. I do not expect many readers will accept them either. Even so, Valdettaro's recording memorializes a cellist creating "a technique of an unusual and original style" by which he "arrives at the production of surprising vocal effects."

Moans as indicators of phrase

Grunts, groans, and moans can wordlessly signal the boundaries of phrase, especially in orchestral and chamber contexts where they can act as a coordinating temporal marker. The interaction between moaning and phrasing can be illustrated by a 1984 recording by Georg Solti and the Chicago Symphony Orchestra of the slow movement from Gustav Mahler's Fourth Symphony.[21] Mahler's marking at the opening of the third movement is *Ruhevoll (Poco adagio)*. Alongside, he asks those members of the cello section who are carrying the melody (the section is divided) to play *espress. sehr gesangsvoll*. Constantin Floros classifies the music at the outset of this twenty-minute double variation movement as a bar form arrangement and characterizes the initial *Stollen* as "a sixteen-measure cantilena of the cellos" (1993, 127). This cantilena flows along in a rather untroubled G major and closes, in m. 16, on a half cadence.

Solti released two studio recordings of Mahler's Fourth Symphony, one with the Concertgebouw Orchestra and soprano Sylvia Stahlmann in 1961, the other with the Chicago Symphony Orchestra and soprano Kiri Te Kanawa

[20] "Kodály vi esprime dei pensieri musicali nuovi con un mezzo nuovo e allo stesso tempo il più semplice possibile, comé quello del violoncello solo. Ed è precisamente la soluzione di questo problema che ha dato occasione al compositore di creare una tecnica di stile insolita e originale: mediante la quale egli giunge a riprodurre effetti vocali sorprendenti, oltre ai quali, sopra ai quali anzi, brilla il valore intrinseco del lavoro come musicalità" (Bartók 1921, 196–97).

[21] I am grateful to Peter Kupfer for introducing me to this recording.

in 1984.[22] In the 1961 recording, no conductor sounds are audible during the slow movement's opening cantilena. By contrast, the 1984 recording captures vivid vocalizations from the podium. Reviewing the original compact disc release, Richard Osborne found Solti's sounded effort notable, while simultaneously providing a glimpse into the historical moment when listeners were acclimatizing themselves to the qualities of this novel medium:

> It is the only CD version of the Fourth available at present in the UK catalogue, and as such can be broadly recommended. The added immediacy of the orchestral image makes the reading seem rather less urbane that it does on LP, but in terms of the articulation of some inner detail the CD is marginally preferable; it is also easier to reproduce clearly. In addition, there is the added advantage of the guarantee of permanently silent surfaces in the slow movement and in the coda of the fourth movement. Offsetting this is the new clarity with which [the] CD points up Solti's anticipatory grunts on upbeats. I still can't hear the second violins at the start of bar 17 of the slow movement. (1984, 223)[23]

Example 4.13 transcribes the location of Solti's audible moans during the opening sixteen-bar *Stollen*, led by the cellos. Following the format of the Dashon Burton analysis in Chapter 2, I have numbered Solti's moans. This allows each one to be characterized individually for, like Burton's inhales, Solti's vocalizations are not all identical. His unwritten moans—there are no fewer than seven in the first sixteen measures—are notable in that they articulate the phrasing of Mahler's opening cantilena. It is telling where they occur, and where they do not. At times, Solti's moans cut across the boundaries of notated slurs and phrase markings, thereby indicating his sense of where phrases originate.

Moan 1 occurs precisely at the beginning of the track and acts as an anacrusis to the G major triad on the first downbeat. John Dunkerley, who worked with James Lock as a sound engineer for Solti's recording, allowed

---

[22] The original 1984 compact disc release on Decca 410 188 2 states that Solti's recording was made in April 1983. Frank Villella, archivist of the Rosenthal Archives of the Chicago Symphony, confirmed to me that the recording took place not in April, but in March, on the 28th and 29th. This places the recording just after the Chicago Symphony's live performances of the work, which took place on March 23–26, 1983 (personal communication, April 30, 2014).

[23] Osborne's quip about not being able to hear the second violins at the start of bar 17 seems spurious, as Solti's moan 7 ends prior to their entrance. Moreover, this moan is one of shortest and quietest in the passage.

Example 4.13 Gustav Mahler, Fourth Symphony, third movement, mm. 1–16, annotating seven moans in the 1984 recording by Georg Solti and the Chicago Symphony Orchestra. See ▶ Audio Example 4.12.

the opening moan to remain on the track. Given the enmeshed nature of moans 2–7, removing moan 1 might, paradoxically, have sounded unnatural. Moan 2 precedes bar 3, its presence setting off the first two measures as a sub-phrase and setting in motion the possibility that the movement will proceed in two-bar units. The expectation of a phrase ending at the end of m. 4 is met with the arrival of moan 3. This third moan makes clear that the cello melody is paramount in Solti's phrasing (as one might expect), given that moan 3 cuts across the slur in the violas, which extends across the bar line. Given the now-established 2 + 2 pattern, one might expect a moan at the end of bar 6. In this case, the cello ascent has quickened and the rising bass motion (reaching a sounding C3 on the downbeat of bar 7) means that there is no phrase segmentation, and no moan.

The pattern of moans at bar lines is broken by moan 4, which arrives not at the *end* of m. 8, but before beat 3. The melody determines Solti's moan placement, as the rising eighth notes on beat 4 act as an anacrusis to the following downbeat. As a result, moan 4 unceremoniously splits the slur in the cello melody that Mahler notates across the entire duration of m. 8. Moan 5 continues this pattern, as Solti's utterance acts as a dividing line between the melodic B that begins the measure and the rising C–D eighth notes that act as an anacrusis to bar 11. Moan 5 is the loudest and most urgent of Solti's grunts and ushers in the passage of greatest harmonic dissonance within the *Stollen*: the applied diminished seventh chord that resolves to the mediant in bar 12. Solti's imploring moan matches Mahler's marking of *im Ausdruck steigernd* (with rising expression). Moan 6 is faint, owing to the volume of the intensifying cello melody; even so, it continues the pattern of three consecutive pre–beat 4 moans in mm. 8, 10, and 12. After this series, one might expect a moan in bar 14, but the melodic and harmonic activity is moving ahead in a fashion analogous to bar 6. Solti's final moan of the passage— moan 7 at 1:16.2—acts as an upbeat to the second *Stollen* and cues the arrival of the second violins (not heard yet in the movement). Taken as a group, Solti's seven moans across the opening sixteen-measure cantilena generate a beat-level phrase segmentation of 8 + 8 + 15 followed by 8 + 8 + 17. The moans provide a window into Solti's sense of Mahler's phrasing.

Grunts unheard

To close the topic of sounded effort, I will venture into admittedly unusual territory. This final section will include no musical examples; instead, I will take up a set of sounds that cannot be heard. I am not attempting to excavate sounds of effort that have been erased from audio tracks before they were released. There lies—scattered around the earth on unreleased master tapes and audio files—a vast archive of sounded effort that goes unaudited. In the case of unused or unreleased takes, the intervention of engineers and musicians has (often sensibly) prevented countless instances of sounded effort from appearing on commercial recordings. Instead, the unheard exertions that I have in mind here were never captured by microphones at all, because they were never made.

Analyzing sounds for which no record exists seems, at best, a daunting task and, at worst, an impossibility. Still, it is imperative that theorists of audio tracks remain cognizant of what it is that they might *not* be hearing, and why they might *not* be hearing it. I am inspired in this investigation by Allyson Nadia Field's "archive of absence." Discussing the (obvious) challenges that accompany analyzing a corpus of nonextant African American films made in the 1910s, Field writes:

> What does it mean to talk about lost film? This requires a necessarily re-
> lational stance. To whom is a film lost? Films and film artifacts that are
> considered lost to us did, of course, once enjoy projection (beyond the fan-
> tasy that our desires might conjure up). Though obvious, it bears reminding
> that just because we can't see a film does not mean that someone else hasn't,
> or didn't, see it. (Field 2015, 24)

Analogous questions might be asked of audio recordings. Shifting the domain of Field's queries: just because I (or we) didn't hear a recording doesn't mean that someone else hasn't or didn't. I divide this section on "unheard grunts" into two parts. First, I address sounds of effort that have been silenced before-the-fact by mentors, teachers, and the classical music recording industry. Second, I will look anew at the purported, cancer-related grunts that played a pivotal role in the legacy of pianist Joyce Hatto.

In Chapter 1, I discussed the fact that non-notated sounds made by men are more likely to be accepted by (predominantly male) critics than similar sounds made musicians of other genders. For example, critic Marc Rochester puts a positive spin on conductor Michel Plasson's grunts in a recording of music by Camille Saint-Saëns with the Toulouse Capitole Orchestra: "This is a tremendously exciting account of the Third Symphony, crackling with supercharged energy and blazing with colour. If the grunts and groans emanating (hopefully) from the conductor's rostrum are anything to go by, Plasson is clearly enjoying himself and inspires some top-notch playing from his orchestra" (1997, 76). Plasson's audible exertions are read as emblems of pleasure and his recording has seemingly transferred that pleasure to Rochester.

Women are not granted the same, charitable "overlooking" of sounded effort. I have come upon few positive reviews of female musicians grunting. Indeed, there are relatively few recordings where they grunt at all. While there are exceptions, including the tracks by Claire Chase and Hélène Grimaud analyzed above, there seem to be fewer instances of sounded effort in recordings by women. It is possible that female conservatory students who grunt, groan, and moan during their lessons are more likely to be told to silence themselves than their male counterparts. What sounds are going unheard? One possible answer is that sounds of effort might have been made but were *discouraged before the musician ever entered the studio*. Women seem to be most impacted by these unwritten rules and least excused when they break them. A more welcoming approach to classical music performance for all students—including and especially those whose natural practice has been heavily curtailed by bias—could produce a generation of recordings that reflect musicians being themselves, be that quiet or loud.

A second "archive of absence" in the realm of unheard grunts is more historically specific. The point I seek to make is delicate and requires a careful separation of fact from fiction. As the case involves extensive duplicity, this is no simple task. Pianist Joyce Hatto was born in London in 1928 and died in Hertfordshire in 2006. According to Eric Drott, Hatto's performing career began in the 1950s and extended until the mid-1970s "when she was forced to retire from the stage on account of a protracted struggle with ovarian cancer" (2010, 65). Beginning in the 1990s, the Concert Artist label began to release recordings in Hatto's name covering much of the core repertoire for her instrument, many of them garnering high praise from the critical community. Nicholas Cook, himself a pivotal figure in the undoing of what turned out to be an elaborate hoax, explains the unique nature of Hatto's post-retirement career:

> But in the 1990s a miracle took place. Concert Artist started releasing recording after recording by the now elderly Hatto, in which she systematically scaled the peaks of the pianistic repertory. From 2003 she was taken up by a number of British music critics associated with the influential monthly journal *Gramophone*, and by the time of her death in 2006 she had become a myth: the story of the reclusive, cancer-defying artist was irresistible, and besides, the recordings were good.

That is because they were taken from existing recordings by a wide range of well-chosen professional pianists. Sometimes an entire album was copied, while at other times tracks were mixed and matched from a number of sources; often the acoustic of the recording was digitally modified, while on occasion the recordings would be slightly speeded up or slowed down. The astonishing thing is that more than a hundred Hatto CDs were issued before the fraud was unmasked. (Cook 2013, 152)

Hatto was not to blame. Cook identifies her husband—the sound engineer and onetime classical music agent William Barrington-Coupe (known socially as "Barry")—as "perpetrator of the celebrated hoax that bears her name" (2013, 151). Barrington-Coupe famously admitted to the deception after the facts against him became too damning. Much of the critical writing related to Barrington-Coupe's fraud has focused on the ways in which hoax came to light—involving a marvelously varied cast including a financial analyst named Brian Ventura, the audio recording identification software Gracenote, scholars from the Centre for the History and Analysis of Recorded Music at the University of London, and Cook himself.[24]

While the hoax is understandably notorious, one fact has attracted less attention. Barrington-Coupe's *mea culpa* stated that his decision to perpetrate the deception in the first place hinged on his wife's grunting. Two complementary accounts of his confession characterize the role of grunts in his decision-making. Writing in the *New Yorker*, Mark Singer reported:

Within a couple of news cycles, Barry confessed—sort of—in a letter to the head of the Swedish label that had released László Simon's Liszt recording. The executive shared excerpts with *Gramophone*, which paraphrased Barry's mea culpa as "I Did It for My Wife"—as if they were both victims of his gallant uxoriousness. "It" referred not to bootlegging entire performances but to having borrowed bits of other recordings to solve technical problems. Hatto had played all the pieces herself, Barry explained, but they had been marred by involuntary grunting noises prompted by the pain from her advancing cancer. So he had searched for recordings by artists with similar styles and spliced patches into her work. "My wife was completely unaware

---

[24] Lisa Giombini (2020) offers a philosophical perspective on the intersection between the Hatto recordings and notions of authenticity.

that I did this," he wrote. "I simply let her hear . . . the finished editing that she thought was completely her own work." (2007, 76, ellipsis in original)

In a dispatch published by *Gramophone* on February 26, 2007, Charlotte Smith revealed that before Barrington-Coupe began lifting entire tracks from other pianists, his editing was designed specifically to patch over his wife's grunts:

> Although she kept up a rigorous practice regime, Barrington-Coupe says that Hatto was suffering more than she admitted, even to herself. Recording session after recording session was marred by her many grunts of pain as she played, and her husband was at a loss to know how to cover the problem passages.
>
> Until, that is, he remembered the story of Elisabeth Schwarzkopf covering the high notes for Kirsten Flagstad in the famous EMI recording of Wagner's *Tristan und Isolde*. Surely something similar could apply here, he reasoned. He began searching for pianists whose sound and style were similar to that of his wife, and once he had found them he would insert small patches of their recordings to cover his wife's grunts. (Smith 2007)

In summary, the most notorious scandal in recent classical music history emerged because Joyce Hatto's ovarian cancer caused her to grunt while she played and—crucially, for our purposes—because her husband, William Barrington-Coupe, could not accept the sound of his wife's grunting as integral to her music-making at that stage of her life.

The reader will no doubt have already surmised how saddened I am by this deception, less for what it produced than for what it obscured. It seems that there might have been recordings of Hatto that included the sound of her grunting, sounds stemming in part from her grave illness. Were Hatto's unedited, grunt-filled recordings to materialize, I would not expect any person, including myself, to automatically laud them. Her interpretations might have been visionary or enervated. Her unedited recordings undoubtedly are (or were) a document of a professional pianist performing at a moment in her life that was marked by the need to grunt. To be able to analyze those recordings—the sounds as they were before Barrington-Coupe began his frenzy of illicit patching—would be fascinating. Having myself heard severely ill musicians perform, I would expect to hear intimate exertions. There might even be a few of the climactic kind. Still others might have inspired a new theoretical category.

Joyce Hatto's ostensibly grunt-filled original tracks stand as emblems of unwritten music. Had the recordings been released commercially, I assume that critical response would have been unfriendly. I expect that Hatto's unedited tracks would have been savaged in some quarters and quietly dismissed in others. Music theorists would likely have ignored them, as they do not document "the pieces" precisely enough. Had this critical dismissal come to pass, the number of Hatto recordings released during the last twenty years of the pianist's life would have been far fewer than the dozens of falsified releases that appeared in their place. There can be no doubt that one disc of Hatto making her own music—grunts and all—would be more historically and musically valuable than Barrington-Coupe's dozens of nefariously mislabeled fakes. Earlier, I stated that there would be no musical examples in this final section. In recognition of Hatto's archive of absence—one might also call it an obfuscated archive—I ask the reader to picture an imaginary "Example 4.14" designed to analyze (and memorialize) a track that recorded the pianist as she was.

5

Surface Noise

Surface noise as music

Of all the ways to describe surface noise, I particularly admire Lionel Salter's "fierce swish."[1] The two words produce a marvelous contrast. *Fierce* connotes the intense and potentially violent nature of the sound, while *swish* grants it an onomatopoetic playfulness. Salter coined the phrase while reviewing one of Arthur Friedheim's recordings of the funeral march from Chopin's Second Piano Sonata, Op. 35. Later in his review, Salter characterized the swish as "really troublesome." Here we part ways. While surface noise can detract from a listener's ability to focus solely on the sound of a performance, it deserves to be studied without praise or reproach. A more neutral analysis of the unwritten music on Friedheim's track would measure the time interval between each swish and discuss when, if ever, the hissing cycles move into synchrony with the meter of Chopin's march. In this chapter, I focus on a specific type of surface noise: the cyclic hiss patterns created by the rotation of phonograph cylinders and early gramophone discs. I will measure when this type of surface noise occurs, gauge what it expresses, and watch the swishes undergo development.

A contrast to Salter's encounter with surface noise is found in Joan Chissell's September 1984 *Gramophone* review of Mitsuko Uchida playing Mozart. The occasion marked the crossing of a technological threshold in Chissell's listening life: "This was the first CD I'd played in my own study and, with eyes shut, the illusion was complete: Mitsuko Uchida was right there, only a few feet away. The total absence of surface noise, whatever the volume, of course helped most to bring her there" (1984, 352). It is not

---

[1] Salter's coinage appears in his August 1993 *Gramophone* review of Friedheim's complete recordings on the Pearl label, where he declares that, "even allowing for the very early recording which all but flattens out tonal gradations, a piano with an extremely weak top octave, and some really troublesome surface noise (at its worst in the Hungarian Rhapsody No. 2, and with a fierce swish in one of two takes of the Chopin Funeral March), Friedheim—who was in his fifties at the time—does not show up at all well in comparison with other Liszt pupils and with the giants of the golden age of pianists" (1993, 89).

the clamor of the surface noise that catches Chissell's attention, but its absence. Her review allows us to eavesdrop on the experience of a music lover encountering a new audio format and feeling a visceral intensification of *presence*. As Chissell listens to Uchida, she credits the lack of surface noise with creating a sensation that the pianist is "right there." The illusion to which Chissell refers has been a goal of sound engineering since the advent of recording. A record has the power to instantiate a kind of séance, placing us in the room with beloved (and sometimes deceased) musicians. This magic trick ostensibly works best when the recording and playback media keep quiet.

It is no simple matter to listen closely to recordings with surface noise. The first obstacle is not so much the audio but the acculturated presumption that "noisy" recordings are undesirable and potentially unlistenable. It is easy to imagine a listener who desires to learn a specific piece dismissing a surface noise-laden recording within the first few seconds. For them, such sounds are obstructions. It becomes a matter of expectation. If one takes an early Berliner gramophone disc to be the record of a piece of music being performed, then any hissing will be understood as a hindrance. If, on the other hand, one recognizes all sounds as integral, then surface noise is simply another component of the mix. The latter perspective is advantageous for theorists who are interested in sound recordings as documents. I consider late nineteenth-century wax cylinders to be as *listenable* as twentieth-century vinyl or twenty-first-century digital tracks. Decades of technological innovation have generated a river of momentum. Records are generally understood to be representations of music-making whose full appreciation is impeded by the presence of surface noise. I will reverse the current of this river to pose a simple question: what happens if we pay attention to the sound of recording and playback machines alongside the sound of the performance that they capture? Put another way: when surface noise is audible, what can it express as part of the totality of the sounding music?

In *Making Sense of Recordings: How Cognitive Processing of Recorded Sound Works*, Mads Walther-Hansen employs a pair of useful metaphors to describe recording practices. The first—called *One Reality*—posits that improvements to recording quality are "a search for *one* future endpoint" (2020, 33, italics in original). There is a sound created by the musician (which Walther-Hansen calls a "pre-recorded sound") and technological advances are designed to create ever-more-faithful captures of that sound.

A contrasting metaphor—called *Multiple Realities*—acknowledges that "recorded sound has other assets than its similarity (or dissimilarity) to pre-recorded sound" (2022, 33). While Walther-Hansen is not concerned with the music of surface noise, his classification of *non*-pre-recorded sounds as "assets" creates a fruitful opening for music theory. While classical recordings have implicitly positioned themselves as capturing primarily "pre-recorded sound," I will treat their surface noise, when it appears, as an "asset."

Considerable intellectual and technical energy has been spent removing surface noise from early recordings. Melle Jan Kromhout's *The Logic of Filtering* chronicles this quest from the early analog era through the noise reduction innovations of Ray Dolby to the "myth of perfect fidelity" in the digital age. Kromhout writes: "Most efforts at improving the sound quality of early phonography, therefore, aimed to reduce this flurry of machinic noises, whether by experimenting with different recording materials, fine-tuning mechanical parts, or improving the design and functionality of inscription surfaces, styluses, and horns" (2020, 18). The collective effort of sound engineers and technologists to maximize the clarity, vibrancy, and presence of audio recordings has moved the state of the art from tin horns and wax inscriptions to today's exquisite contemporary sound capture and diffusion techniques. Joseph Auner characterizes these advancements using the analogy of a cold war:

> The story has been dominated by the dialectic of music and noise, with the battle lines drawn over frequency range, distortion, scratches and pops, hiss and rumble. Yet rather than a battle, it was more of a cold war: reducing and eliminating these imperfections was a major concern, but it was never possible. Listeners have always had to learn to listen past these sounds, to filter them out, to keep the medium distinct from the message. (Auner 2000)

Why exactly is it that "listeners have always had to learn to listen past these sounds"? Must we automatically filter them out? What if the sounds of the recording medium are understood *as part of the message*? The immediate answer to these questions seems obvious: we filter to hear the performance that is, after all, the recording's *raison d'être*. But this does not have to be the case.

Evidence of a "cold war" against surface noise is found on records themselves. As early recordings were transferred onto modern formats, labels including Andante and Pearl made a point of preserving surface noise on their transfers. On multiple releases, including their 2002 three-disc set of early recordings of Maurice Ravel's orchestral works, Andante (which sometimes stylized their name with a lowercase "a") includes a thoughtful disclaimer that reads in part: "andante has chosen to follow a strict policy of minimal surface noise elimination. By doing so, we achieve an optimal balance between clarity of recorded sound and faithfulness to the expressive musical detail that is the hallmark of a great performance" (Ravel 2002, xiii). Pearl's reputation for so-called honest transfers is well documented. Reviewing Pearl's compact disc release of Fritz Busch's 1936 Glyndebourne recording of *Don Giovanni*, Alan Blyth writes: "That said, it is the kind of honest picture of the original as is to be found on most Pearl issues, and your ear soon accustoms itself to the 'frying-tonight' sounds" (1991, 1740). The high point of disdain for surface noise seems to have followed the arrival of the compact disc in the 1980s. A 1987 Music & Arts CD transfer of a 1939 recording of Ernest Bloch's Violin Concerto by Joseph Szigeti and the Amsterdam Concertgebouw bears a memorable paragraph on its back cover: "WARNING: This rare 'live' performance was recorded in the pre-tape era on lacquer discs. Despite careful digital reprocessing, some distortion, crackle, and surface noise remain on the CDs. Released because of their extraordinary artistic value, these CDs are not recommended to sound enthusiasts" (1987). I consider myself a "sound enthusiast" and admire this recording of Bloch's concerto *as it is*. Music & Arts' marketing language hints at the anxiety felt by the recording industry about the existence of "noisy" media when "silent" digital environments were becoming the norm.

Tracks that have audible evidence of their own recording process comprise a relatively small proportion of classical music recordings. Even so, they document pivotal figures in the history of interpretation. The singer Elizaveta Lavrovskaya and the pianist Paul Juon made their only recordings on Edison phonographs. Their sounding legacies are therefore enmeshed within the cyclic threshing of a spinning cylinder. A day will come when audio technology will be able to fully suppress the surface noise on early formats. When that day arrives, the original recordings will still exist, as will their various transfers to analog and digital media. Many listeners—including celebrated musicians from across the twentieth century—were profoundly influenced by recordings that were blanketed with "fierce swishes" from tip to tail.

Listening *with*

Early recordings have long been studied to reveal historically significant ways of playing, shedding light on vanished (or vanishing) modes of interpretation.[2] When encountering a recording from the age of phonographs and gramophones, a performance analyst is, sensibly, trying to listen *through* the surface noise to study the musician's way of playing a given score. As an alternative practice, I recommend listening *with* (listening *inclusive of*) the sound of surface noise as it runs alongside the sounds of performance.[3] Surface noise is foreign to classical scores but integral to certain recording formats. This binary is adapted from Ragnhild Brøvig-Hanssen and Anne Danielsen's *Digital Signatures: The Impact of Digitization on Popular Music Sound*. Discussing the audio fingerprints of recording and playback media, they write: "While listeners were used to listening *through* the medium signatures of musical equipment and recording technology, digital technology's elimination of sonic colorization demanded that they start listening *to* those sounds" (2016, 68, italics in original). The track-specific analyses in this chapter are designed to extend Brøvig-Hanssen and Danielsen's notion of "digital signatures" into the analog domain.

The practice of listening *through* surface noise has a long history. Gramophone enthusiasts took up the practice early on. The November 1, 1923, issue of *The Musical Times* includes an article authored by Feste that uses the ableist metaphor of "turning a deaf ear" to describe this very act: "For example, you are not a gramophonist very long before you easily acquire the knack of turning a deaf ear to any surface noise; and a little later you find yourself mentally supplying deficiencies in the clearness of bass instruments" (1923, 767). An inspiring, if indirect, refutation of Feste's approach comes from film studies. In *Sound Theory, Sound Practice*, Rick Altman lays the groundwork for a theory of sound that has a kinship with my own:

---

[2] Writings that connect early recordings and performance practice include Robert Philip *Early Recordings and Musical Style: Changing Tastes in Instrumental Performance* (1992), Rebecca Plack "The Substance of Style: How Singing Creates Sound in Lieder Recordings 1902–1939" (2008), and Roy Howat *The Art of French Piano Music: Debussy, Ravel, Fauré, Chabrier* (2009). The influence of recording on classical performers is discussed in Robert Philip *Performing Music in the Age of Recording* (2004).

[3] Composers have long been asking listeners to pay attention to the music of recording and playback machines. Pauline Oliveros's *A Little Noise in the System* (1968) might be called the apotheosis of surface noise. The piece, made at the University of California San Diego Electronic Music Studio, presents and then develops a cyclic hissing pattern across its 30:25 duration. In *The Cambridge Companion to Music and Digital Culture*, Paul Sanden discusses my sextet *La fille dérivée* (2012), which is based on a microtiming of Alfred Cortot's 1931 recording of Debussy's prelude "La fille aux cheveux de lin." Sanden writes: "Beaudoin has the pianist use sandpaper blocks, while the wind players blow through their instruments in rhythmically recurring patterns to create a sort of dilated echo of the cyclical hissing of the phonograph. This is a piece of music that refers not only to Debussy's iconic piano prelude, but also to its specific instantiation as recorded by Cortot in London on 2 July 1931" (2019, 189–90).

Most listeners have learned to concentrate on the aspects of sound events that are most faithfully rendered by recordings and to pay little attention to the aspects introduced or transformed by the recording process. A proper theory of sound will accept no such selective deafness. It will pay special attention to those very points where confusion is possible, recognizing in such moments of imprecision, indecision, or incoherence the very place where sound seizes the opportunity to take an active role in the definition and exploitation of culture. (Altman 1992, 30)

While our goals are not identical, I hear in Altman's words a refrain pertinent to this chapter and, indeed, this book. Surface noise is introduced by processes of recording and playback and is commonly disregarded as not being part of "the music."

Redirecting Altman's language: a proper theory of recording analysis will set aside listening *through* surface noise and instead suggest that we listen *with* it. Surface noise creates complicated chains of agency. It is not controlled by the composer, the score, or the performer. Paying attention to it *as music* unearths expressive and otherwise invisible musical connections. This mode of listening takes patience. It is natural to mentally filter out the scratchy veneer of early recordings and focus on the piece being performed. My practice recommends widening the perceptive window, reserving a portion of attention for the sounds of the performance and a portion for the sounds of the recording and playback media. It requires that listeners cede some attentive bandwidth to the surface noise in order that all sounds be allowed to coexist and commingle as music.

Recordings as *carta*

The last page of the *libri secundi* of Robert Fludd's *Utriusque cosmi maioris scilicet et minoris metaphysica, physica atque technica historia in duo volumina secundum cosmi differentiam diuisa* (1617, 308) uses an illustration of a sighting grid to demonstrate the benefits of optical perspective when creating a realistic drawing. Reproduced as Figure 5.1, the image can be read from right to left. In the upper right corner is the *civitatis pars* (a part of the city). Two dotted lines emerge from its architecture: one from the rightmost base of the tower and another from near the tip of its spire. These two lines flow from the *civitatis pars* down to a wooden table on which rest

Figure 5.1 Illustration of a sighting grid from Robert Fludd *Utriusque cosmi maioris scilicet et minoris metaphysica, physica atque technica historia in duo volumina secundum cosmi differentiam diuisa* (1617).

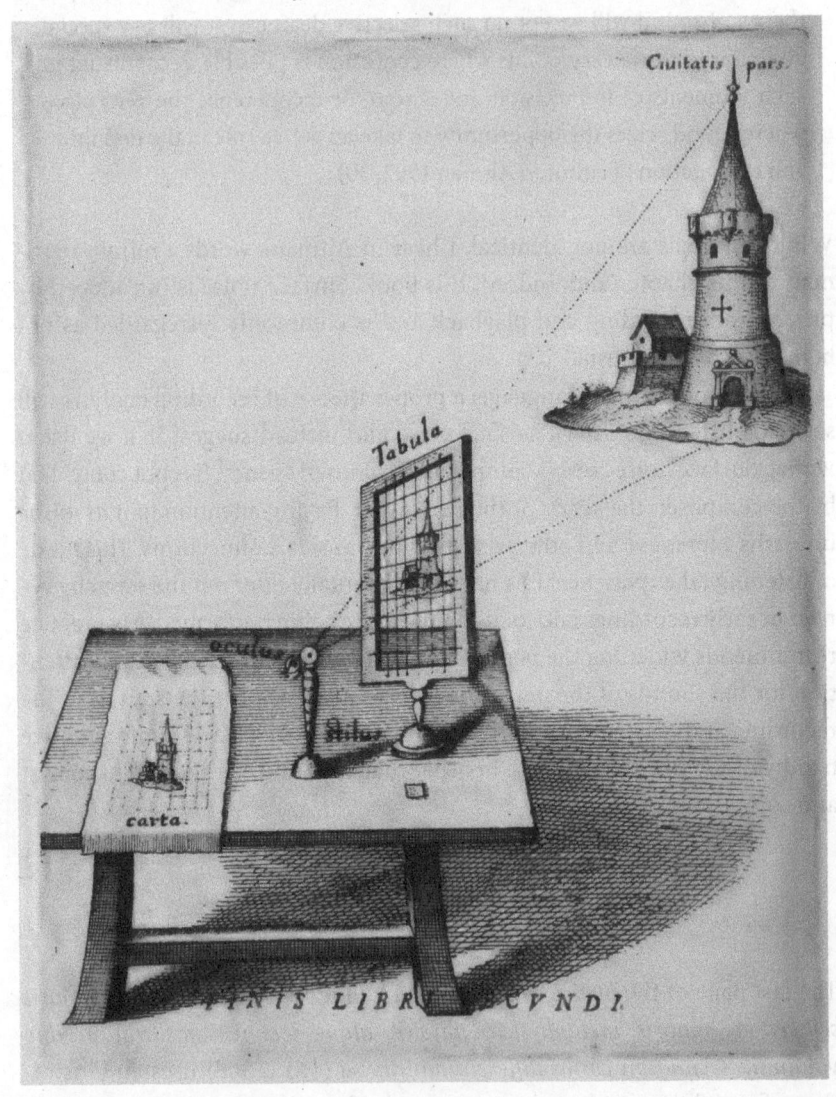

three objects: a rectangular *tabula* (board) resting on a hemispherical base, a slender object housing an *oculus* (eye) and a *stilus* (writing implement) that also rests on a hemispherical base, and a *carta* (drawing) whose lower section hangs slightly over the edge of the table.

Following the path of light, the lines emerging from the *civitatis pars* converge into the *oculus*. Before they meet, they pass through the *tabula*, which has an unexpected feature. The center of the *tabula* is cut away, making it akin to an empty picture frame. This void is strung up with a grid of wires; six are vertical and nine are horizontal. Together with the inner edge of the *tabula*'s frame, they produce a grid of seventy units. Hovering mysteriously in this grid is an image of the *civitatis pars*, its numerous curvilinear details held in proper proportion. The drawing on the left side of the table represents the product of the implied equation: *civitatis pars + tabula + oculus + stilus = carta*. Critically, the *carta* not only reproduces the image of the *civitatis pars* that was hovering in the *tabula*, but also reproduces the grid lines.

The relationship between the objects in Fludd's illustration can be mapped onto audio recordings, particularly those from the early phonograph and gramophone eras, where it is common to hear a regular, hissing pattern of surface noise. Let the *civitatis pars* represent the "pre-recorded sound" of a performance. Let the *tabula* represent the mode of intake by the recording machine. The *oculus* and *stilus* represent modes of translating sound waves onto a given recording medium. Finally, the *carta* is the recording itself. The key detail lies in the grid lines that appear in the *tabula* and on the *carta*. These grid lines are not part of the *civitatis pars*, yet they find their way onto the drawing. The grid on the *carta* is akin to the hissing and clicking cycles heard on early recording media. They form an embedded, grid-like pattern within the sonic image. After producing a *tabula*-aided drawing, a visual artist might erase the penciled-in grid, leaving only the image of the *civitatis pars*. By analogy, a recording engineer might attempt to remove the surface noise from a recording. These attempts can only go so far. In the case of phonographs and early gramophones, the grid is so prominent—so deeply enmeshed in the grooves—as to be nearly impossible to erase. Innovations in recording technology can be understood as an ongoing attempt to remove the grid lines in the *tabula*, so that the only item on the *carta* is a pristine image of the *civitatis pars*.

Six modes of interaction

The fierce swish imparted by the rotations of early recording media can produce an audible pulse stream whose pattern is normally asynchronous with the meter of the piece being played. John Roeder put forth a theory that "represents rhythmic polyphony as two or more concurrent 'pulse streams' created by regularly recurring accents. These pulse streams are considered to be distinct continuities, not 'levels' or groupings of each other" (1994, 232–33). In the case of recordings from the pre-tape era, two concurrent pulse streams can often be clearly delineated: the performed music—often exhibiting generous *rubato*—runs alongside the clock-like *swoosh* of the revolving phonograph cylinder or gramophone disc. Paying attention to the rhythm of the revolutions alongside the meter of the score being performed, three basic interactions emerge: asynchrony, synchrony, and development. Asynchrony is the normative state. As its name suggests, it occurs when the metric pacing of the performance and the swishing surface noise are out of phase with one another. It is admittedly difficult to consciously track two pulse streams at the same time.[4] This does not mean that the activity is not exciting or worthwhile. Synchrony is rarer, occurring when the rhythm of revolutions falls into phase with the meter of the performed music for an appreciable length of time. While such a state is both temporary and serendipitous, it can produce spectacular coincidences of accent, especially if the synchronization arrives during a climactic phrase in the piece being recorded. Finally, surface noise can undergo changes during a single track. When this occurs in recordings of vocal music, it can ramify the meaning of a lyric.

From these basic categories can be built a diagram—seen in Figure 5.2— that presents six modes of interaction between sounds of performance and sounds of surface noise. The continuum ranges from recordings where the performance is prominent and the surface noise is faint or missing (mode 1), to recordings where that relationship is inverted (mode 6). In between these extremes lies a set of modes where performance sounds and surface noise coexist and interact. I will illustrate each mode via an analysis of a representative recording.

Performance-centric recordings—mode 1—are the norm. Surface noise is nominal or absent and the sound of the performance is clear throughout. This mode is exemplified by Icy Simpson and Artina McCain's 2012 recording of Margaret Bonds's "Dream Variation." Mode 2—*narrative asynchrony*—occurs when asynchrony between the surface noise and the

---

[4] See Ève Poudrier and Bruno Repp (2013) for experimental evidence pertaining to a listener's ability to track two different beat patterns simultaneously.

Figure 5.2 Six modes of interaction between the sounds of performance and the sounds of surface noise.

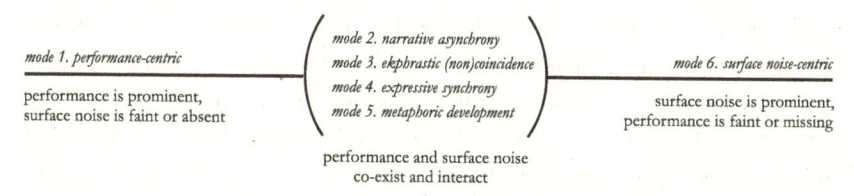

mode 1. performance-centric

performance is prominent,
surface noise is faint or absent

mode 2. narrative asynchrony
mode 3. ekphrastic (non)coincidence
mode 4. expressive synchrony
mode 5. metaphoric development

performance and surface noise
co-exist and interact

mode 6. surface noise-centric

surface noise is prominent,
performance is faint or missing

performance generates patterns that aid in the narration of the work or, in the case of a vocal work, its lyric. *Narrative asynchrony* will be demonstrated by an analysis of Enrico Caruso and Salvatore Cottone's 1902 recording of Gaetano Donizetti's aria "Una furtiva lagrima." Mode 3—*ekphrastic (non) coincidence*—is heard when synchrony, asynchrony, or their combination works in dialogue with an artwork outside the recording. This multimedia mode is portrayed by Enrique Granados's 1912 improvisation on his own *El pelele: Escena goyescas*, itself inspired by Francisco de Goya's 1791–1792 painting *El pelele*. Mode 4—*expressive synchrony*—occurs when the pulse patterns between the surface noise and the performance move into synchrony for an appreciable length of time. An example of this rare mode is found on the 1894 wax cylinder that captured Anton Arensky recording "Strophe alcéene" from his piano cycle *Essais sur les rythmes oubliés*, Op. 28. Mode 5—*metaphorical development*—comes about when the surface noise undergoes changes within a single recording. This mode is exemplified by Anna Krushelnytska's 1904 recording of Mykola Lysenko's song "Z moho tiazhkoho sumu." *Surface noise-centric* recordings—mode 6—are perhaps the least audited type of classical music recording. The category results when surface noise takes over a track, obscuring the performance so completely that it becomes faint or inaudible. This mode will be discussed in the context of the 1889 wax cylinder that captured—among other things—the sound of Johannes Brahms playing the piano.

Performance-centricity

Performance-centric recordings (mode 1) are the most common across the entirety of recorded history. In this category, the sounds made by performers are clear and surface noise is minimal or absent. The category might seem self-evident, as "noise-reduction" has been a goal of recording engineers for over a century. Example 5.1 presents an excerpt from a *performance-centric* track. The score being performed is "Dream Variation," the second song from Margaret Bond's *Three Dream Portraits* (1959) setting poems by Langston Hughes. The recording is by soprano Icy Simpson and pianist Artina McCain, from their 2012 compact disc *I, Too*. The track was recorded and mixed by Andy Murphy at the Butler School of Music Recording Studio and produced by Simpson, McCain, and Murphy. The example provides an excerpt of mm. 21–25 of Bonds's score as well as a spectrogram of the same passage as it appears on Simpson and McCain's recording.

The score and spectrogram of Example 5.1 reveal separate inscriptions of sound. Bonds's staff notation prescribes her harmonic, melodic, and rhythmic design. For example, in bar 23 the bass motion that accompanies the lyric "tall, slim tree" outlines a descending augmented triad $A_\natural$–$F_\natural$–D.[5] The spectrogram offers an image of what was happening when Simpson and McCain performed this bar. Recorded digitally and engineered by Alexander Cross, the track has no surface noise of the type found in the phonograph or early gramophone eras. The suspended tonality of Bonds's passage—as voiced by Simpson and played by McCain—plays out clearly in the foreground of the track. There is little to obscure the sounds made by the musicians.

A viewer of the spectrogram can appreciate countless details of Simpson's vocal interpretation. The foreground features the undulating marks created by Simpson's vibrato and the horizontal bars that denote McCain's piano tones. Its background reveals an undisturbed light gray wash. Salter's "fierce swish" is nowhere to be found. The darker bands between 8,000–9,000 Hz display the formants of Simpson's voice. Also visible are her four expressive inhales at 1:10, 1:18, 1:25, and 1:38, as well as the twelve vibrato oscillations as she holds the $C_\natural$ of "tree." The recording and playback devices have remained out of the way. In the analogy of recording-as-*carta*, Simpson and McCain's recording of "Dream Variation" has no visible grid lines.

---

[5] Donald Ivey (1982, 121) notes certain ambiguities related to accidentals in the 1959 edition of Bonds's "Dream Variation." For the sake of clarity, the accidentals in Example 5.1 match those heard in the 2012 recording by Icy Simpson and Artina McCain.

Example 5.1 (*top*) Margaret Bonds, "Dream Variation" from *Three Dream Portraits*, mm. 21–25; (*bottom*) spectrogram of the passage in the 2012 recording by Icy Simpson, soprano, and Artina McCain, piano. See ▶ Audio Example 5.1.

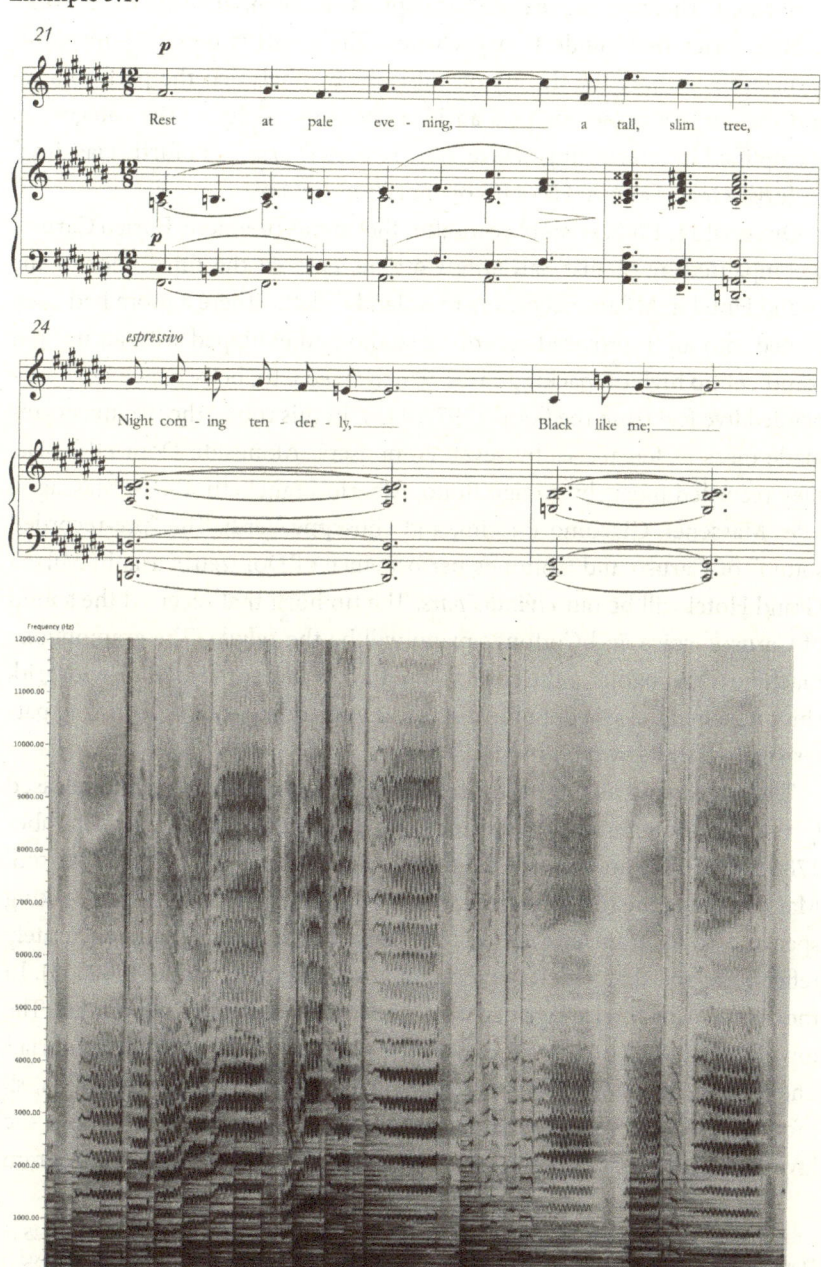

Narrative asynchrony

Surface noise is usually out of sync with the meter of the work being performed. This normative state has expressive potential when vocal works include lyrics that allude to asynchrony. The result is mode 2—*narrative asynchrony*—where the duality of pulse streams between the performance and the surface noise portrays an idea latent in the lyric. The category is exemplified by a recording of Gaetano Donizetti's aria "Una furtiva lagrima" (A furtive tear) from Act II of his opera *L'elisir d'amore*.

On April 11, 1902, seventy years after the opera's premiere, Enrico Caruso, accompanied by pianist Salvatore Cottone, entered the third floor of the Grand Hotel in Milan. According to Roland Gelatt, "There a room had been turned into an improvised recording studio and equipped with an upright piano, set up high on packing cases, which faced a tin bell-shaped horn suspended five feet from the floor" (1977, 115). In this room, the two musicians made discs of ten pieces by seven composers. Alongside Donizetti's aria, they recorded music by Arrigo Boito, Alberto Franchetti, Pietro Mascagni, Jules Massenet, Giacomo Puccini, and Giuseppe Verdi. The "pre-recorded sound" of Caruso and Cottone's performance of Donizetti's aria in Milan's Grand Hotel will be our *civitatis pars*. The tin horn that received the sound of Caruso's voice and Cottone's piano will be the *tabula*. The gramophone machine is analogous to the *oculus-stilus* pair as well as the *tabula*'s wire grid, since it etched the aria onto the disc while embedding the cyclic hissing pattern caused by its own rotation.

The *carta* in our analogy is the recording of "Una furtiva lagrima" released by the Gramophone and Typewriter Company, Ltd. (G&T) as matrix number 1786 B-GC52346 and transferred to compact disc in 2000 by Ward Marston. Marston made the transfers from mint-condition, original pressings, taking special care to "transfer each disc at the proper speed so that it accurately reflects the speed at which the recording was originally made" (2000, 5). In the case of "Una furtiva lagrima," that speed is 73 revolutions per minute. The top of Example 5.2 presents the vocal score of mm. 20–25 of Donizetti's aria.[6] The lyric in these six measures reads: "Che più cercando io vo? M'ama, sì, m'ama, lo vedo, lo vedo" (What more need I look for? She loves me! Yes, she loves me, I see it, I see it). The bottom of Example 5.2 presents a spectrogram

---

[6] Caruso and Cottone begin their recording on the downbeat of bar 9. As a result, mm. 20–25 in Donizetti's score correlate to mm. 12–17 in their recording. For the sake of clarity, I will refer exclusively to the measure numbers in Donizetti's score.

Example 5.2 (*top*) Gaetano Donizetti, "Una furtiva lagrima," vocal score of mm. 20–25, from *L'elisir d'amore*, Act II; (*bottom*) spectrogram of the passage in the 1902 recording by Enrico Caruso, tenor, and Salvatore Cottone, piano. See ▶ Audio Example 5.2.

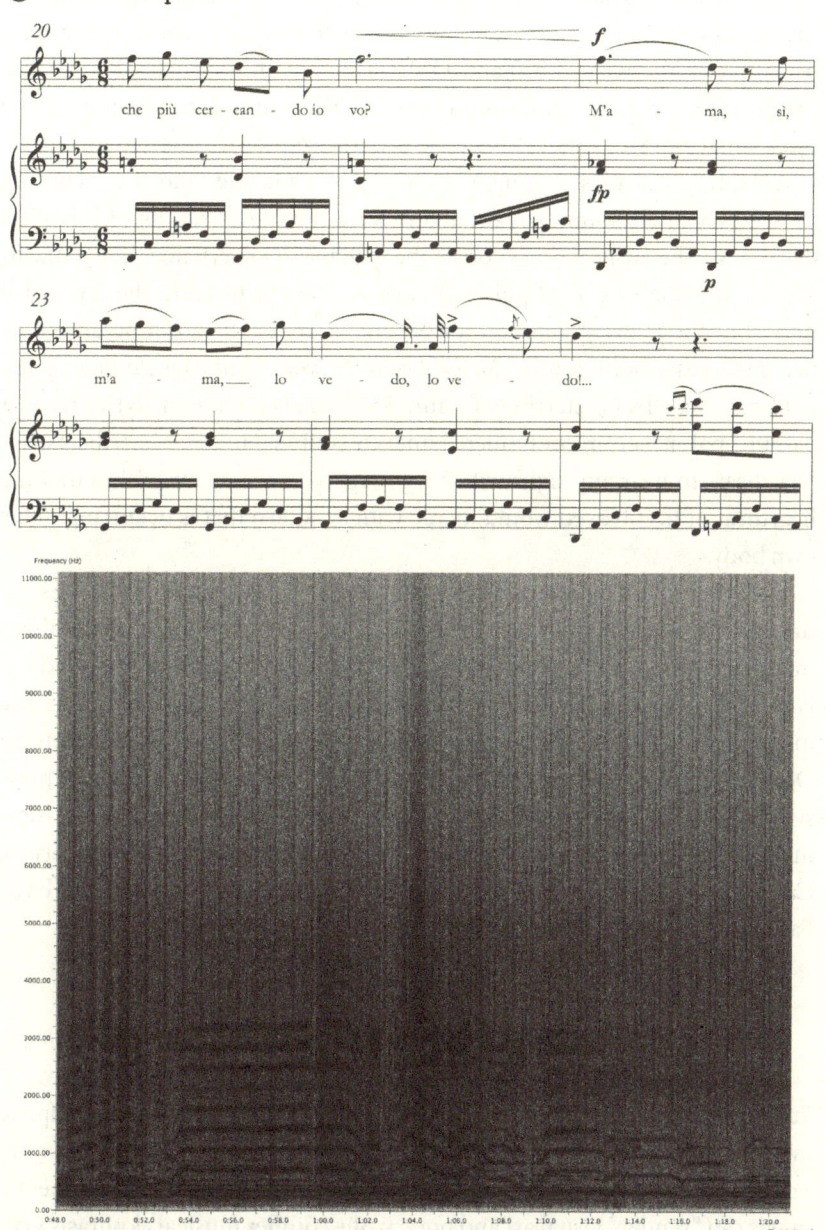

of these same measures as they appear in Marston's transfer of the original gramophone recording. The spectrogram "draws" Caruso and Cottone's recording, including the dark vertical bars that represent sounding rotations of the recording/playback device. The vertical lines in the spectrogram denote the peak of each of the forty audible surface noise cycles. These lines are especially vivid between 4,000 and 11,000 Hz, though they extend lower and impact the vocal and piano spectra as well. Akin to the *carta* in Figure 5.1, the track superimposes Donizetti's music with the sounds required to record it.

Accepting Caruso's singing, Cottone's piano playing, and the recording device as a single sound stream allows for a revealing reading of this 1902 G&T disc. The surface noise forces the listener to experience the Donizetti aria as if through a grid of pulsing hisses. As the aria unfolds, the expressive impact of the gramophone sounds become more explicit, not because they become louder but because *Caruso begins to sing about asynchronous pulse patterns*. The effect is startling. In mm. 35–38, Felice Romani's lyrics read: "I palpiti, i palpiti sentir, confondere i miei co' suoi sospir" (Her heartbeats, her heartbeats to hear, my sighs with hers to merge). The tenor wishes that the heartbeat of his beloved would merge with a pattern that is occurring in his own body.

Listening *with* the surface noise, the recording takes on a new expressive dimension, one not found in the score. Caruso's impassioned verse about merging sighs and heartbeats recasts the asynchrony between the fluid *rubato* of the aria and the regular pulse patterns of the gramophone disc. The mapping is auspicious. The recording reinforces themes that are latent in Donizetti's piece. The *rubato* of the sung melody is analogous to expressive sighing, while the gramophone rotations have the regular-but-not-mechanistic pattern of heartbeats. The sonic interaction between Caruso, Cottone, and the recording device sonifies a central metaphor in the lyric. Far from being a nuisance, this asynchrony is narrative.

Ekphrastic (non)coincidence

Surface noise can be ekphrastic. In general, *ekphrasis* refers to descriptive evocations of visual art. In *Musical Ekphrasis: Composers Responding to Poetry and Painting*, Siglind Bruhn investigates ways in which instrumental music can "render" visual art and poetry. She codifies musical ekphrasis via a checklist: "Correspondingly, what must be present in every case of what I will refer to as *musical ekphrasis* is (1) a real or fictitious scene or story, (2) its representation in a visual or verbal text, and (3) a rendering of that presentation in musical language" (2000, 8). Orit Hilewicz suggests that "musical ekphrasis calls listeners to treat artworks as further resources in analysis" (2018).[7] Furnished with Bruhn's definition, I take up Hilewicz's call, considering the ekphrastic relationship between Enrique Granados's 1912 gramophone recording "Improvisation on No. 7 (*El pelele*)" and the artwork that inspired it: Francisco de Goya's oil painting *El pelele* (1791–1792). The comparison provides an example of mode 3—*ekphrastic (non)coincidence*. In this mode, the interaction between the performance and the surface noise connects a track with another artwork. The relationships generated by Granados's recording are especially rich, given that his score is also ekphrastic.

Reproduced as Figure 5.3, Goya's *El pelele* (The Straw Man) depicts four women using a blanket to toss a doll in the air. According to Adrienne Laskier Martin, "The tossing of dogs, cats, and stuffed figures (*peleles*) in blankets was a traditional Carnival activity in Spain and is best depicted on Goya's cartoon 'El Pelele'" (2021, 265). Anyone who has played this game will know that it requires coordination among the blanket-holders to send an object—be it a dog, a cat, or a doll—aloft. When the game begins, the first few attempts will likely be uncoordinated, and the object will flop about. Goya's painting is about timing. The implications of the game it depicts are portrayed by Victor Stoichita and Anna Maria Coderch:

> What we are witnessing is a rite of ludic reversal, which is also a rite of punishment *in effigie*. Four young women are tossing a puppet with broken joints up into the air by means of a sheet. They do not, it is true, allow him to crash to the ground and break, but neither will they allow him to rest. Flying so as not to be destroyed, the simulacrum will always be in a state of between-the-two, a perpetual state of uncoordinated reversal: he can no longer control his limbs; his masked head has swung round his neck, but, dumbfounded, still gazes up at the sky. It is quite obvious that the puppet will soon fall, face down, legs pointing into infinity, even though for the present they still form a large circumflex accent highlighted by the huge grin of one of the women mocking him. (Stoichita and Coderch 1999, 75)

---

[7] For further discussion of musical ekphrasis, see Lydia Goehr "How to Do More with Words. Two Views of (Musical) Ekphrasis" (2010), 389–410.

Figure 5.3 Francisco de Goya y Lucientes, *El pelele*, 1791–1792, oil on canvas, 267 cm × 160 cm, Museo del Prado, Inventory number P000802, public domain.

Goya's painting presumes a synchronicity has taken place. For the straw man to assume the airborne position seen in the image, the four women must have aligned their collective effort when the blanket was at a low point before slinging the doll skyward in unison. According to the implied movement in the painting, the straw man reached an even higher apex on this toss and is now falling, as the blanket has already moved from its convex throwing position (with the center toward the sky) to its concave catching position (with the center toward the ground). The subject of Goya's *El pelele* is, in essence, entrainment.

Granados's solo piano work *El pelele: Escena goyescas* is generally considered as one of the composer's *Goyescas*, even though it was not published with the six scores that comprise the piano cycle proper. Goya's art was a fecund source of inspiration for the composer. Alongside the piano music, it inspired Granados's one-act opera—also called *Goyescas*—premiered at the Metropolitan Opera in New York on January 28, 1916. Since the track I am studying records Granados playing the piano piece prior to its publication, it makes sense to delineate the various versions of the work. According to Walter Aaron Clark (2006), the manuscript of Granados's *El pelele (Escena goyesca)* is undated; it was premiered at the Escola Coral in Terrassa, Spain, on March 29, 1914, and published by G. Schirmer, New York, in 1915. Describing the occasion of Granados's recorded improvisation, Clark writes: "In 1912 he had made some acoustic recordings on double-sided ten-inch discs for Odeon in Barcelona. Since these could hold only a few minutes of music, longer works could not be recorded, and the repertoire on these recordings includes some of the *Danzas españolas*, a Scarlatti transcription, and an improvisation" (2006, 174–75). The last item on Clark's list is the subject of my analysis.[8]

Before turning to Granados's 1912 improvisation, a word about the published score. *El pelele: Escena goyescas*, as published by G. Schirmer in 1915, is classically ekphrastic. The score fulfills Bruhn's definition of musical ekphrasis on all counts: the traditional blanket-doll game is the story, Goya's painting represents that story as a visual text, and Granados's composition renders Goya's representation in musical language. I hear the doll's bouncing as sonically depicted from the outset. The symbols that populate

---

[8] Granados commonly improvised on his own compositions, both before and after they appeared in print. According to Douglas Riva, "The composer's daughter, Natàlia Granados de Carreras, says that in the family home her father improvised constantly, especially in his own compositions, continually refining them" (1986, 103).

Example 5.3 Enrique Granados, *El pelele: Escena goyescas*, mm. 1–6, as notated in the 1915 G. Schirmer edition.

the score represent characteristics of Goya's painting, a relationship that Lydia Goehr calls "notational ekphrasis" (2010, 408). Example 5.3 shows mm. 1–6 of Granados's score as it appears in the Schirmer edition. Clark describes how the notated music buoyantly expresses the game: "In fact, the rhythmic gesture of a broad trill on beat three in tandem with the ascending melodic contour at the beginning of the piece evokes the physical act of hurling the comically helpless *pelele* aloft" (2006, 139). Each measure participates in the sonification. The rising and falling gestures in bars 1–2 and bars 5–6, respectively, could be read as representing the flight of the straw manikin.

The *notational* ekphrasis only goes so far. The score portrays the game but does not explicitly address the synchrony and asynchrony exhibited by the women who are playing it. Granados's 1912 recorded improvisation, on the other hand, brings a new dimension to the ekphrasis via the inclusion of the repetitive hissing patterns that superimpose a regular *swish* over the piano music. Simple probability suggests that surface noise patterns are bound to intersect with the performed music, but this does not preclude such random intersections from accruing meaning. The implied periods of synchronization and asynchronization between the four women in Goya's *El pelele* are depicted, sonically, by the dueling pulse streams in Granados's 1912 recording. The surface noise hiss pattern—replete with a click at the peak of each cycle—runs mostly out of sync with Granados's performed meter.

Example 5.4 Transcription of 0:00–0:14.5 from Enrique Granados's 1912 "Improvisation on No. 7 (*El pelele*)," annotating the timing of each downbeat and the eighteen surface noise cycles. See ⊙ Audio Example 5.3.

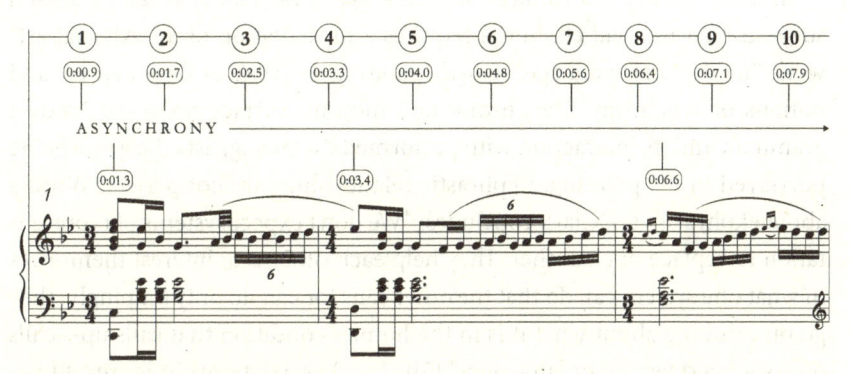

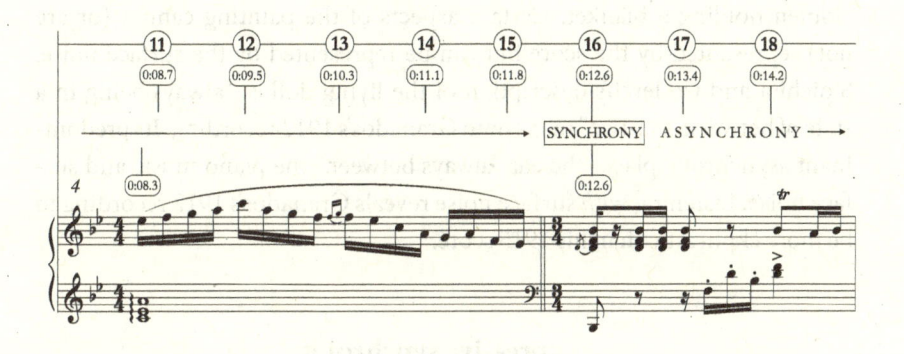

Example 5.4 illustrates the relationship between the cycles of surface noise and the performed meter in the piano music.[9] Note that Granados is not playing the music seen in his 1915 score; this is a recorded improvisation based on the material that would later coalesce into the published version. The measurements demonstrate the general asynchrony between the mechanistic sounds and the piano music. This asynchrony is to be expected. What

---

[9] The surface noise pattern during the first fifteen seconds of Granados's 1912 recording consists of a series of prominent swishes. Two-thirds of the way between each main swish sits a quieter one that, when added to the main swish, generates a triple meter in the surface noise. The surface noise cycles denoted in Example 5.4 mark only the main swishes that define each cycle.

is unexpected (and rather elegant) is a single coincidence of accent at 0:12.6 between the surface noise and the piano music. They arrive together at the very moment that would become, in the 1915 published score, the *Andantino quasi allegretto* seen in bar 3 of Example 5.3.

Granados's 1912 recording exemplifies *ekphrastic (non)coincidence*. Bruhn suggests that musical ekphrasis requires a presentation of an external art-work "in musical language." Goya's painting *El pelele* is designed around notions of synchrony, asynchrony, and motion. Surface noise has its own grammar, and its interaction with performed meter suggests the game being portrayed in the painting. Ekphrastic relationships are not perfect. Writing about ekphrasis, T. J. Clark concludes: "We don't expect systems of representation to replace one another. They help each other out; interest themselves in what one system can do that the other can't, or can do only limpingly; they go on thinking about what it is in the human condition that calls up—calls on—such a diversity of languages" (2022, 31). A relationship is created between three recording systems: Granados's score, his gramophone recording, and Goya's eighteenth-century painting of a straw doll thrown aloft by four women holding a blanket. Certain aspects of the painting cannot (or are not) represented by the score but can be represented by the surface noise. Stoichita and Coderch's description of the flying doll as "always being in a state of between-the-two" maps onto Granados's 1912 recording. Its predominant asynchrony places the ear "always between" the piano music and surface noise. Listening *with* surface noise reveals Granados's 1912 recording to be more ekphrastic than his 1915 score.

Expressive synchrony

Among the earliest recordings of classical music is a wax cylinder made in Moscow on December 20, 1894, which preserves traces of a performance by the composer and pianist Anton Arensky. The recording was made by Edison phonograph enthusiast Julius Block, whose celebrated collection of cylinders constitutes "the earliest surviving recordings ever made of music by Bach, Wagner, Chopin, Schumann, Donizetti, Bizet, Tchaikovsky, Verdi, and others" (Maltese and Benko 2009, 20). Cylinder 119 in Block's archive captures Arensky playing the third and fifth of his six *Essais sur les rythmes oubliés* [Essays on Forgotten Rhythms], Op. 28. His recording of No. 5, "Strophe alcéene" [Alcaic Stanza], is a rich document for theorists interested in rhythm and superimposed meter. Arensky's 1893 score, notated in 6/8, is based on an ancient Greek metric structure—the *alcéene* of the title refers to a poetic form named after Alcaeus. Arensky's 1894 recording applies extremes of rubato to his score's alcaic phraseology. The contents of the Block cylinder—as heard on the 2008 compact disc transfer by Ward Marston—embeds the recording machine's cyclical, hissing groove across the surface of Arensky's spirited performance. At an auspicious moment outside the control of Alcaeus, Arensky, Block, or Marston, the meter of the culminating phrase of "Strophe alcéene" comes into momentary synchrony with the cylinder's hissing pattern, allowing for a coincidence of accent between the score, the pianist, and the surface noise. Arensky's composition emphasizes a specific aspect of the alcaic's metric design, and his performance of it sets off a cascade of metric resonances that extend beyond the score and onto the phonograph cylinder. Properly teasing out the enmeshed layers of rhythmic and metric intrigue requires patient analysis. I will provide a series of examples that reveal a brilliant synchrony that links Alcaeus' ancient Greek poetic meter, Arensky's notated alcaics, and the groove of Block's Edison machine.

The Lesbian alcaic descends from Alcaeus of Mytilene, a poet who lived ca. 625–ca. 580 BCE and was a contemporary of Sappho. John Talbot reports that the alcaic, "like most classical meters, is based on vowel quality—the succession of long and short syllables—not, as in English verse, on the succession of stressed and unstressed syllabus" (2004, 201). Denys Page (1955, 321) summarizes the stanza's generalized four-line structure using "–" to denote a long syllable, "◡" to denote a short syllable, and "x" to denote an *anceps* (a syllable of indeterminate quality, which can be short or long):[10]

$$x - ◡ - x - ◡◡ - ◡ -$$
$$x - ◡ - x - ◡◡ - ◡ -$$
$$x - ◡ - x - ◡ - x$$
$$- ◡◡ - ◡◡ - ◡ - x$$

Talbot clarifies the characteristic recapitulatory design of the alcaic stanza: "This is to say that the fourth line constitutes a kind of return to the metrical motive announced and established in the first two lines, abandoned

---

[10] Page (1955) uses a different sign to denote *anceps*. Following the practice seen in Talbot (2004), I denote *anceps* with an "x."

in the third, and picked up again in the middle of the fourth" (2004, 202). The most conspicuous metric event in an alcaic stanza is the "– ‿ ‿" element, which is embedded in lines 1–2, missing entirely from line 3, and recalled twice at the outset of line 4.

Since Arensky composed his work nearly 2,500 years after Alcaeus's poetic paradigm, it would be useful to know how the composer himself interpreted alcaic meter, in particular the *anceps*, which can either be long or short. In the front matter of his 2005 P. Jurgenson edition of the *Essais sur les rythmes oubliés*, V. Samarin reports that, in the original 1893 edition, "the music is preceded with schemes of different forms of ancient versification used by the composer in the rhythmic patterns of his pieces" (2005, 71). The page to which Samarin refers can be seen in Figure 5.4. It describes, in both Russian and French, the poetic meters used by Arensky in his six *Essais*. The explanatory heading can be translated as: "The six piano pieces which constitute this work present essays on some of the rhythms that one finds in the poetry of the ancient Greeks, the Romans, and other peoples." The metric diagram under the heading "No. 5. (Ré maj.)—Strophe alcéenne" (*sic*) provides a key to the poetic meter as employed by Arensky. Each of the *anceps* is interpreted as short (‿). The commentary also includes demarcations of phrasing, denoted with vertical lines (|). The complete alcaic stanza diagrammed in the front matter of the early edition of Arensky's *Essais* reads:

$$\cup | - \cup - \cup | - \cup \cup | - \cup -$$
$$\cup | - \cup - \cup | - \cup \cup | - \cup -$$
$$\cup - \cup - \cup | - \cup - \cup$$
$$- \cup \cup | - \cup \cup | - \cup - \cup$$

Arensky's use of the alcaic stanza is plain to see (and hear). Every bar of "Strophe alcéene" articulates the ancient Greek metrical structure. Example 5.5 presents the complete fifty-eight-measure score, identifying the alcaic stanzas throughout.[11] The piece presents four complete alcaics: the first in mm. 1–14, the second in mm. 15–25, the third in mm. 26–40, and the fourth in mm. 41–51. Following a dramatic silence in bar 52, Arensky rhythmically reprises the meter of the stanza's final couplet to create an emphatic

---

[11] Audio Example 5.4 presents the beginning of Arensky's recording. Readers are invited to audit the complete track on *The Dawn of Recordings: The Julius Block Cylinders* (Arensky 1894/2008).

Figure 5.4 Front matter from the first edition of Anton Arensky's *Essais sur les rythmes oubliés*, Op. 28, displaying the poetic rhythms that govern each piece in the set.

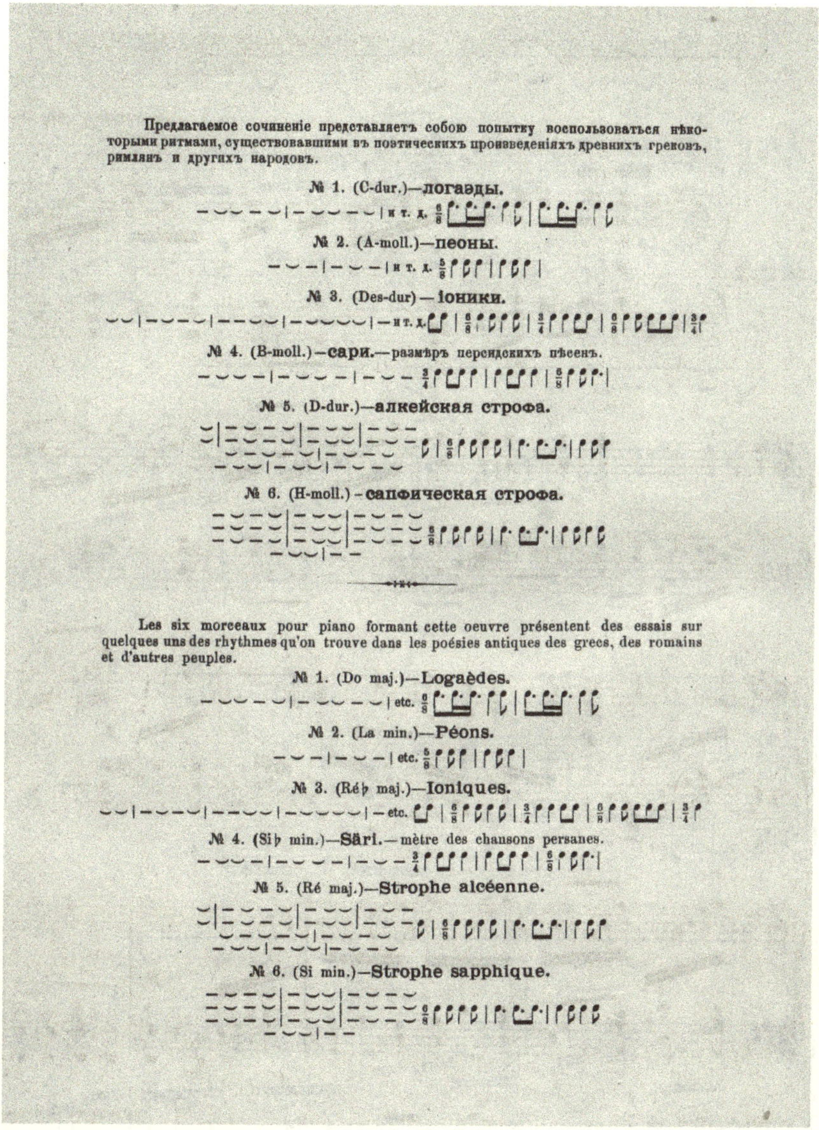

Example 5.5 Anton Arensky, "Strophe alcéene," from *Essais sur les rythmes oubliés*, Op. 28, annotating the Alcaic stanzas that govern its design. See  Audio Example 5.4.

Example 5.5 Continued

SECOND ALCAIC

line 1

line 2

line 3

line 4

Example 5.5 Continued

Example 5.5 Continued

concluding phrase in mm. 52–58.[12] The example intentionally incorporates measures that extend over system breaks (e.g., bars 5, 8, and 14) in an effort to clarify the alcaic structure. In total, Arensky's "Strophe alcéene" sounds four and a half alcaic stanzas: four full iterations plus a final couplet. This piece of solo piano music is, as such, a wordless eighteen-line poem.

My identification of bars 52–58 as the rhetorical climax of "Strophe alcéene" contextualizes a detail, noticed by Samarin, in the autograph manuscript housed at the M. I. Glinka State Central Museum of Musical Culture: "Initially, the piece comprised 51 bars. The final 7 bars (52–58) were written with different ink; in all probability, the composer added them later" (Arensky 2005, 71). Arensky's concluding couplet, beginning in bar 52, marks the first *fortissimo* in the score, breaks the pattern of complete alcaics, and features a new, descending bass line in octaves that passes through a perilous minor subdominant toward the final D major cadence.

Turning from Arensky's score to his recording, we can listen to these alcaic stanzas alongside the prominent surface noise pattern. There are 159 sounding cylinder revolutions during the 1:23 duration of Arensky's 1894 recording of "Strophe alcéene." (The complete track has a duration of 1:35, the remaining twelve seconds comprised by faint sounds of speech, during which the cylinder revolutions continue at the same pace.) The interonset interval between each surface noise peak is about 542 milliseconds. Subtle variations in this timing are evident throughout and are likely a result of physical characteristics of the cylinder and the challenge of precisely marking the onset of a whirring hiss.

Mapping the dual pulse streams of the piano sounds and cylinder revolutions is complex to visualize but simpler to describe. As one might expect, surface noise swishes remain largely out of sync with Arensky's performed meter across the entire recording. There is, however, a significant exception. During the rhetorical climax of "Strophe alcéene" in bars 53–54— the very music that, according to Samarin, Arensky added to the manuscript

---

[12] There is one small difference between the metric diagram published in the front matter of the 1893 score and Arensky's application of it in his "Strophe alcéene." It pertains to the duration of the *anceps*. Comparing Page's 1955 designation of the alcaic with the first edition of Arensky's score, most of the original *anceps* are interpreted as short (◡). Exceptions include the last notes in m. 25 and m. 51, respectively, which fall on short syllables but whose fermatas mark them as long, as well as the downbeat of m. 58, which is both long and stressed but which, according to Arensky's formula in the front matter, carries the designation of short. Recognizing the difference, I have placed the "◡" in bar 58 in brackets.

Example 5.6 Anton Arensky, "Strophe alcéene," from *Essais sur les rythmes oubliés*, Op. 28, mm. 53–56, annotating the synchrony and asynchrony between surface noise cycles 134–43 and each half bar in the composer's 1894 recording. See ▶ Audio Example 5.5.

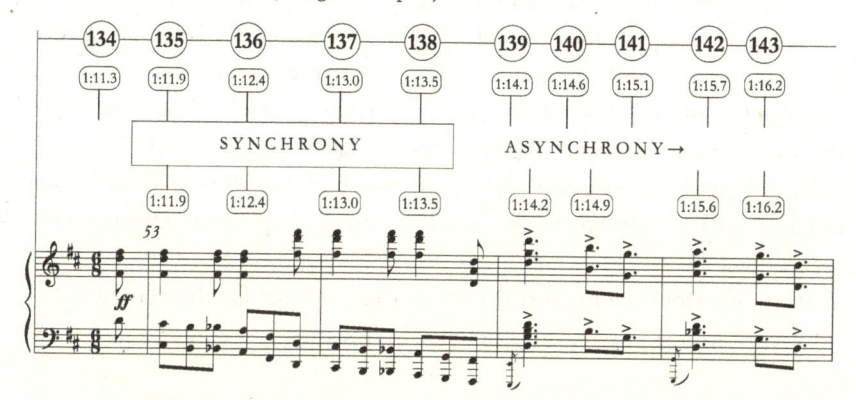

in a different ink—*the meter of Arensky's performance synchronizes with the oscillations of Block's Edison phonograph for four full beats.* Example 5.6 illustrates this arresting synchrony, presenting the timing of cylinder cycles 134–43 and the piano music in mm. 53–54. Along the top of the diagram are the onset times of each surface noise peak. Along the bottom are timings of each half-bar in Arensky's interpretation. Timing the revolutions is a rather inexact science, since Block's wax cylinder does not utter a precise click each time it goes round. The measurements are taken from the peak hiss within each revolution. The synchrony between the recording machine and the piano begins on the downbeat of bar 53 and continues until they part ways at the downbeat of bar 55. In the score, these measures inaugurate the closing couplet and mark the rhetorical climax of Arensky's composition. The cylinder sounds come into phase with the onset of the closing couplet—which breaks the pattern of complete alcaic stanzas that extends all the way back to bar 1—and coincides with the composition's first notated *fortissimo*. Recalling Fludd's illustration of the sighting grid, it is as though architectural elements of the *civitatis pars* have aligned with the crosshatch of the sighting grid.

The momentary synchronicity between Arensky's piano music and Block's cylinder rotations interweave several historical and metrical pasts. These few seconds capture Block's Edison phonograph on December 20, 1894, as it records Arensky's performance of his own 1893 composition, which itself makes use of a metric pattern derived from Alcaeus's poetic meter from circa 600 BCE. In the context of the fifty-eight-measure piece, the synchrony arrives in step with a pivotal break in the prevailing metric structure and acts as a pivot between the four complete alcaic stanzas and the concluding couplet. Bar 53 is the most emphatic agogic accent in the composition. Its rhetorical effect is amplified when the machinic whirr of Block's Edison machine moves into momentary synchrony with Arensky's interpretation. The result illustrates mode 4—*expressive synchrony*. It is both an Alcaic and Edisonian synchronicity, a metric fusion between the sound of a piano and the machine recording it.

Ward Marston, the mastering engineer responsible for the compact disc transfer of Arensky's recording, detailed his process:

> In preparing these recordings for publication, I first removed thousands of transient noises, commonly known as clicks and pops, which interfered with the flow of the music. I then experimented with various degrees of noise reduction to determine how the music was affected. Some reduction of the surface noise undoubtedly helped to bring the music forward, but in every case, I used less reduction than I had expected. (Marston 2008, 58–59)

Thanks to Marston's judicious touch, the Arensky track drawn from Cylinder 119 remains imbued with the sounds of the rotating cylinder. As Marston continues his note, he makes a point that—from an engineer's perspective—is sensible, but which describes a mode of listening that differs from my own. Offering guidance to a contemporary listener acclimatizing to these Edison-era recordings, Marston writes:

> I recommend using high-quality headphones for optimal results. Eventually, one's brain will begin to filter out the noise, and the musical aspects of each performance will emerge with unexpected vividness. What may start out sounding like noise with no musical content can end up providing the listener with hours of fascinating discovery. It may take some effort, but the rewards are worth the trouble. (Marston 2008, 59)

While it is true that "one's brain will begin to filter out the noise," I encourage *denying* one's brain the pleasure of such an erasure. I agree with Marston's exhortation, but its contrary is also viable. The contributions made by the re-cording machine and playback device—undoubtedly part of the track—can be heard as one music. Eventually, one's brain can be taught to *preserve* what many call "noise." This inclusive mode of analysis—listening *with* rather than *through* surface noise—offers hours of fascinating discovery. Moreover, my analysis would be unavailable to listeners who allow their brains to "filter out the noise."

Metaphoric development

One might reasonably assume that the mechanical sounds of recording devices are uniform across a given recording and that, once the hissing pattern starts, it remains regular. If this were indeed the case, the playback of an Edison-era phonograph would pit the fluid, dynamic, and develop-mental music played by the performer against the inert, mechanistic, and non-developmental sound of the cylinder. Such an assumption turns out to be incorrect. Surface noise patterns are not generally uniform across the entirety of a recording. While their pacing might remain somewhat stable, the sounding rhythm can morph, suggesting different subdivisions and meters. The opportunity thereby exists for *metaphoric development* (mode 5), where changes in the surface noise across a given track con-tribute layers of developmental, expressive content to the piece that it accompanies.[13]

Metaphoric development takes center stage in Anna Krushelnytska's June 1904 recording of Mykola Lysenko's 1893 song "Z moho tiazhkoho sumu" ("From my great sorrows"). The recording was captured on a 17.5cm cyl-inder in Lviv by G&T Red Label.[14] This cylinder—whose embedded histories

---

[13] Music theorists are accustomed to explicating the rhythmic and metric designs of lieder, illuminating compositional choices that reflect and ramify a poetic text. For example, Yonatan Malin's analysis of Fanny Hensel's "Nachwanderer" (Night Wanderer), Op. 7, No. 1 (setting a poem by Joseph von Eichendorff), draws a connection between the poem's "chaotic surging" and the lied's metric terrain. Describing a particularly turbulent passage, Malin writes that "all we have to latch onto met-rically is the change of harmonies, the snippets of vocal declamation, and the overlapping piano responses" (2010, 92). Listening to unwritten music adds surface noise to the existing categories of "what we have to latch onto."

[14] The measurements of Krushelnytska's recording were taken from the 2003 compact disc *The First Opera Recordings (1895–1902): A Survey, Part II*, released as Symposium Records 1320, which is a transfer from a record owned by Sir Paul Getty. Contrary to the compact disc's subtitle, the Krushelnytska cylinder dates from 1904.

are accompanied by a few ambiguities, including the identity of the singer—exemplifies the extent to which recording machines can contribute to a sounding artwork.[15] The poem Krushelnytska sings in "Z moho tiazhkoho sumu" originates not with Lysenko but with Heinrich Heine. Heine's poem "Aus meinen grossen Schmerzen" was published in his *Buch der Lieder* in 1827 and translated into Ukrainian sometime around 1890 by Maksym Slavynskyi. The following presents four versions of the poem: Heine's original, Slavynskyi's version, a transliteration of Slavynskyi's version, and an English version of the transliteration:

> Aus meinen grossen Schmerzen
> Mach' ich die kleinen Lieder;
> Die heben ihr klingend Gefieder
> Und flattern nach ihrem Herzen.
>
> Sie fanden den Weg zur Trauten,
> Doch kommen sie wieder und klagen,
> Und klagen, und wollen nicht sagen,
> Was sie im Herzen schauten.

> З мого тяжкого суму складаю я пісні,
> Я їм даю крилечка, легенькі, голосні.
> На крильцях тих легеньких летять вони усі
> У серце до моєї дівчиноньки краси.
>
> Пісні назад вернулись
> і жалібно бринять,
> Що бачили у серці
> не хочуть розказать.

---

[15] The unsigned liner notes that accompany Krushelnytska's recording (on Symposium 1302) suggest a degree of ambiguity about the identity of the singer: "Anna Kruszelnicka is reported to have been a sister of Salomea Kruszelnicka, but little is known of her. If she was, then by inference, she was born at Tysiv, near Lemberg [Lvov] circa 1870, studied initially with Wysocky in Lvov, and continued to study whilst accompanying her sister in Italy. The records, labelled 'Ruthenian Soprano,' indicate a voice so remarkably similar to that of Salomea that some have attributed the records to her" (2003, 5). A stronger attribution to Anna Krushelnytska is provided in Katarzyna Janczewska-Sołomko and Michał Pieńkowski *Dyskopedia poloników do roku 1918: Suplement*. They catalog Recording No. 1823 as "Anna KRUSZELNICKA (m-sopr.), Kompozytor niezidentyfikowany *Z moho Tiażho sumu*, 1823. GR 23566, mr 451 d. Nagr. 06.1904 Lwów. Płyta ø 17,5 cm" (2021, 66).

Z moho tiazhkoho sumu skladaiu ya pisni,
I yim daiu krylechka, lehenki, holosni.
Na kryltsiakh tykh lehenkykh letiat vony usi
U sertse do moiei divchynonky krasy.

Pisni nazad vernulys
I zhalibno bryniat,
Shcho bachyly u sertsi
Ne khochut rozkazat.

From my great sorrows I make small songs,
I give them little wings, light and sound.
On their delicate wings, all these songs
Flutter towards her heart, the heart of my beauty.

The songs came back
Strumming in their grief,
Yet they will not say
What they saw in her heart.

Slavynskyi's translation preserves the tone and general content of Heine's original while lending greater emphasis to the fluttering wings that the poetic narrator gives to his songs. Whereas Heine's poem first mentions the feathered plumage in line 3 ("Gefieder") and their fluttering in line 4 ("flattern"), Slavynskyi's version introduces the wings earlier, in line 2 ("krylechka"), repeating the word in line 3. Heine's second stanza does not mention the wings by name, focusing instead on the lament of the returning songs ("klagen" in both lines 6 and 7) and their reticence ("und wollen nicht sagen, / Was sie im Herzen schauten" in lines 7–8). Slavynskyi's version, on the other hand, includes a sonification of strumming ("bryniat" in line 6), an allusion to the movement of wings.[16]

With all the attention on "fluttering" in Slavynskyi's translation, it might be surprising to learn that Lysenko's 1893 setting does not take the opportunity to introduce wing-related word-painting in either the vocal part or the piano accompaniment. (By contrast, Hugo Wolf's 1878 setting of Heine's

[16] There is an additional Heine association in the song: Lysenko's "Z moho tiazhkoho sumu," which sets a Ukrainian translation of Heine's "Aus meinen grossen Schmerzen," also includes an allusion to the melody from the fifth song of Schumann's *Dichterliebe*, which itself sets Heine's "Ich will meine Seele tauchen."

original poem—published as the fourth song of his *Liederstrauß*—includes a vividly fluttering piano part.) Lysenko's lied, marked *Andante non troppo*, has more to do with the grieving lament for the incommunicative lover than any avian messengers. It emphasizes the "great sorrows" of the poem's first

Example 5.7 Transcription of Anna Krushelnytska's 1904 recording of Mykola Lysenko's "Z moho tiazhkoho sumu," annotating the 145 surface noise cycles. See ▶ Audio Example 5.6.

Example 5.7 Continued

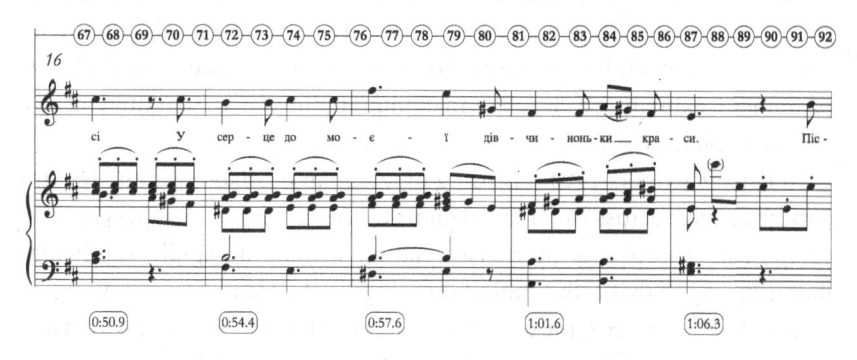

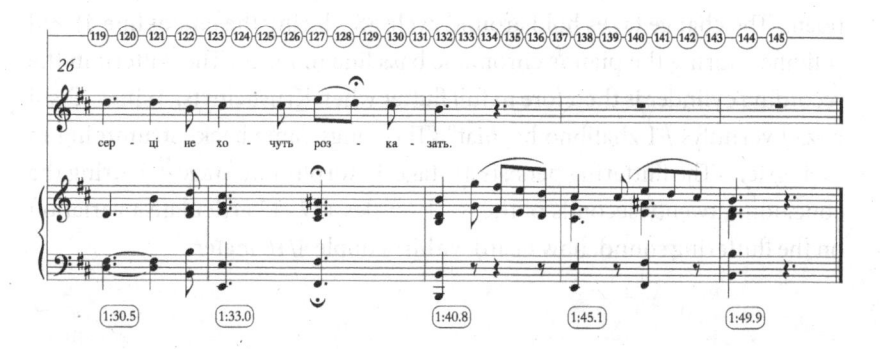

line more than the quick movements of "little wings." This imagistic gap between the poem and the score is precisely where the surface noise becomes integrally expressive. Example 5.7 provides a transcription of the complete 1904 recording.[17] In addition to Krushelnytska's singing and the playing of

---

[17] Audio Example 5.6 presents the beginning of Krushelnytska's recording of "Z moho tiazhkoho sumu." Readers are invited to audit the complete track on *The First Opera Recordings: 1895–1902, A Survey* (Krushelnytska 1904/2003).

her anonymous accompanist, the example transcribes all 145 surface noise cycles during the 1:51.6 track.[18] The example also includes the timing for each of the score's thirty performed downbeats. The surface noise cycles are prominent, exhibiting a click or a maximum point of hiss each time the cylinder completes a turn.

In Krushelnytska's 1904 recording of "Z moho tiazhkoho sumu," the hiss patterns evolve across the track, demonstrating a kind of unsupervised development. The phases of transformation include a rapidly subdivided fluttering sound that calls to mind the wings in the Heine/Slavynskyi poem. As seen in Example 5.8, the cylinder sounds on this track can be divided into four distinct stages.[19] During the last two stages, the surface noise is—quite literally—fluttering. The cylinder sounds in stage 1 (cycles 1 through 37) articulate a clear triple meter, with click-like events on beats 1 and 3. There is no suggestion of wings in this rhythm, only the creation of a meter that is out of phase with both the 6/8 of Lysenko's score and the *rubato* of Krushelnytska's phrasing. After cycle 37, the cylinder sound begins to morph. By the beginning of stage 2 (which lasts from cycle 50 to cycle 73), the triple meter gives way to duple waves that could be described as *amorphous shushing*. Stage 3 is rather astonishing. The cylinder articulates a vivid, rhythmically subdivided 3/16 pattern akin to the rapid shuffling of cards. As it develops, this shuffling sound takes on the characteristics of fluttering wings, the topic of the poem. The change takes hold around cycle 88 (during the end of line 4) and solidifies during the piano's chromatic bass line in m. 24. The pattern in the recording cylinder is therefore in full flutter when Krushelnytska sings "Pisni nazad vernulys / I zhalibno bryniat" (The songs came back, Strumming in their grief). The fluttering persists as stage 3 morphs into stage 4. During the concluding twenty seconds of the track, cycles 127–45 articulate a variation on the fluttering sound, now heard within a duple 4/16 meter.

---

[18] Dynamics and character markings present in the printed score of "Z moho tiazhkoho sumu" are not included in the transcription in Example 5.7. The original score (which appears in Lysenko 1953) is notated in C minor, whereas Krushelnytska's recording is in B minor. The recording includes some notable divergences with the score, such as the absence of the octave that begins the motive in mm. 1, 5, and 21, the pianist's improvised ornament in m. 7, and the fact that Lysenko writes the cadence in m. 20 to the major subdominant (F major) with a vocal resolution on its third scale degree (A), whereas Krushelnytska resolves instead to the subdominant's root (F, sounding as E given that the recording is a half-step lower than the original score). Krushelnytska's resolution removes the score's emphasis on a brightened, major sonority on "krasy" (beauty), instead creating a hollow sonority wherein the voice reinforces the piano octaves rather than the chordal third.

[19] Audio Example 5.7 presents, in succession, all four stages of the cylinder rhythm: stage 1 (0:06–0:11), stage 2 (0:38–0:43), stage 3 (1:04–1:10), and stage 4 (1:41–1:48).

Example 5.8 The four-stage evolution of the cylinder rhythms in Anna Krushelnytska's 1904 recording of Mykola Lysenko's "Z moho tiazhkoho sumu." See ▶ Audio Example 5.7.

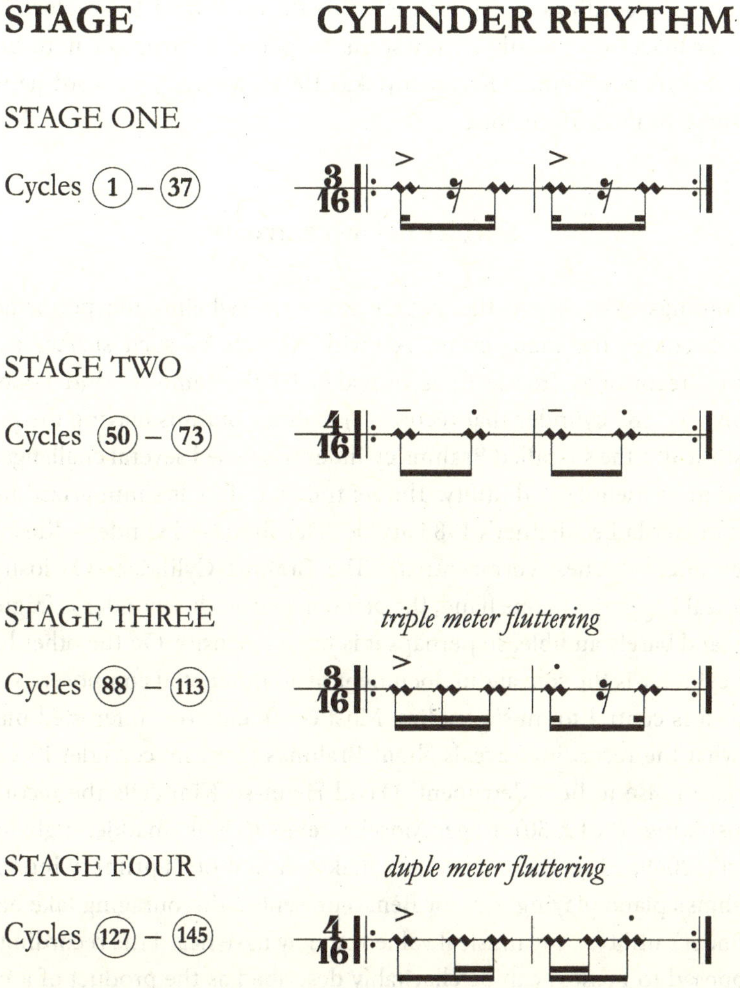

STAGE   CYLINDER RHYTHM

STAGE ONE

Cycles ①–㊲

STAGE TWO

Cycles ㊿–㊳

STAGE THREE   *triple meter fluttering*

Cycles ㊳–⑬

STAGE FOUR   *duple meter fluttering*

Cycles ⑰–⑭

Listening *with* the surface noise, the fluttering in stages 3 and 4 is uncanny. The cylinder sound—which began the track in a firmly etched triple meter—comes to life as a flickering, subdivided pattern at the very moment the vocal melody tells of the return of the winged songs. The cylinder's flutter then morphs from 3/16 to 4/16 during the final vocal phrase, providing the listener with dozens of motivic recollections of the sound of wings. It is no simple matter to ascribe compositional agency. This example of mode 5—metaphoric *development*—owes debts to Heine, Slavynskyi, Lysenko, Krushelnytska, her anonymous pianist, and the cylinder itself. Few other recordings so captivatingly fuse the notational, the performative, and the machinic. Lysenko's score seems to ignore the imagistic fluttering in Slavynskyi's poem but, in Krushelnytska's 1904 recording, the word-painting is "sung" by the surface noise.

Surface noise–centricity

Recordings exist where the surface noise overwhelms the performance and becomes the main event. A vivid example of such *surface noise-centric* recordings (mode 6) is provided by the famous—and famously "noisy"—1889 cylinder that recorded Johannes Brahms playing the piano. Historically, the so-called Brahms cylinder has posed several challenges related to its identity and utility. The central quandary is summarized in the title of Gerda Lechleitner's 1985 article "Der Brahms-Zylinder—Kuriosität oder musikalisches Vermächtnis" (The Brahms Cylinder—Curiosity or Musical Legacy). On one hand, the piano music on the cylinder is fragmentary and barely audible, so perhaps it is just a curiosity. On the other hand, the cylinder is the sole audio document of an influential composer, so perhaps it is central to music studies. Most commentators, interested mainly in what the recording reveals about Brahms's pianism, consider its heavy surface noise to be a detriment. David Hyun-su Kim calls the recording "frustrating" (2012, 50). Roger Moseley refers to it as "maddeningly indistinct" (2009, 138). These adjectives make sense if one's primary interest is Brahms's piano playing. Gregor Benko presents a discouraging take on the cylinder's utility: "Any musical value you may have heard the recording was supposed to possess can be charitably described as the product of a pathological imagination" (1977). How Brahms played the piano is a pressing question for all of us who love his music, but it is not the *only* question posed by the cylinder. While I run the risk of personifying Benko's diagnosis of possessing a "pathological imagination," it is worth asking: what if we studied the Brahms cylinder *as it is*, rather than as we wish it to be? What sounds are found there in addition to the faint fragments of a person playing the piano?

The question of the cylinder's utility can be redrawn if Brahms's pianism is decentralized. Part of the purported problem with the recording—and with tin and wax cylinders in general—is that the *illusion* that Joan Chissell experienced in 1984 while listening to Mitsuko Uchida has disappeared. Uchida, on compact disc, is present, while Brahms, on wax cylinder, isn't (or isn't enough). We are separated from the musician by the sound of the very machine that allows us to hear them. There has been considerable research into the cylinder, including a significant piece of audio archeology by Jonathan Berger and Charles Nichols (1994) who, by means of elaborate filtering, brought the traces of Brahms's playing into clearer focus. But Brahms's piano is not the only sound on the cylinder. Indeed, for long stretches, the piano is unheard amid the hissing cycles of surface noise. Alexander Rehding gets to the heart of the matter, distinguishing what the Edison device that captured Brahms's playing *is*, and what the cylinder itself might be useful *for*:

> Each time the cylinder was played, the quality of the groove deteriorated somewhat. This point is acutely brought home in Brahms's famous 1889 recording. He was introduced by a speaker with a distinct sense of urgency, who shouted into the sound funnel and whose words are now identified as "Haus von Doktor Fellinger, Achtzehnhundertneunundachtzig. Bei mir ist Doktor Brahms, Johannes Brahms" ("Dr. Fellinger's house, 1889. I have Dr. Brahms, Johannes Brahms with me"). This aural date and signature, albeit "ghostwritten," is followed by what can barely be recognized as some measures from Brahms's Hungarian Dance no. 1. It is ironic and unfortunate that Brahms was as popular as he was: through the many playings of this famous document, the sound quality over the thirty seconds of the recording decayed to such a degree that for the longest time it was considered virtually useless for purposes of performance analysis. (2005, 126)

Rehding's observation about the cylinder's long period of *uselessness* to the field of performance analysis hints at the possibility that it might be *useful* elsewhere, such as the field of recording analysis.

In the case of the Brahms cylinder, it becomes essential to clarify which recording we are studying. Due to its age, import, and fragility, the original object has birthed families of recordings. The lineage born from the "prerecorded sounds" made by Brahms in 1889 includes the original cylinder before it was ever played back, the cylinder after it had been replayed numerous times, Ward Marston's 1977 vinyl transfer *Landmarks of Recorded*

Pianism: Volume 1, the 1997 Symposium compact disc *About a Hundred Years: A History of Sound Recording*, the 1998 Piano Library compact disc *Brahms Plays Brahms*, and the group of LCT denoised versions created by Jonathan Berger as part of the Brahms restoration project at Stanford University's Center for Computer Research in Music and Acoustics. These recordings can be studied and theorized individually or in groups. I will inventory an excerpt from another member of this family to demonstrate a track where surface noise overwhelms the performance sounds.

Example 5.9 presents a spectrogram of a ten-second segment (1:50–2:00) from the 1997 re-recording (*Übertragung*) of the Brahms cylinder. The recording—issued by Verlag der Österreichischen Akademie der Wissenschaften—is called *Historische Stimmen aus Wien, Volume 5: Brahms spielt Klavier, Aufgenommen im Hause Fellinger 1889, The Re-recording of the Complete Cylinder*, and the track title is "Ungarischer Tanz und

Example 5.9 Spectrogram of 1:50–2:00 from the 1997 Österreichischen Akademie der Wissenschaften re-recording of the 1889 Brahms cylinder. See ⊙ Audio Example 5.8.

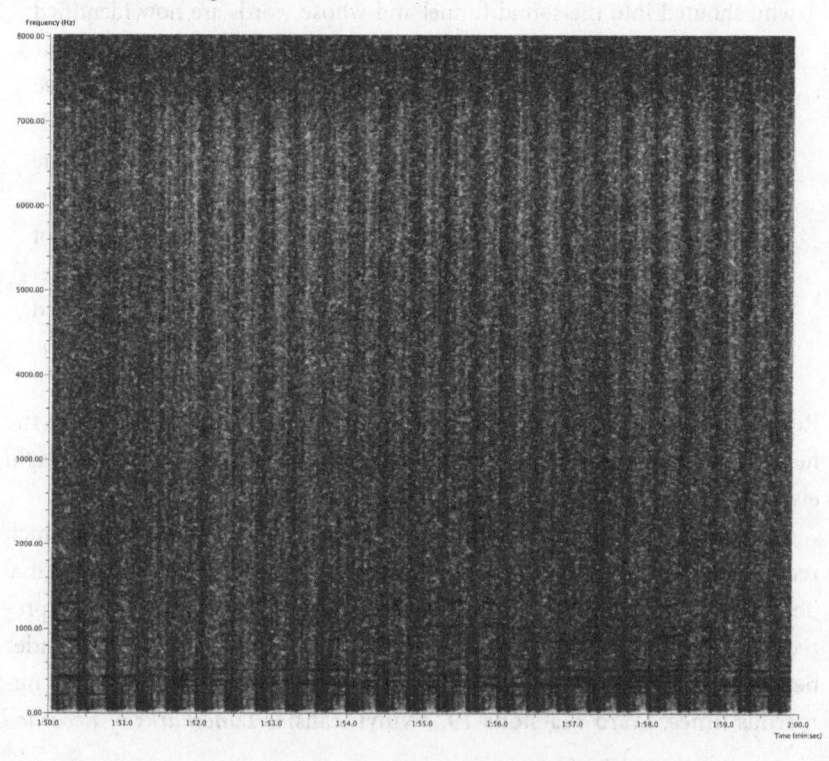

Walzerfragment (Original-Walze, Übertragung 1997)." The excerpt comes from the latter portion of the track, when Brahms is apparently playing a fragment of Josef Strauss's *Die Libelle, Polka-Mazurka für das Pianoforte*, Op. 204. The piano takes on the role of backdrop to the surface noise. In this ten-second span, there are twenty-four surface noise cycles, or one cycle about every 416 milliseconds. This 1997 re-recording foregrounds surface noise. The piano music is faint. During certain spans, it is inaudible.

The spectrogram in Example 5.9 looks like a piece of corrugated tin. Its undulations record the *fierce swishes* that blanket this track. Listeners familiar with other transfers of the Brahms cylinder might question my choice. Why study the 1997 re-recording, which is one of the noisiest versions available, when there are others—such as Marston's 1977 vinyl transfer—in which the piano music is considerably clearer? My choice is intentional. Due to the fragility and age of the cylinder, the 1997 re-recording exemplifies mode 6 exceedingly well. The scholars and sound engineers who participated in the re-recording were faced with an object that was deteriorating before their eyes. The state of the cylinder at the time of the re-recording produced a track that offers itself as an extreme—and ideal—case of *surface noise–centricity*. Franz Lechleitner, who worked on the re-recording, describes the situation:

> Strange though it may seem, the copy of the re-recording from 1935 sounds clearer than that of the modern recording, despite the seemingly limitless possibilities afforded by modern recording technology. However, when the 1935 recording was made, the physical condition of the original cylinder was much better than in 1983. The cylinder has deteriorated further still between 1983 and the present, and we have discovered an additional crack and further loss of signal. (Lechleitner 1997, 12–13)

I appreciate Lechleitner's frankness. He acknowledges that the cylinder sounded better when it was newer. Its age and repeated playings have brought it to a literal breaking point. Even as the compact disc bears the title *Brahms spielt Klavier*, the recordists were not making a recording of Brahms playing the piano as much as they were capturing the sounds imprinted on a fragile, wax object. The 1997 re-recording stands as an exemplar of a *surface noise–centric* track.

The Brahms cylinder is one of the earliest audio recordings of classical music. It is fitting that we encounter it now, as the last analysis in this book. While theorists of historical performance might have little use for its abrasive sonic foreground, the 1997 track is a fruitful object for recording analysis. Its scant traces of Brahms's playing are awash in some of the fiercest swishes I have encountered. The surface noise—not notated in the scores that Brahms was playing—has become the track's foreground. Its steady encroachment calls to mind a letter by Rainer Maria Rilke, one of several that the poet penned to Magda von Hattingberg on February 11, 1914. Rilke is ruminating on an object that was dear to him: a daguerreotype of his father, taken when he was a young man.[20] Rilke came upon the photograph after his father's death and had become increasingly concerned about its deterioration:

> I must have seen it once among my father's papers when I was a child, later it was as if lost for years, it was no use asking about it. Then one day I found it as I went through his estate, framed in ancient faded red velvet in the manner of miniatures, unhurt, and of course I realized at the moment of recognition how profoundly it had been grafted into my heart. On closer scrutiny, a few tiny metal green specks became visible near one of the eyes, as though something were corroding the plate. Concerned that the condition might deteriorate further, I had a case made, lined inside and outside with black suede, to shut out completely any further effects of the light. Occasionally I asked for the opinion and advice of people who seemed to know all about such things—oh, my dear one, need I tell you the rest?—all this, all this just so that suddenly, again years later, at a time of complete unpreparedness, I would rip open the back of the frame and hurriedly try to correct matters with a wretched wad of cotton, of course aggravating the timid little defect to the point of real destruction. (Rilke 1987, 37–38, translated by Joel Agee)[21]

[20] Rilke invokes this photograph in his 1906 poem "Jugend-Bildnis meines Vaters" (Youthful Portrait of My Father). According to Stephanie Harris, "Rilke is said to have carried the daguerreotype with him at all times" (2006, 146).

[21] „In meiner Kindheit musste ichs einmal zwischen Papieren meines Vaters gesehen haben, später wars jahrelang wie verschollen, es half nichts, danach zu fragen—, dann eines Tages fand ich's in seinem Nachlass, von altem rothverglühten Sammet in Art der Miniaturen gerahmt, unverletzt, und merkte nun freilich an meinem Wiedererkennen, wie unsäglich mirs ins Herz gebildet gewesen war. Nun zeigte sich bei näherem Zusehen, dass in der Gegend des einen Auges ein paar winzige metallgrüne Punkte entstanden waren, als ob etwas an der Platte sich zersetzte, besorgt, es möchte jener Zustand Fortschritte machen, ließ ich ein Etui, außen und innen aus schwarzem Wildleder, dafür herstellen, den weiteren Einfluss des Lichtes völlig auszuschließen, fragte auch wohl gelegentlich der Meinung und dem Rathe von Leuten nach, die sich in solche Sachen zu verstehen schienen—oh Liebe, muß ichs Dir noch sagen?—alles das, alles das, um plötzlich, wieder nach Jahren, in dazu ganz unvorbereiteter Stunde, das nieeröffnete Rähmchen hinten aufzureißen und rasch, mit einem unseligen Stück Watte, einzugreifen: den ängstlichen kleinen Schaden natürlich zur wirklichen Zerstörung vergrößernd" (Rilke 2000, 62–63).

The metallic specks on the photograph of Rilke's father are a kind of surface noise. They get in the way of what Rilke—as a son—wants to see. While the specks inhibit the portrait's ability to seem movingly real, they contribute new expressive content.

Rilke feared that the specks would spread and corrode the image. He had a protective case made, akin perhaps to the digitization of a wax cylinder. Continued deterioration was inevitable. Something similar has happened, and will continue to happen, to the Brahms cylinder. A photographic portrait has a history as both a document of a person and an independent, two-dimensional object. The same duality applies to musicians and their recordings. Early recordings memorialized performances on tubular cylinders and flat discs. We might seek out a record from that era to hear a certain musician playing a certain work. The musician has a history, as does the score that they perform. A recording—be it preserved in tin, wax, vinyl, plastic, or bytes—has a separate history. At the conclusion of this study of surface noise, reading Rilke's poetic evocation creates in me an unexpected desire. While the original was no doubt interesting, I would prefer to see the photograph as it appeared to Rilke in 1914, in the black suede case, with the tiny green specks near one of the eyes.

6
Inclusive Track Analysis

The preceding chapters on sounds of breath, touch, effort, and surface noise unfold the central categories of my study. In them, I invite the reader to flex their attention across the contours of written and unwritten music alike. It is useful, now, to draw a line. Not just any line, but a *vinculum*, a mathematical term referring to a horizontal placed over multiple quantities to indicate that are to be operated on as a single entity. I hereby draw a vinculum over the first five chapters and use this final one to harness their shared energies. Their lessons are distilled into a music theory—*inclusive track analysis*—whose hallmark is the recognition of all sounds that appear on a given recording. After acknowledging the influence of Pauline Oliveros's concept of *attentional flexibility* and Walter Benjamin's notion of *reading what was never written*, I unfold the tenets of inclusive track analysis, a practice informed by early pragmatist thought, especially William James's conception of *theory-as-instrument*. While my methodology was developed in the context of classical recordings, I offer glimpses of its utility beyond classical music (in popular songs) and beyond music altogether (in poetry readings and auditory psychology). The book concludes with a discussion of the meaning and source of its title.

Attentional flexibility

On April 3, 2012, Pauline Oliveros was a guest in my Introduction to Composition course at Harvard University. She sat with my students and me, in a circle, at the center of Room 4 in the Music Building, and together we sang her *Tuning Meditation*. Oliveros was approaching her eightieth birthday and I remember her vocal timbre set against the voices of my undergraduate students. The intensity of her attention was palpable. She seemed aware of each sound as it was born into the space, exerted its presence, and departed. Music theory can learn a great deal from Oliveros, who calls on musicians to create and receive sound in both its grandest and most granular

Sounds as They Are. Richard Beaudoin, Oxford University Press. © Oxford University Press 2024.
DOI: 10.1093/oso/9780197659281.003.0007

forms. In *Software for People*, she composed a sentence that could run as a chyron below each page of this book: "Good attentional flexibility is essential for participation in music no matter what one's role is" (1984, 190). At its best, music theory incorporates the same hypervigilant *noticing* that Oliveros championed across her lifetime of participation in music. In both her music and writings, she counsels the ear, and the mind, to accept the totality of audible events, whether they be on tracks or in the world. Everyone involved in audio recordings—including instrument builders, composers, sound engineers, listeners, musicologists, performers, publishers, students, teachers, technologists, and theorists—benefits by practicing *Oliverosian attentional flexibility*.

Paying close attention can be revelatory and upsetting in equal measure. Oliveros's awareness—her Deep Listening—should not be confused with passive perceiving. The sound of the word *attention*, after all, includes (and subsumes) the sound of the word *tension*. John Dewey addressed this dual nature of awareness, writing: "Awareness means *attention*, and attention means a crisis of some sort in an existent situation; a forking of the roads of some material, a tendency to go this way and that. It represents something the matter, something out of gear, or in some way menaced, insecure, problematical and strained" (1908, 73, italics in original). I appreciate the edge that Dewey sharpens into awareness's blade. He understands the complexity of paying close attention: "But awareness means inquiry as well as doubt—these are the negative and positive, the retrospective and the prospective relationships of the thing" (1908, 76). While my analyses require precise documentation of audible events, they also stir up clouds of interpretive dust that require time to settle. When unwritten sounds are allowed to be heard *as music*, certain truths pertaining to the score are overturned. Items considered plainly factual by score-based theories—such as where a phrase begins or how many sounds are occurring at a given moment—become contingent and difficult to predict. When a theorist pays careful attention, track analysis becomes a lesson in humility.

Attention is a central preoccupation of Oliveros's work. Again and again, she asks people to heighten their awareness of their own sounding lives. One section of her score *The Witness* is titled "Attention All Over." It reads, in part: "Expand your field of attention, as far as possible, to include any environmental sound, movement, or dramatic action as part of this unity" (1989, 4). Oliveros's philosophy of extending one's attention "as far as possible" is simultaneously a request to listen *as close as possible*, the far/close dichotomy working together toward a shared goal of heightening sensitivity to one's environment. My mode of inquiry asks listeners to likewise expand their attention, placing it as close as possible to a track's surface. "Oh! what a crowded world one moment may contain!" reads a line by Felicia Hemans (1836, 116). Listening to tracks in detail puts a theorist face-to-face with such crowded moments. Encountering the entangled layers of written and unwritten music, it is tempting to withdraw back into the safety of more well-theorized areas: structural forms, notated harmonies, performed tempi. My method of track analysis is designed to plunge theory back into the complexities and idiosyncrasies that populate tracks.

The Oliveros-Dewey connection demonstrates their shared interest in the contemporary moment. In Dewey's formulation: "Better it is for philosophy to err in active participation in the living struggles and issues of its own age and times than to maintain an immune monastic impeccability, with relevancy and bearing in the generating ideas of its contemporary present" (1908, 80). Something similar might be said of music theory. Making analytical sense of complex assemblages requires a collaboration between intellect and imagination. New assemblages appear each day, made by new musicians playing new instruments whose sound is captured by new equipment and diffused by new speakers. It is incumbent upon music theory to resist the safety of "immune monastic impeccability" and grapple with the "generating ideas" of present-day music-making, even when the music being made is based on scores from past centuries.

Reading what was never written

In a November 1974 interview she gave to *Essence* magazine, Roberta Flack described her compositional practice: "Music comes first from my heart and then goes upstairs to my head where I check it out before letting it out" (Ebert 1980, 294). Music theory is no stranger to Flack's multi-stage process. A theorist might first experience a piece via a recording, a film, a performance, a score, or a combination of these. The music then moves up to the mind for careful examination. During this transfer, unwritten music commonly gets left behind. Sounds not prescribed by the score have regularly been detained at our collective aesthetic checkpoints. In the analyses that populate the preceding chapters, I have attempted to demonstrate the expressive categories that emerge when tracks—in their entirety—are allowed "up-stairs" to be "checked out" using music theory's manifold instruments.

As a student, I recall being puzzled when a professor claimed that, after a harmonic analysis, a phrase was fully understood or, in British parlance, *sorted*. One can feel this way only if strict (and often unspoken) boundaries are set. Take Debussy's Sonata for Violin and Piano. One might make claims about the piece based on its score. (Even then, there is the question of which edition.) Recordings of the sonata often add unwritten music whose placement and function challenges score-based conclusions. In the case of the sonata's first eight measures, there are recordings with no breath sounds,[1] one inhale,[2] multiple inhales,[3] multiple inhales and exhales,[4] chair creaks,[5] piano pedal sounds,[6] and surface noise.[7] Analyzing any one of these recordings requires a theorist to acknowledge the entanglement of both the written and the unwritten. It necessitates reading score and spectrogram together, while cultivating an appreciation for their inherent contradictions.

André Monglond made a provocative analogy between historiography and photography: "The past has left images in literary texts that are comparable to those that light imprints on a sensitive plate. The future alone possesses developers strong enough to delve into these plates" (1930, xii).[8] Transposing this sentiment into the language of track analysis, it can be said that the past has left in audio recordings something comparable to that which light imprints on a photographic plate. Recordings might be considered *sound-sensitive plates*. Patient and energetic developers of these plates can reveal latent details. In this analogy, music theorists—and all listeners—become the "strong developers" whose attention can reveal the image in all its complexity. Spectrograms aid in this work, as do scores. I encourage literacy in both. Like photographs, spectrograms provide the viewer with a static picture of what was once fluid. These pictures foreground certain aspects while suppressing others. Delving into these "sensitive plates" reveals how much sonic activity is waiting to be heard if one is attuned to accept it.

---

[1] Kyung-Wha Chung and Radu Lupu (Chung 1998).
[2] Ginette Neveu and Jean Neveu (Neveu 1948).
[3] Renaud Capuçon and Bertrand Chamayou (Capuçon 2017).
[4] Janine Jansen and Itamar Golan (Jansen 2010).
[5] Sigiswald Kuijken and Piet Kuijken (Kuijken 2000).
[6] Tamsin Waley-Cohen and Huw Watkins (Waley-Cohen 2014).
[7] Jacques Thibaud and Alfred Cortot (Cortot 1929).
[8] « Le passé a laissé de lui-même dans les textes littéraires des images comparables à celles que la lumière imprime sur une plaque sensible. Seul l'avenir possède des révélateurs assez actifs pour fouiller parfaitement de tels clichés. » (Monglond 1930, xii).

An avid practitioner of Oliverosian attentional flexibility, *avant la lettre*, was Walter Benjamin. Among the writings unpublished at the time of his death was a paragraph-long parenthetical from 1940, written as part of his "Paralipomena to 'On the Concept of History.'" In it, Benjamin refers to Monglond's statement about "strong developers" and offers his own provocative extension: "The historical method is a philological method based on the book of life. 'Read what was never written,' runs a line in Hofmannsthal. The reader one should think of here is the true historian" (2003, 405, translated by Edmund Jacott and Howard Eiland). Fusing the historical and the philological, Benjamin's statement resonates with my methodology. A music theory devoted to *tracks-as-documents* embodies a philological method based on the literature of captured sound. I take Benjamin's statement as an invitation to engage in music theory. Interpreting all the audible events on a given track allows a theorist to "read what was never written." In the context of recordings of notated classical music, sounds of breath, touch, effort, and surface noise are unwritten music. Historically, their *unwrittenness* led to their being suppressed as audible phenomena (by producers and sound engineers) and as objects for analysis (by theorists). I encourage music studies to *read* unwritten music, bringing it into balance with the notated sounds with which it is expressively intertwined.

Inclusive track analysis: A pragmatic framework

The vinculum placed over the preceding chapters can now be activated. Their collective energy can be funneled into the practice of *inclusive track analysis*. The basis of this practice can be defined rather simply: inclusive track analysis (hereafter ITA) recognizes all sound events on a given track. This methodology applies to recordings of both notated and non-notated music, regardless of genre. ITA pays attention to all sounds, no matter their origin or author. A contrary approach—one might call it *exclusive track analysis*—would analyze only a subset of audible events, such as melody, harmony, rhythm, or interpretative details such as tempo. Exclusive analyses ignore certain classes of sound. To be sure, exclusive approaches are not always undesirable. Ignoring specific sounds can allow light to be shed on others. My practice, however, is founded on paying attention to the totality.

ITA opens the floodgates to new categories of sonic objects. The practice unfolds in three stages: (1) attending to all audible events on a given recording or section of it; (2) measuring the rhythmic position of both written and unwritten music; and (3) analyzing the expressive function of the totality. The practice neither predicts nor prescribes any particular result, but pragmatically encourages the recognition of all events. Extrapolating from the analyses that populate the preceding chapters, I offer a methodology for ITA. The first stage involves making a proper *census* of all sounds within a given passage. Depending on the purview of the theorist, this window can be as large as a whole track and as small as a single moment. The second stage involves measuring the *location* of each sound in time. Note that I emphasize the sound's location over its source. It is not always possible to identify the precise source of unwritten music. Even so, its existence means that it has a function. Once locations are charted, the focus moves to familiar territory for music theory: illustrating the *relationship* between sounds.

In recordings of notated music, the three main rhythmic positions for unwritten sounds are before, simultaneous with, or after a notated sound. Chapters 2–5 provided numerous examples. Breath sounds appeared as anacruses, on-beat additions, and post-beat adornments. Touch sounds— which by their nature are often coincident with note-production—often appeared as simultaneous with pitch onset. Sounded effort likewise appears in all three positions: recall the *early* grunt lead, the *coincident* climactic moan, and the *chord-extending* growl. Listening *with* surface noise requires that attention be paid to the synchrony and asynchrony between its pulse stream and that of the performance, as well as any changes to its patterning across the track.

ITA is inspired by ideas from pragmatism, a philosophy that, in the words of William James, "does not stand for any special results. It is a method only" (1907, 51). If it does not stand for any special results, then what does pragmatism offer? James replies: "No particular results then, so far, but only an attitude of orientation, is what the pragmatic method means. *The attitude of looking away from first things, principles, 'categories,' supposed necessities; and of looking towards last things, fruits, consequences, facts*" (1907, 54–55, italics in original). The pragmatic method welcomes the idea that new facts unsettle certainty. It decentralizes preordained, generalizing categories and encourages open-ended inquiry. It offers a reminder that the work of philosophy is never done because the mind is persistently brought into contact with an ever-evolving present. The same holds true in music. Music theory's work remains necessarily—and fruitfully—unfinished in the face of unpredictable sounds: new scores, new performances, new recordings, new technology, new engineering, and new listeners.

Invoking pragmatism, I am not wedding ITA to the whole of pragmatist thought. Like all branches of philosophy, pragmatic literature is rife with internal contradictions and generational divides. I would, therefore, like to be specific. My engagement with pragmatist ideas stems primarily from James's "What Pragmatism Means," which appears as Lecture II in *Pragmatism, A New Name for Some Old Ways of Thinking* (1907, 43–81). I have already invoked, in Chapter 1, the words of pragmatism's founding author, Charles Sanders Peirce, and, earlier in this chapter, its most public practitioner, John Dewey. Below, I will call upon more contemporary pragmatist commentaries by Richard Rorty and Cornel West. But it is James, above all, who speaks directly to matters that connect pragmatism to music studies.

Music theory is at its best when it widens its metaphorical ears. Key developments in the discipline came about when once-ignored categories of sound were given a seat at theory's proverbial table. When theory expands the notion of what *counts* as music, it becomes more generous, providing new ways to activate one's analytic imagination. This is precisely the spirit that characterizes pragmatism. Setting the parameters of the pragmatic method, James considered words such as *matter*, *reason*, and *the Absolute* to be hollow monikers that close off, rather than inspire, metaphysical quests:

> But if you follow the pragmatic method, you cannot look on any such word as closing your quest. You must bring out of each word its practical cash-value, set it at work within the stream of your experience. It appears less as a solution, then, than as a program for more work, and more particularly as an indication of the ways in which existing realities may be *changed*.
>
> *Theories thus become instruments, not answers to enigmas, in which we can rest.* We don't lie back upon them, we move forward, and, on occasion, make nature over again by their aid. Pragmatism unstiffens all our theories, limbers them up and sets each one at work. Being nothing essentially new, it harmonizes with many ancient philosophic tendencies. (1907, 53, italics in original)

ITA operates along similar lines. It exemplifies the Jamesian notion of *theory-as-instrument* and harmonizes well with existing theories of meter, harmony, form, and timbre, be they ancient or modern.

Reflecting on the pragmatist project, Richard Rorty writes: "Rather, the pragmatists tell us, it is the vocabulary of practise rather than of theory, of action rather than contemplation, in which one can say something useful about truth" (1982, 162). In the preceding chapters, I presented just such a *vocabulary of practice*, one designed to encourage others to study recordings. Attached to this vocabulary is a set of symbols—the noteheads and objects that signify inhales, exhales, fingernail clicks, fingerfalls, squeaks, valve clacks, podium stamps, damper pedal engagements, grunts, moans, groans, growls, and the fierce swish of surface noise—that are designed to be useful and non-cumbersome. While these symbols have been carefully chosen and employed, I do not expect them to become standard, nor am I naïve enough to think that they account for the complete spectrum of non-notated sounds. In a pragmatist spirit, I look forward to their expansion and revision. ITA does not rely on a prescriptive set of formulas. Such a design would be anti-pragmatic. Instead, like pragmatist philosophy itself, it is a *mode of inquiry* designed to join and augment theory's existing instruments.[9]

Recording analysis is a natural partner for pragmatism. In the words of Arved Ashby, "The recording has pragmatic potential because, unlike the ed-ited score, it does not aim to preclude other versions" (2010, 116). A basic tenet of ITA is that tracks are not improved or marred by unwritten music. The presence (or absence) of such sounds should not analytically privilege one recording over another. ITA is designed to *serve* musicians and sound engineers by paying careful attention to their tracks alongside scores, performances, and a host of other associated objects. In this way, track anal-ysis becomes a tool for theorists who wish to widen the landscape of musical objects under their consideration. Consider Vivian Luong's constructive critique of a Mozart analysis by Marion Guck. Guck's 1997 article "Music Loving, Or the Relationship with the Piece" puts forth an analysis of what, in her words, "one piece does to me" (1997, 348). The piece, in this case, is the *Adagio* from Mozart's Piano Concerto in A major, K. 488. Guck writes: "What I want to understand is why we are so entranced; what makes each moment seem so special? What gives it this power to attract?" (1997, 349). Guck's object is Mozart's "piece," though the term is not fully defined. Guck refers

---

[9] A precursor of ITA is found in "Die Analyse von Tonaufnahmen" (The Analysis of Sound Recordings), Olivier Senn's 2007 dissertation at the University of Zürich. Senn devotes hundreds of pages to semiotic, phonetic, timbral, and micro-rhythmic analyses of Sarah Vaughan's July 18, 1961, recording of Rodgers and Hammerstein's "My Favorite Things." The track he studies appears on Vaughan's album *After Hours*, released on LP in 1961 and reissued on compact disc in 1996. The record, produced by Teddy Reig, features Mundell Lowe on guitar and George Duvivier on bass.

mainly to Mozart's score and the hands of the solo pianist interpreting it. Luong's "Rethinking Music Loving" calls on Guck—and music theory more generally—to expand the objects under consideration. She writes: "In Guck's account of the Mozart concerto movement in 'Music Loving,' for example, interactions with performers, instruments, recordings, and other publications, named mostly in the footnotes, all contribute to her relationship with the piece" (2017). ITA provides a framework for heeding Luong's call, foregrounding as it does tracks in all their fine detail. It adds recordings to the list of objects that we might, in a Guckian sense, love. (Other emotions are also possible.) ITA encourages theorists to pinpoint what recordings "do to them," regardless of whether the sounds in question appear in the score being recorded, or whether the piece has a score at all.

As an example of the implications of a pragmatic music theory of tracks, recall, from Chapter 2, Kim Kashkashian's 2018 ECM recording, made with producer Manfred Eicher and Tonmeisterin Judy Sherman, of the Gigue from Bach's Suite in C minor, BWV 1011. Multiple published analyses of the first part of the gigue claimed that it unfolded as three eight-measure phrases: 8 + 8 + 8. Kashkashian's breath sounds—their location, their duration, and (to borrow a phrase from pragmatism's progenitor, Charles Sanders Peirce) their particular "Quality of Feeling"—generate phrase lengths of 7 + 7 + 3 + 3 + 4. A positivist music theory that treats recordings mainly as sonic demonstrations of score-based structures might claim a *disjuncture* between Bach's gigue and Kashkashian's recording of it. From that vantage, her breath sounds are inopportune because they are "not the piece." As a pragmatist music theory, ITA *accepts* the particularities of the track and goes about analyzing how all the sounds—notated or not—work together. It recognizes tracks as collaborative efforts, their content comprising sounds from varied sources, including the score, the instrument, the body of the performer(s), and the recording/playback devices.

A critic might argue that ITA evades proper music theory altogether. The same accusation was levied at pragmatism itself. The point is succinctly made by the title of Cornel West's *The American Evasion of Philosophy: A Genealogy of Pragmatism* (1989). West charts the pragmatic tradition's move away from positivist, Cartesian certitude and toward a philosophy of continual revision based on newly encountered facts. He writes: "Rather, the claim is that once one gives up on the search for foundations and the quest for certainty, human inquiry into truth and knowledge shifts to the social and communal circumstances under which persons can communicate and cooperate in the process of acquiring knowledge" (1989, 213). Declining a quest for certainty in favor of a communal mode of knowledge-sharing leads West to his own *prophetic pragmatism,* which "rests upon the conviction that the American evasion of philosophy is not an evasion of serious thought and moral action. Rather such evasion is a rich and revisable tradition that serves as the occasion for cultural criticism and political engagement in the service of an Emersonian culture of creative democracy" (1989, 239). In the spirit of West's prophetic pragmatism, ITA is not an *evasion* of serious thought, but an *exhortation* to treat the content of tracks with more seriousness—more completely *as tracks*—than before.

A great deal of work lies ahead. Once sounds of breath, sounds of touch, sounds of effort, and surface noise are analyzed as integral—not only in classical tracks but in all sound recordings—the sheer scale of the project to document their expressive function comes into view. Pragmatist philosophers experienced a similar reckoning concerning the complexity (and workload) implied by their stance. The pragmatic method, valuing as it does the *particular* over the *general,* places a great deal into the laps of its adherents. But pragmatists, it seems, are not put off by complexity. With lively eloquence, James contrasts the pragmatist philosopher with the rationalist one, favoring the fullness of the former's purview:

> See the exquisite contrast of the types of mind! The pragmatist clings to facts and concreteness, observes truth at its work in particular cases, and generalizes. Truth, for him, becomes a class-name for all sorts of definite working-values in experience. For the rationalist it remains a pure abstraction, to the bare name of which we must defer. When the pragmatist undertakes to show in detail just *why* we must defer, the rationalist is unable to recognize the concretes from which his own abstraction is taken. He accuses us of *denying* truth; whereas we have only sought to trace exactly why people follow it and always ought to follow it. Your typical ultra-abstractionist fairly shudders at concreteness: other things equal, he positively prefers the pale and spectral. If the two universes were offered, he would always choose the skinny outline rather than the rich thicket of reality. (James 1907, 68, italics in original)

Transposed onto music theory, the passage inspires me toward a confession. Experiencing music studies as a discipline for some years, I have encountered a surfeit of rationalist theories. Our field has for decades been marked by attempts to clear away the brambles of sounding peculiarities in favor of formal schemas and corpus studies. While such approaches are illuminating, even thrilling, I imagine James judging them to be "skinny outlines" when placed alongside the totality of sonic experience. ITA asks music studies to engage with the "rich thicket" of recorded sounds, be they written or unwritten. James's horticultural metaphor calls to mind Steven Rings's portrayal of the relationship between music and theory: "For surely the best way we can value music is to acknowledge that it will always exceed the manicured gardens of our theories" (2011, 506). ITA welcomes the unmanicured and asks music theory to accept the unkempt, the overgrown, and the tousled.

Beyond classical tracks

I have focused on classical tracks because it is there that unwritten music is least resolved and most often dismissed. The utility of attending to sounds of breath, touch, and effort extends beyond classical music. ITA proves useful in contexts where no score is present. Consider three widening rings of resonance. First, ITA can be applied to tracks in other genres, such as popular songs. Second, it can be used to analyze tracks that capture sound not normally considered music, such as poetry readings. Third, ITA has a tangential link to the psychological theory of Auditory Scene Analysis. I discuss each in turn.

As a track-centric art form, popular music has a healthier relationship with sounds of breath, touch, and effort than does classical music. Indeed, applying ITA to popular music generates enough material for a separate monograph. Taking here an intentionally narrow view, I identify expressive breath sounds in six songs released between 1987 and 2019. These are not analyses, but rather glimpses of moments that exemplify the expressive impact of audible breathing.

Suzanne Vega's "Tom's Diner" (1987) includes twenty-six inhales, all of which are naturalistic (occurring as part of the singing and not recorded separately).[10] These inhales lend Vega's track a *right-there-with-her* presence

---

[10] "Tom's Diner" was composed and performed by Vega, produced by Steve Addabbo and Lenny Kaye, and appears on the album *Solitude Standing* (1987).

and support the quotidian nature of the lyric.[11] By contrast, Tracy Chapman's "Behind the Wall" (1988) has almost no audible inhales.[12] Those that are heard are faint; many have been summarily removed. Given that the song addresses police indifference to violence, Chapman's "missing" inhales generate expressive tension. Naturalistic breaths are withheld. The effect is powerfully and effectively unsettling.

Toni Braxton expands the typology of breath sounds. At 2:59 of "Un-break My Heart" (1996), she produces a fluttering inhale after the word *pain* on the second iteration of the lyric "Don't leave me in all this pain, Don't leave me out in the rain."[13] The psychological state implied by Braxton's trembling inhale is one of keenly felt emotion. Imogen Heap's "Hide and Seek" (2005) is notable for its quasi-robotic atmosphere, generated via a digital harmonizer.[14] I count forty-nine breaths on Heap's track. One inhale-exhale pair occurs at 3:27, just after the lyric "Ransom notes keep falling out your mouth." This breath pair was recorded separately from the singing and serves a rhythmic and groove-based function.

The last sound on Fiona Apple's "Hot Knife" (2012) is a decisive inbreath.[15] The song's final downbeat consists of a single, unaccompanied word ("you") followed by a rapid inhale. Given that this track ends the album, Apple's inhale imparts a feeling of (potentially) unending anticipation. Her syncopated breath prepares the listener for a sound that never arrives. Finally, Solange's "Things I Imagined" (2019) preserves a breath that plays with expectation and meaning.[16] The track includes a hesitating inhale at 0:24, during which the listener is unsure of what they will hear next, or when they will hear it.

Imagine recording a cover of any one of these six tracks. Specifically, a *mimic cover*, which Cristyn Magnus, P. D. Magnus, and Christy Mag Uidhir define as one that aims to reproduce "the arrangement and interpretation

---

[11] Jonathan Sterne (2012, 174–76) relates the role that Vega's track played in the development of the MPEG audio format.

[12] "Behind the Wall" was composed and performed by Chapman, produced by David Kershenbaum, engineered and mixed by Kevin W. Smith, and appears on the album *Tracy Chapman* (1988).

[13] "Un-break My Heart" was composed by Diane Warren, produced and arranged by David Foster, and appears on Braxton's album *Secrets* (1996). I am grateful to Celia Douville Beaudoin for drawing my attention to this track.

[14] "Hide and Seek" was produced by Heap and appears on the album *Speak for Yourself* (2005).

[15] "Hot Knife" was composed by Apple, who co-produced the track with Charley Drayton. It appears on *The Idler Wheel Is Wiser than the Driver of the Screw and Whipping Cords Will Serve You More Than Ropes Will Ever Do* (2012), an album with enough breath-related material for its own ITA-centered monograph.

[16] "Things I Imagined" was produced by Solange, Christophe Chassol, and John Key and appears as the opening track on the album *When I Get Home* (2019).

of the canonical version" (2013, 362). An artistic decision would need to be made: do you preserve the location and duration of the breath sounds, or do you leave them out? To my mind, a strict *mimic cover* would reproduce all (and only) the breaths that are audible on the original recording.

ITA need not be limited to recordings of music. Recorded poetry readings, for example, include paralinguistic sounds produced by the reciter that are not present in the printed poem. While poems are experientially and functionally different from scores, both are written documents that give rise to sonic performances. Charles Bernstein has theorized the relationship between poems and their recitation, positing that a poem's identity is inclusive of all readings of it. The case he makes resonates with ITA:

> The relation of script to performance, or performance to script, is necessarily discrepant, hovering around an original center in a complex of versions that is inherently unstable. Poetry readings proliferate versions of the poem, each version displacing but not replacing every other. As such, close listening presents an ongoing challenge to readings that, in their intolerance of ambiguity, associative thinking, and abstraction, reduce the poem to a single level of meaning, banishing from significance—as stray marks or noises—all but the literal or concrete. (2009, 148)

Bernstein's invocation of "stray marks or noises" to define what is lost when we define a poem solely by its printed form is energizing. For example, some recordings of Stravinsky's *Sérénade en la* for solo piano include a great deal of unwritten music. Some do not. Bernstein asks us to accept that the notated composition, plus all recordings of it, together form an ever-growing entity called "*Sérénade en la*" whose score is but part of a greater whole.[17] While I will not here embark upon the (re)definition of a musical work, I suggest that the recognition of unwritten music will put pressure on some existing definitions of work identity.

---

[17] Stravinsky's four-movement piano work *Sérénade en la* owes its duration to the physical limitations of a recording format. The impetus for the piece "came not from the concert platform but a recording contract with Brunswick, with each movement designed to fit snugly on one side of a ten-inch 78rpm disc" (Dingle 2000, 3). In the composer's own words: "In America I had arranged with a gramophone firm to make records of some of my music. This suggested the idea that I should compose something whose length should be determined by the capacity of the record. I should in that way avoid all the trouble of cutting and adapting. And that is how my *Sérénade en La pour Piano* came to be written" (Stravinsky 1975, 123–24).

Equally inspiring is Aleksandra Kremer's *The Sound of Modern Polish Poetry: Performance and Recording after World War II* (2021). Kremer analyzes recordings of poets reading their own work, using spectrograms to highlight the expressive role of paralinguistic events. I understand my book to be a cross-disciplinary companion to hers. In one illuminating analysis, Kremer studies two recordings of Tadeusz Różewicz reading his poem "List do Ludożerców" (Letter to the Cannibals). One recording was made in the 1960s, the other in 1998. Kremer takes account of the tempo and pacing differences. In the earlier reading, Różewicz reads roughly twenty-eight syllables in a 7.5 second span; in the later reading, he utters thirteen syllables within the same duration (2021, 236). While my approach largely mirrors Kremer's, there are divergences. Analyzing a pause in the earlier reading, Kremer concludes that it "results from Różewicz's need to take a breath, which can be heard in the recording. This break in pitch has nothing to do with the poem's semantics, it is purely accidental" (2021, 236). Whether or not an inhale bifurcates the semantic wholeness of a poetic phrase does not require that it be characterized as "accidental." While it might be correct to say that inhales have "nothing to do with the poem's semantics," they have everything to do with the poet in the act of reciting. An ITA approach to Różewicz's audible mid-line inhale would classify his breath not as an *accident*, but rather as *integral* to a recording that, in a Bernsteinian sense, is itself part of a potentially limitless set of objects collectively called "List do Ludożerców."

A final implication of ITA beyond classical music emerges from the field of psychology, in particular Albert Bregman's theory of Auditory Scene Analysis (ASA), codified in his 1990 book of the same name. ASA has been summarized as "the ability of human listeners to parse complex acoustic scenes into coherent objects, such as a single talker in the middle of a noisy babble, or, in music, a single melody in the midst of a large orchestra" (Pressnitzer, Suied, and Shamma 2011, 1). While ASA has connections to music, its compass is wider, acting as a framework for understanding how the mind parses sonic phenomena within any given listening experience. In the terminology set forth by Bregman, one tenet of ASA is *exclusive allocation*, which holds that the mind, in the act of making sense of various sound sources, allocates an audible event as either *belonging* or *not belonging* to a given sound stream (1990, 12–13). Bregman's distinction activates many strands of ITA's methodology, as unwritten music on classical tracks has long been categorized by theorists as *not belonging* to the music. Reflecting on recent developments to his theory, Bregman unveils a critical realization concerning the temporality of the listening experience:

> I believe, instead, that there is an initial bias toward hearing all incoming acoustic energy as deriving from a *single* source. Only when evidence builds up that there is more than one source of sound does auditory scene analysis (ASA) begin to hear more than one stream. So it is not as if it favors the hearing of multiple sources. It is built to hear whatever is actually happening in the world, be that a single dominant source of sound or multiple sources. (Bregman 2015, 13, italics in original)

I encourage music studies to consider Bregman's statement in the context of track analysis. Historically, when a theorist listens to a recording that includes unwritten music, a seemingly automatic parsing kicks in. Sounds denoted in the score are placed in a favored stream called *music*. Sounds not denoted in the score are allocated to a separate stream called *non-music*. The former has received the lion's share of analytical attention while the latter has been ignored, even derided. ITA is designed to reposition music theory toward Bregman's "initial bias," a state in which the listener widens their attention to "hear whatever is actually happening" on the track and where "all incoming acoustic energy" is counted as expressive music.

Les sons tels qu'ils sont

Regarding this book's title: one might ask how the words *as they are* pertain to sounds? The plainest reading, and the one that has guided me throughout, is as a reminder that tracks are documents in and of themselves. ITA attends to notated chords and rhythms alongside sounds that are not notated—nor even implied—by the score. *Sounds as They Are* functions, then, as encouragement to study tracks *in toto*. A misreading of the title would be one that hears "as they are" to mean "as they always were and always will be." The reader will no doubt recognize how antithetical such an interpretation is to the spirit and content of my analyses. Even so, such a misreading deserves a moment of reflection. As a discipline, music theory finds great energy in disagreements. What is the structural function of a given sound? What are the origins of a certain sonority? What did a composer mean by a unique notation? ITA allows greater refinement to enter into these debates.

The practice of ITA is not meant to settle any facts for all time, but rather to *unsettle* aspects of theory that have begun to take on the veneer of certainty. For example, phrases that repeat (in the score) are often plainly different when recorded, not only in terms of tempo and ornamentation, but in the realm of unwritten music. Likewise, a theorist who claims that a given piece begins, say, with a major triad might pause. The statement might be true of the score, but false in the context of many (even most) recordings. On a track, the chord might be preceded by an inhale, or the sound of a finger being placed. The triad itself might be enveloped in the sound of an exhale. It is no simple matter to pin down precisely which sounds are occurring at a given moment in a recording without vigilant attention to the written and the unwritten alike.

Attentiveness to what recordings *are* implies an acceptance that we cannot predict what they *might become*. My title is therefore not about static notions of being, but about sounds as they appear to each listener individually.[18] Listeners, including myself, are not stable entities. Attention has built-in temporal aspects. I am reminded of a claim by Stanley Fish: "Disagreements are not settled by the facts, but are the means by which the facts are settled. Of course, no such settling is final, and in the (almost certain) event that the dispute is opened again, the category of the facts 'as they really are' will be reconstituted in still another shape" (1980, 338–39). Just because a score suggests a pair of four-bar phrases does not mean that breath sounds will not impart a feeling of three plus five, or that fingernail clicks will not shift the perception of a downbeat, or that synchronous surface noise will not give a phrase new significance.

The unpredictability of human and machine sounds can, at times, force a reconstitution of accepted facts about the piece being recorded. It is for this reason that ITA is couched as a method of *finding out*, not as a prescription for what one will find. Recall what Hilary Putnam wrote of Dewey's pragmatism: "For Dewey, social problems are not resolved by telling other people what to do. Rather, they are resolved by releasing human energies so that people will be able to act for themselves" (1995, 200). Problems in music theory are no different. ITA is not prescriptive, it is attentive. Its vocabulary and symbols were devised to invite others to extend the depth of their own perception into—and of—tracks.

---

[18] In "Music Theory, Music History, and Quicksand," Lawrence Zbikowski situates music theory as a discipline in which "the role of the listener is defined not by a particular set of competencies but as a position within a set of interpersonal exchanges" (2011, 227).

The last three words of this book's title—*as they are*—were inspired by an anecdote about Marcel Proust. The story turns out to be a face-saving embellishment, but its veracity is beside the point. Since his death in 1922, Proust has been called a "neuroscientist,"[19] a "social satirist,"[20] a "lover of pastiche,"[21] a "gourmand of feeling,"[22] a "world-class sufferer,"[23] a "master of the art of flattery,"[24] a "committed Wagnerian,"[25] an "accomplished amateur philologist,"[26] and a "great novelist who suffered from severe asthma."[27] I would add that Proust had the attentive spirit of a music theorist. *À la recherche du temps perdu* (*In Search of Lost Time*), his novel in seven volumes published between 1913 and 1927, includes hundreds of characters, each drawn with exquisite authorial attentiveness. One of these is Jupien, a tailor who runs a male brothel. The fictional Jupien was based on the real Albert Le Cuziat, who opened a similar establishment in Paris, on the rue de l'Arcade, in 1917. Proust spent time at Le Cuziat's place—he clandestinely observed clients and was a client himself—and certain scenes in his novel owe their authenticity to these visits.

Céleste Albaret was Proust's housekeeper, secretary, nurse, and confidante during the last years of his life. Apparently, she did not approve of his visits to the rue de l'Arcade. In her 1973 memoir of their time together, Albaret claimed that Proust's motivation for visiting Le Cuziat's place was writerly research and *rien d'autre* (nothing more). She composed a scene in which she expressed her concerns to Proust and authored his noble reply:

> The strange thing is that every time he [Proust] came back from rue de l'Arcade he would talk to me about the visit just as if he'd come back from an evening at Count de Beaumont's or Countess Greffulhe's. What interested him was the spectacle he'd seen, nothing else. When I said, with my usual forthrightness, that I couldn't understand how he could let Albert [Le Cuziat] come to see him, still less go there, he said:

[19] Jonah Lehrer (2007, ix).
[20] Raymond Riva (1968, 219).
[21] Maria Paganini-Ambord (1994, 110).
[22] John Romano (1978, 101).
[23] Frank Gannon (1997, 25).
[24] Leon Edel (1984, 518).
[25] Duncan Large (1993, 612).
[26] Allan Pasco (1994, 275).
[27] Harold L. Levitan (1978, 144).

"I know, Céleste. You can't imagine how much I dislike it. But I can only write about things as they are, and to do that I have to see them." (Albaret 2003, 196, translated by Barbara Bray)[28]

In Albaret's telling, Proust visited the brothel to witness things *as they are* in order to write about them. Adapting the phrase for my title, I welcomed its implied neutrality. *Sounds as They Are* sets out not to *judge* recordings, but to be *attentive* to them.

This book was written to be useful to all who participate in audio recordings, including and especially listeners. During my research, I encountered tracks that I loved alongside some that (to borrow Barbara Bray's turn of phrase) you can't imagine how I disliked. But music theory is not about what one *likes*, but what *is*. Along the way, I have learned that unwritten music is not as sordid as its reputation suggests. Listening closely, I have experienced the unique beauty of breaths, fingerfalls, moans, and the fierce swish of surface noise. I have heard exhales that extend chordal resonance and pedal flutters that made me breathless. I came to understand that audio tracks can brim with activity even when their overall mood is calm. Across this study, I have tried to appraise each track with a clear eye and an attentive ear. Studying sounds *as they are* demands Oliverosian attentional flexibility. It calls on theorists to examine the convergence of sounds with heterogeneous origins. It asks the field of music studies to read what was never written. Paying attention to a track in its wholeness requires concentration and repetition. Patience and openness are encouraged. When unwritten music appears, I propose measuring its location, studying its context, and elucidating its expressive function. So begins an inclusive track analysis. Unwritten music—so plentiful once you bend your awareness in its direction—calls out for recognition. This book invites listeners to savor the rich thicket of sounded intricacies that greet them each time they press play.

[28] « Ce qui est frappant, c'est que, chaque fois qu'il en revenait, il m'en parlait sur le même ton que s'il était rentré d'une soirée chez le comte de Beaumont ou chez la comtesse Greffulhe. C'était le tableau de ce qu'il avait vu qui l'intéressait. Rien d'autre. Quand je lui faisais remarquer, avec mon franc-parler, que je ne comprenais pas comment il pouvait recevoir Albert chez lui, ni encore moins aller là-bas, il me disait :
 – Je sais, Céleste. Vous n'imaginez pas comme cela m'embête et comme je n'aime pas cela. Mais je ne peux écrire les choses que telles qu'elles sont, et pour cela il faut que je les voie. » (Albaret 1973, 239–40).

Discography

Aimard, Pierre-Laurent, pianist. 2018. *Messiaen: Catalogue d'oiseaux*. Pentatone PTC5186 670, 3 compact discs.

Alban Berg Quartet. 1986. *Debussy, Ravel, Stravinsky*. EMI Digital CDC 7 47347 2, compact disc.

Apple, Fiona. 2012. *The Idler Wheel Is Wiser than the Driver of the Screw and Whipping Cords Will Serve You More than Ropes Will Ever Do*. Clean Slate/Epic 88691978632, compact disc.

Archilés, Ana, guitarist. 2019. "Adelita," by Francisco Tárrega. On *Tárrega . . . de la guitarra d'Ana al plectre de "La Tárrega."* Lemon Songs, streaming audio. Accessed October 11, 2021. Qobuz.

Arensky, Anton, pianist. 1894. *The Dawn of Recordings: The Julius Block Cylinders*. Marston Records 53011-2, 2008. 3 compact discs.

Argerich, Martha, pianist. 1986. *Chopin: Preludes, Op. 28, Op. 45, Op. posth.; Barcarolle Op. 60; Polonaise Op. 53; Scherzo No. 2 Op. 3*. Deutsche Grammophon 415 836-2, compact disc.

Arnold, Sheila, pianist. 2000. *Miniaturen für Klavier*. Edition Zeitklang ez-10003 403282400030, compact disc.

Arrau, Claudio, pianist. 1964. *Beethoven: The Complete Piano Sonatas and Concertos*. Philips 462 358-2, 1998, 14 compact discs.

Arrau, Claudio, pianist. 1992. *Wolfgang Amadeus Mozart*. Philips Arrau Edition 432 306-2PM7, 7 compact discs.

Ax, Emanuel, pianist. 1986. *Chopin: The Four Ballades, Sonata No. 2 in B-flat Minor*. RCA RCA1-7069, compact disc.

Balestracci, Guido, pardessus de viole. 2015. *Jean Barrière, Volume 2*. Bruno Cocset and Les Basses Réunies. Alpha Classics 220, compact disc.

Bassingthwaighte, Sarah, flutist. 2006. *Stalks in the Breeze*. CD Baby, compact disc.

Beauregard, Lawrence, flutist. 1984. *Varèse: Amériques, Ionisation, Density 21.5, Offrandes, Arcana, Octandre, Intégrales*. Pierre Boulez. Sony Classical SK 45844, compact disc.

Berezovsky, Boris, pianist, Dmitri Mahktin, violinist, and Alexander Kniazev, cellist. 2005. *Rachmaninov and Shostakovich: Piano Trios*. Warner Classics 2564 61937-2, compact disc.

Bernstein, Leonard, conductor. 1984. *Symphonie No. 3 "Eroica" and "Egmont" Overture*. Wiener Philharmoniker. Deutsche Grammophon 413 778-2, compact disc.

Bertrand, Emmanuelle, cellist. 2011. *Le violoncelle parle*. Harmonia Mundi HMC 902078, compact disc and digital video disc.

Blomstedt, Herbert, conductor. 1980. *Beethoven: Complete Symphonies*. Staatskapelle Dresden. With Helena Döse, Marga Schiml, Peter Schreier, and Theo Adam. Berlin Classics 0301524BC, 2020, 5 compact discs.

Borodin String Quartet. 1989. *Debussy and Ravel: String Quartets.* Virgin Classics VC 7 91077-2, compact disc.

Borodin Trio. 1983. *Shostakovich: Piano Quintet in G minor and Piano Trio No. 2 in E minor.* Chandos CHAN8342, compact disc.

Brahms, Johannes, pianist. 1889a. *Historische Stimmen aus Wien,* Vol. 5: *Brahms spielt Klavier, Aufgenommen im Hause Fellinger 1889, The Re-recording of the Complete Cylinder.* Verlag der Österreichischen Akademie der Wissenschaften OEAW PHA CD 5, 1997, compact disc.

Brahms, Johannes, pianist. 1889b. *Landmarks of Recorded Pianism,* Vol. 1: *Acoustic Recordings 1889–1924.* Desmar IPA 117, 1977, 33⅓ rpm.

Braxton, Toni. 1996. *Secrets.* LaFace Records 73008-26020-2, compact disc.

Bream, Julian, guitarist. 1970. *Julian Bream: Romantic Guitar.* BMG Music 6798-2-RB, 1991, compact disc.

Brown, Ray, bassist. 1957. *Bass Hit!* Verve Records 314 559 829-2, 1999, compact disc.

Brown, Velvet, tubist. 2003. *Music for Velvet.* Crystal Records CD 693, compact disc.

Burton, Dashon, bass-baritone. 2015. *Songs of Struggle and Redemption: We Shall Overcome.* Nathanial Gumbs, pianist. Acis APLO8685, compact disc.

Busch, Fritz, conductor. 1936. *Mozart: "Don Giovanni," The Glyndebourne Recording of 1936.* Pearl GEMM CDS 9369, 1989, 3 compact discs.

Capuçon, Renaud, violinist. 2017. *Debussy: Sonatas and Trio.* Bertrand Chamayou, pianist. Erato 0190295773960, compact disc.

Caruso, Enrico, tenor. 1902a. *The Complete Recordings of Enrico Caruso, Volume 1.* Salvatore Cottone, pianist. Naxos Historical 8.110703, 2000, compact disc.

Caruso, Enrico, tenor. 1902b. *Enrico Caruso: The Complete Recordings.* Salvatore Cottone, pianist. Bayer DaCapo BR 200 010-23, 1990, 16 compact discs.

Casals, Pablo, cellist. 1936. *Bach: The Six Cello Suites.* EMI Classics 724356261723, 2003, 2 compact discs.

Casals, Pablo, cellist. 1945. *Elgar, Casals, Sammons: Cello and Violin Concertos.* Avid Master Series, AMSC 587, 1997, compact disc.

Casals, Pablo, cellist. 1953. *Robert Schumann: Cello Concerto, Piano Trio No. 1, 5 Stücke im Volkston.* Prades Festival Orchestra. Eugene Ormandy, conductor. Pablo Casals Edition, Sony Classical SMK 58993, 1993, compact disc.

Casals, Pablo, cellist. 1954. *Schumann: Cello Concerto and Showpieces.* Prades Festival Orchestra. Eugene Ormandy, conductor. Sony Music Labels SICC 1859, 2016, compact disc.

Casals, Pablo, cellist. 1961. *Ludwig van Beethoven: Piano Trios and Cello Sonatas.* Philips 438 520-2PM3, 1993, 3 compact discs.

Chapman, Tracy. 1988. *Tracy Chapman.* Elektra 9 600774-2, compact disc.

Chapman Nyaho, William, pianist. 2020. *Kete: Piano Music of the African Diaspora.* MSR Classics MS 1708, compact disc.

Chase, Claire, flutist. 2013. *Density.* New Focus Recordings FCR135, compact disc.

Chase, Claire, flutist. 2020. *Density 2036 (2016–2017).* Corbett vs. Dempsey CvsD CD076, 2 compact discs.

Chase, Claire, flutist. 2023. *Density 2036 (2019, 2020, 2021).* New Focus Recording FCR353, 3 compact discs.

Chung, Kyung-Wha, violinist. 1998. *Franck, Debussy: Violin Sonatas; Chausson: Poème.* Radu Lupu, pianist. Decca 460 006-2, compact disc.

Chung, Lucille, pianist. 2022. *Alexander Scriabin: Piano Works*. Dynamic CDS 416, compact disc.

Cortot, Alfred, pianist. 1929. *Alfred Cortot: The Master Pianist*. Jacques Thibaud, violinist. EMI 2173042, 2008, 7 compact discs.

Davis, Colin, conductor. 2003. *Dvořák: Symphony No. 7*. London Symphony Orchestra. LSO Live LSO0014, compact disc.

Davis, Colin, conductor. 2004. *Sibelius: Symphonies Nos. 3 and 7*. London Symphony Orchestra. LSO Live LSO0051, compact disc.

Dylan, Bob. 2018. *More Blood, More Tracks: The Bootleg Series, Vol. 14*. Columbia/Legacy 19075858982, compact disc.

Friedheim, Arthur, pianist. 1918. *The Complete Recordings*. Pearl GEMM CD 9993, 1993, compact disc.

Goode, Richard, pianist. 1991. *Beethoven: The Op. 10 Piano Sonatas*. Electra Nonesuch 9 792130-2, compact disc.

Goode, Richard, pianist. 2018. "Masterclass with Richard Goode." Directed by Marcos Pereiro. Recorded on July 26, 2018. Medici.tv. Accessed on March 11, 2021. https://www.medici.tv/en/masterclasses/master-class-richard-goode/.

Gould, Glenn, pianist. 1965. *Glenn Gould Plays Beethoven Piano Sonatas: Opus 10 Complete*. Columbia Masterworks ML 6086, 33⅓ rpm.

Gould, Glenn, pianist. 1965. *Glenn Gould Plays Schoenberg: The Glenn Gould Collection Volume 16*. Sony Classical 88725413642-01, 2012, compact disc.

Gould, Glenn, pianist. 1968. *Arnold Schoenberg: Oeuvre pour piano*. CBS 75675, 33⅓ rpm.

Granados, Enrique, pianist. 1912. *Composers in Person: Manuel de Falla, Enrique Granados, Federico Mompou, Joaquín Nin*. EMI Classics 0777 7 54836 2 8, 1993, compact disc.

Grimaud, Hélène, pianist. 1999. *Hélène Grimaud: The Warner Recordings*. Erato/Warner Classics as 0825646227372, 2014, 6 compact discs.

Guarneri Quartet. 1993. *Schubert: String Quintet in C, D. 956*. Bernard Greenhouse, cellist. Philips Digital Classics 432 108-2, compact disc.

Guarneri Quartet. 1996. *Arriaga: The String Quartets*. Philips 446 092-2, compact disc.

Hagen Quartett. 2004. *Mozart: String Quartets K. 499, 589, 590*. Deutsche Grammophon B0003454-02, compact disc.

Harlem Quartet. 2020. *Cross Pollination*. Harlem Quartet Recordings, compact disc.

Hartzell, Valerie, guitarist. 2011. *Ex Tenebris Lux*. Soundset Recordings SR 1036, compact disc.

Heap, Imogen, 2005. *Speak for Yourself*. RCA Victor 82876 72532-2 RE-1, compact disc.

Hewitt, Anthony, pianist. 2016. *Alexander Scriabin: Complete Piano Preludes*. Champs Hill Records, CHRCD072, 2 compact discs.

Jansen, Janine, violinist. 2002. *24 Capriccios for Violin from the Netherlands*. NM Classics NM 92120, 2002, 2 compact discs.

Jansen, Janine, violinist. 2010. *Beau Soir*. Itamar Golan, pianist. Decca 478 2256, compact disc.

Kameníková, Valentina, pianist. 1991. *Chopin: Ballades and Impromptus*. Supraphon 11 1009-2, compact disc.

Kashkashian, Kim, violist. 2018. *J. S. Bach: Six Suites for Viola Solo*. ECM New Series ECM 2553/54, 2 compact discs.

Keller String Quartet. 1994. *Debussy and Ravel: String Quartets*. Erato 4509-96361-2, compact disc.

Kissin, Evgeny, pianist. 1997. *Piano Works by Liszt and Schumann*. Revelation Records RV10031, compact disc.

Kissin, Evgeny, pianist. 2004. *Schubert: Piano Sonata in B-flat, Op. posth.; Schubert-Liszt: Four Songs; Liszt: Mephisto Waltz No. 1*. RCA Red Seal 82876-58420-2, compact disc.

Krushelnytska, Anna, soprano. 1904. *The First Opera Recordings: 1895–1902, A Survey*. Symposium 1320, 2003, compact disc.

Kuijken, Sigiswald, violinist. 2000. *Claude Debussy: La musique de chambre*. Piet Kuijken, pianist. Arcana A 303, compact disc.

Lehmann, Lotte, soprano. 1928. *Schumann: Legendary Song Cycle Recordings*. Frieder Weissmann, conductor. Pearl GEMM CD 9119, 1994, compact disc.

Lupu, Radu, pianist. 1971. *Brahms: Two Rhapsodies, Op. 79; Three Intermezzos, Op. 117; Six Piano Pieces, Op. 118; Four Piano Pieces, Op. 119*. Decca 417 599-2, 1987, compact disc.

Mengelberg, Willem, conductor. 1939. *Mengelberg as Accompanist*. Concertgebouw Orchestra of Amsterdam. Music & Arts CD 270, 1987, compact disc.

Nelsova, Zara, cellist. 1959. *Zara Nelsova: Cello Concertos, Sonatas & Suites*. Audite 21.433, 2015, 4 compact discs.

Neveu, Ginette, violinist. 1948. *Ginnette Neveu: The Complete Recordings*. Jean Neveu, pianist. Warner Classics 0190295490485, 2019, 4 compact discs.

Nézet-Séguin, Yannick, conductor. 2010. "Tchaikovsky: The Nutcracker—Rotterdams Philharmonisch Orkest—Complete Concert in HD." Rotterdam Philharmonic Orchestra. Recorded on December 23, 2010. Posted by AVROTROS Klassiek channel on January 18, 2011. Accessed on July 1, 2021. https://www.youtube.com/watch?v=tk5Uturacx8.

Ólafsson, Víkingur, pianist. 2022. *From Afar*. Deutsche Grammophon 486 1681, 2 compact discs.

Oliveros, Pauline. 2022. *Reverberations: Tape & Electronic Music: 1967–1970*. Important Records IMPREC 352, 12 compact discs.

Pahud, Emmanuel, flutist. 2018. *Solo*. Warner Classics 9029 57017-5, 2 compact discs.

Plasson, Michel, conductor. 1997. *Saint-Saëns: Symphonie No. 3 "Avec Orgue," Cyprès et Lauriers, La Foi*. Orchestre du Capitole de Toulouse. EMI Classics 7243 5 55584 2 8, 2 compact discs.

Pletnev, Mikhail, conductor. 2009. *Shostakovich: Symphony No. 15*. Russian National Orchestra. Pentatone PTC5186331, compact disc.

Quartetto Italiano. 1972. *Mozart: String Quartets, Complete Mozart Edition, Vol. 12*. Philips 422 512-2, 1991, 8 compact discs.

Quatuor Debussy. 2014. *Debussy: Quatuor et Dances*. Timpani 1C1207, compact disc.

Quatuor Mosaïques. 1996. *Joseph Haydn: Quatuors Opus 33 Nos. 5, 3, and 2*. Auvidis Astrée E 8569, compact disc.

Quatuor Végh. 1973. *Beethoven: Les Quatours 5*. Auvidis Valois V 4405, 1986, compact disc.

Ravel, Maurice, conductor. *Maurice Ravel: Orchestral Works*. Orchestre des Concerts Lamoureux. Andante AND 3990, 2002, 3 compact discs.

Sado, Yutaka, conductor. 1998. *Chabrier and Ravel: Hommage à L'Orchestre Lamoureux*. Orchestre des Concerts Lamoureux. Erato 3984-27321-2, compact disc.

Say, Fazıl, pianist. 2001. *Tchaikovsky: Piano Concerto No. 1, Liszt: Sonata in B Minor.* St. Petersburg Philharmonic Orchestra. Yuri Temirkanov, conductor. Teldec Classics 8573 87009-2, compact disc.

Say, Fazıl, pianist. 2020. *Beethoven: Complete Piano Sonatas.* Warner Classics 0190295380243, 9 compact discs.

Sempé, Skip, harpsichordist. 1995. *Henry Purcell: Airs and Instrumental Music.* Capriccio Stravagante, Deutsche Harmonia Mundi 05472 77419 2, compact disc.

Simpson, Icy, soprano. 2012. *I, Too.* Artina McCain, pianist. Longhorn Music LHM2012001, compact disc.

Sinopoli, Giuseppe, conductor. 1992. *Richard Strauss: Ein Heldenleben, Don Juan.* Staatskapelle Dresden. Deutsche Grammophon 435 790-2, compact disc.

Slenczynska, Ruth, pianist. 1960. *Chopin: Four Ballades; Liszt: Six Chants Polonaises.* Decca DL 710029, 33⅓ rpm.

Slenczynska, Ruth, pianist. 2020. *Ruth Slenczynska: The Complete American Decca Recordings.* Deutsche Grammophon 484 1302, 10 compact discs.

Solange. 2019. *When I Get Home.* Columbia/Saint Records 19075944041, 33⅓ rpm.

Solti, Georg, conductor. 1961. *Mahler: Symphony No. 4.* Concertgebouw Orchestra. Sylvia Stahlman, soprano. London 417 745-2, 1988, compact disc.

Solti, Georg, conductor. 1984. *Mahler: Symphony No. 4.* Chicago Symphony Orchestra. Kiri Te Kanawa, soprano. Decca 410 188-2, compact disc.

Toscanini, Arturo, conductor. 1939. *Toscanini: Beethoven, Mozart, and Cherubini.* BBC Symphony Orchestra. BBC Legends BBCL 4016-2, 1999, 2 compact discs.

Tysman, Hélène, pianist. 2013. *Chopin, Vol. 2: Ballades.* Oehms Classics OC 894, 2 compact discs.

Uchida, Mitsuko, pianist. 1984. *Mozart: Two Sonatas: KV 331, KV 332; Fantasie KV 397.* Philips 412 123-2PH, compact disc.

Valdettaro, Giambattista, cellist. 2014. *Cello Solo: Zoltán Kodály, Bernhard Cossmann, Luigi Dallapiccola.* Velut Luna CVLD250, compact disc.

Vaughan, Sarah, vocalist. 1961. *After Hours.* Roulette Jazz CDP 7243 8 55468 2 2, 1996, compact disc.

Vega, Suzanne. 1987. *Solitude Standing.* A&M Records CD 5136, compact disc.

Waley-Cohen, Tamsin, violinist. 2014. *1917: Works for Violin and Piano.* Huw Watkins, pianist. Signum Records SIGCD376, compact disc.

Walker, George, pianist. 1997. *George Walker Plays Bach, Schumann, Chopin, and Poulenc.* Albany Records TROY 252, compact disc.

Walker, George, pianist. 2001. *American Virtuoso: George Walker Plays Haydn, Mozart, Schubert, Chopin, Debussy, and Liszt.* Albany Records TROY 411, compact disc.

Walker, George, pianist. 2005. *George Walker: Composer, Pianist.* Albany Records TROY 697, 2005, compact disc.

Walter, Bruno, conductor. 1962. *Mahler: Symphony No. 9, Rehearsal and Performance.* Columbia Symphony Orchestra. Sony Classical SM2K 64 452, 1994, 2 compact discs.

Wand, Gunter, conductor. 1996. *Gunter Wand Conducts Beethoven.* NDR Sinfonieorchester. With Edith Wiens, Hildegard Hartwig, Keith Lewis, and Roland Hermann. RCA Red Seal 19075818872, 2018, 5 compact discs.

Wispelwey, Pieter, cellist. 1998. *Johann Sebastian Bach: 6 Suites per violoncello solo senza basso.* Channel Classics CCS 12298, 2 compact discs.

Yepes, Narciso, guitarist. 1983. *Francisco Tárrega: Recuerdos de la Alhambra, Lágrima, Danza Mora, Adelita, Pavana, Jota.* Deutsche Grammophon 410 655-2, 1987, compact disc.

Zee, Zee, pianist. 2021. *Franz Liszt: Sonata in B minor Plus Other Piano Works.* The BBC Music Magazine Collection, BBCMM467, compact disc.

Zimerman, Krystian, pianist. 1988. *Chopin: 4 Balladen, Barcarolle, Fantasie.* Deutsche Grammophon 423 090-2, compact disc.

Works Cited

Abbate, Carolyn. 2004. "Music: Drastic or Gnostic?" *Critical Inquiry* 30 (3): 505–36.

Achenbach, Andrew. 2003. "Dvořák's Symphonic Masterpiece Catches Davis and His Band on Expansive, Eloquent Form." Review of Sir Colin Davis, *Dvořák: Symphony No. 7*, London Symphony Orchestra, LSO Live LSO0014, *Gramophone*, June 2003.

Agawu, V. Kofi. 1984. "Structural 'Highpoints' in Schumann's Dichterliebe." *Music Analysis* 3 (2): 159–80.

Ahmed, Sara. 2000. "Whose Counting?" *Feminist Theory* 1: 97–103.

Ahmed, Sara. 2012. *On Being Included: Racism and Diversity in Institutional Life*. Durham, NC: Duke University Press.

Albaret, Céleste. 1973. *Monsieur Proust: Souvenirs recueillis par Georges Belmont*. Paris: Éditions Robert Laffont.

Albaret, Céleste. 2003. *Monsieur Proust*. Translated by Barbara Bray. New York: New York Review of Books.

Altman, Rick. 1992. *Sound Theory, Sound Practice*. London: Routledge.

Angus, James, and David Howard. 2013. *Acoustics and Psychoacoustics*. London: Taylor & Francis.

Arensky, Anton. 1893. *Essais sur les rythmes oubliés*. Moscow: P. Jurgenson.

Arensky, Anton. 2005. *Selected Works for Piano*. Edited by V. Samarin. Moscow: P. Jurgenson.

Arensky, Anton. 2012. *Près de la mer and Other Collected Suites for Piano*. Selected and edited by Sara Davis Buechner. Mineola, NY: Dover Publications.

Ashby, Arved. 2010. *Absolute Music, Mechanical Reproduction*. Berkeley: University of California Press.

Attali, Jacques. 1985. *Noise*. Minneapolis: University of Minnesota Press.

Auner, Joseph. 2000. "Making Old Machines Speak: Images of Technology in Recent Music." *Echo: A Music-Centered Journal* 2 (2).

Bach, Johann Sebastian. 1984. *Six Suites for Violoncello Solo, BWV 1007–1012*. Edited by Egon Voss. München: G. Henle Verlag.

Badura-Skoda, Paul. 2012. "Should We Play A-natural or A-sharp in Beethoven's 'Hammerklavier' Sonata, Opus 106?" *Notes* 68 (4): 751–57.

Bain, Kimberly. 2017. "Lose Your Breath: A Theory and Praxis of Black Breath." Paper presented at the Princeton Department of African American Studies Graduate Conference, Princeton University, April 21, 2017.

Bain, Kimberly. 2020. "On Black Breath: A Theory and Praxis." PhD diss., Princeton University.

Bakker, Nienke, and Nicole R. Myers, eds. 2021. *Van Gogh and the Olive Groves*. New Haven, CT: Yale University Press.

Barrière, Jean-Baptiste. 1740. *Sonates pour le Pardessus de Viole avec la Basse Continue*. Paris: Leclerc.

Barth, George. 1992. *The Pianist as Orator: Beethoven and the Transformation of Keyboard Style*. Ithaca, NY: Cornell University Press.

Barthes, Roland. 1973. *Le plaisir du texte*. Paris: Seuil.

Barthes, Roland. 1975. *The Pleasure of the Text*. Translated by Richard Miller. New York: Hill and Wang.

Barthes, Roland. 1977. "The Grain of the Voice." In *Image-Music-Text*, edited and translated by Stephen Heath, 179–89. London: Fontana.

Barthes, Roland. 1980. *La chambre claire: Note sur la photographie*. Paris: Gallimard Seuil.

Barthes, Roland. 1981. *Camera Lucida: Reflections on Photography*. Translated by Richard Howard. New York: Hill and Wang.

Bartók, Béla. 1921. "Della musica moderna in Ungheria." *Il Pianoforte* II (7): 193–97.

Bartók, Béla. 1976. *Essays*. Lincoln: University of Nebraska Press.

Bascom, William. 1955. "Verbal Art." *Journal of American Folklore* 68 (269): 245–52.

Bazzana, Kevin. 2004. *Wondrous Strange: The Life and Art of Glenn Gould*. New York: Oxford University Press.

Beaudoin, Richard. 2021. "Gould's Creaking Chair, Schoenberg's Metric Clarity." *Music Theory Online* 27 (1).

Beaudoin, Richard. 2022. "Dashon Burton's Song Sermon: Corporeal Liveness and the Solemnizing Breath." *Journal of the Society for American Music* 16 (1): 1–23.

Beaudoin, Richard. 2023. "Micro-temporal Measurements of Two Early Debussy Recordings as the Foundation for New Music." In *Early Sound Recordings: Academic Research and Practice*, edited by Eva Moreda Rodriguez and Inja Stanović, 118–36. London: Routledge.

Beethoven, Ludwig van. 1980a. *Klaviersonaten, Band I*. Edited by Bertha Antonia Wallner. München: G. Henle Verlag.

Beethoven, Ludwig van. 1980b. *Klaviersonaten, Band II*. Edited by Bertha Antonia Wallner. München: G. Henle Verlag.

Benjamin, Walter. 2003. "Paralipomena to 'On the Concept of History.'" In *Walter Benjamin: Selected Writings*, Vol. 4: *1938–1940*, edited by Howard Eiland and Michael W. Jennings, 401–11. Cambridge, MA: Harvard University Press.

Benko, Gregor. 1977. Liner notes. *Landmarks of Recorded Pianism*, Vol. 1: *Acoustic Recordings 1889–1924*. Desmar IPA 117.

Bent, Margaret. 1983. "*Resfacta* and *Cantare Super Librum*." *Journal of the American Musicological Society* 36 (3): 371–91.

Berger, Jonathan, and Charles Nichols. 1994. "Brahms at the Piano: An Analysis of the Data from the Brahms Cylinder." *Leonardo Music Journal* 4: 23–30.

Bernstein, Charles. 2009. "Hearing Voices." In *The Sound of Poetry. The Poetry of Sound*, edited by Marjorie Perloff and Craig Dworkin, 142–48. Chicago: University of Chicago Press.

Bevan, Clifford. 1997. "The Low Brass." In *The Cambridge Companion to Brass Instruments*, edited by Trevor Herbert and John Wallace, 143–56. Cambridge: Cambridge University Press.

Bijsterveld, Karin. 2008. *Mechanical Sound: Technology, Culture, and Public Problems of Noise in the Twentieth Century*. Cambridge, MA: MIT Press.

Blaukopf, Kurt. 1979. "The Sociography of Musical Life in Industrialised Countries—A Research Task." *The World of Music* 21 (3): 78–86.

Blum, David. 1980. *Casals and the Art of Interpretation*. Berkeley: University of California Press.

Blyth, Alan. 1991. "Mozart: *Don Giovanni*." Review of Fritz Busch, *Don Giovanni*, Glyndebourne Festival Orchestra, Pearl GEMM CDS 9369, *Gramophone*, March 1991.

Böckenhoff, Ludger. 2015. Liner notes. *Cello Concertos, Sonatas & Suites*. Zara Nelsova, cello. Audite 21.433.

Bonds, Margaret. 1959. *Three Dream Portraits*. Milan: G. Ricordi & Co.

Borish, Martin L. 1976. Liner notes. *Acoustic Research Demonstration Record*, Vol. 1: *The Sound of Musical Instruments*. Madrid: Discos Ensayo.

Bregman, Albert S. 1990. *Auditory Scene Analysis*. Cambridge, MA: MIT Press.

Bregman, Albert S. 2015. "Progress in Understanding Auditory Scene Analysis." *Music Perception: An Interdisciplinary Journal* 33 (1): 12–19.

Broesche, Garreth. 2015. "The Intimacy of Distance: Glenn Gould and the Poetics of the Recording Studio." PhD diss., University of Wisconsin–Madison.

Brooks, Christopher A., and Robert Sims. 2014. *Roland Hayes: The Legacy of an American Tenor*. Bloomington: Indiana University Press.

Brooks, Tom. 2004. *Lost Sounds: Blacks and the Birth of the Recording Industry, 1890–1919*. Champaign: University of Illinois Press.

Brøvig-Hanssen, Ragnhild, and Anne Danielsen. 2016. *Digital Signatures: The Impact of Digitization on Popular Music Sound*. Cambridge, MA: MIT Press.

Brower, Candace. 1997. "Pathway, Blockage, and Containment in 'Density 21.5.'" *Theory and Practice* 22/23: 35–54.

Bruhn, Siglind. 2000. *Musical Ekphrasis: Composers Responding to Poetry and Painting*. Hillsdale, NY: Pendragon Press.

Bush, Andrew. 2019. "Introduction." In *Breath Sounds: From Basic Science to Clinical Practice*, edited by Kostas N. Priftis, Leontios J. Hadjileontiadis, and Mark L. Everard, 1–14. Cham, Switzerland: Springer International.

Camille, Michael. 1992. *Image on the Edge: The Margins of Medieval Art*. Cambridge, MA: Harvard University Press.

Camp, Marc-Antoine, Lorenz Kilchenmann, Thomas Volken, and Olivier Senn. 2011. "On Measuring and Interpreting Microtiming." In *Five Perspectives on Body and Soul: And Other Contributions to Music Performance Studies*, edited by Claudia Emmenegger and Olivier Senn, 95–110. Zurich: Chronos Verlag.

Cheng, William. 2020. *Loving Music Till It Hurts*. New York: Oxford University Press.

Chesky, Jane. 1941. "Indian Music of the Southwest." *Kiva* 7 (3): 9–12.

Chion, Michel. 2016. *Sound: An Acoulogical Treatise*. Translated by James A. Steintrager. Durham, NC: Duke University Press.

Chissell, Joan. 1984. "Mozart Piano Works." Review of Mitsuko Uchida, *Mozart: Two Sonatas: KV 331, KV 332; Fantasie KV 397*, Philips 412 123-2PH, *Gramophone*, September 1984.

Chissell, Joan. 1994. "Beethoven Chamber Works." Review of Pablo Casals, *Ludwig van Beethoven: Piano Trios and Cello Sonatas*, Philips 438 520–2PM3, *Gramophone*, March 1994.

Chopin, Fryderyk. 1983. *Etüden*. Edited by Ewald Zimmermann. München: G. Henle Verlag.

Clark, Philip. 2009. "An Over-Literal Approach to the Fifteenth That Leaves You Asking 'Why?'" Review of Mikhail Pletnev, *Shostakovich: Symphony No. 15. Russian National Orchestra*, Pentatone PTC5186331, *Gramophone* Awards Issue, 2009.

Clark, Suzannah. 2019. "Patterns of Exclusion in Schenkerian Theory and Analysis." *Journal of Schenkerian Studies* 12: 141–52.

Clark, T. J. 2022. "Painting and Poetry: What Is the Burglar After?" *London Review of Books* 44 (19): 29–32.

Clark, Walter Aaron. 2006. *Enrique Granados: Poet of the Piano*. New York: Oxford University Press.

CNN.com. 2005. "Ruthless Sharapova Cruises Through." January 21, 2005. Accessed July 13, 2022. http://www.cnn.com/2005/SPORT/01/21/tennis.women/index.html.

Cohn, Richard. 2012. *Audacious Euphony: Chromaticism and the Triad's Second Nature*. New York: Oxford University Press.

Common. 2016. "Common: Black America Again ft. Stevie Wonder." Uploaded on November 4, 2016. YouTube video, 21:49 min. https://www.youtube.com/watch?v=WMNyCNdgayE.

Cook, Nicholas. 2001. "Theorizing Musical Meaning." *Music Theory Spectrum* 23 (2): 170–95.

Cook, Nicholas. 2009. "Changing the Musical Object: Approaches to Performance Analysis." In *Music's Intellectual History*, edited by Zdravko Blažeković, 775–90. New York: RILM.

Cook, Nicholas. 2013. *Beyond the Score: Music as Performance*. Oxford: Oxford University Press.

Corbett, John, and Terri Kapsalis. 1996. "Aural Sex: The Female Orgasm in Popular Sound." *Drama Review* 40 (3): 102–11.

Corredor, J. Ma. 1958. *Conversations with Casals*. Translated by André Mangeot. New York: E. P. Dutton & Co., Inc.

Cowan, Robert. 1994. "Sony Classical Casals Edition." Review of *Robert Schumann: Cello Concerto, Piano Trio No. 1, 5 Stücke im Volkston*, Pablo Casals Edition, Sony Classical SMK 58993, *Gramophone*, May 1994.

Cowan, Robert. 1999. "Toscanini and the BBC Symphony Orchestra in London." Review of Toscanini: *Beethoven, Mozart, and Cherubini*, BBC Legends BBCL 4016–2, *Gramophone*, December 1999.

Cypess, Rebecca. 2007. "Evidence about the *Lira da Braccio* from Two Seventeenth-Century Violin Sources." *Galpin Society Journal* 60: 147–60.

Dahlhaus, Carl. 1974. "Schoenberg and Schenker." *Proceedings of the Royal Musical Association* 100: 209–15.

Darden, Robert. 2014. *Nothing but Love in God's Water*, Vol. 1: *Black Sacred Music from the Civil War to the Civil Rights Movement*. University Park: Pennsylvania State University Press.

Davis, Audrey. 1960. "Pablo Casals at Home." *The Guardian*, July 28, 1960.

Dayme, Meribeth Bunch. 2009. *Dynamics of the Singing Voice*. Wien: Springer-Verlag.

Debussy, Claude. 2012. *String Quartet*. Edited by Ulrich Krämer. München: G. Henle Verlag.

De Lerma, Dominique-René, Doreene McKenzie, and Leroy Vlaun. 1984. "A Concordance of Scores and Recordings of Music by Black Composers." *Black Music Research Journal* 4: 60–140.

Denk, Jeremy. 2012. "The Pure and the Impure." Review of *Reinventing Bach*, by Paul Elie, *The New Republic*, December 6, 2012.

De Souza, Jonathan. 2017. *Music at Hand: Instruments, Bodies, and Cognition*. New York: Oxford University Press.

Dett, R. Nathaniel. 1913. *In the Bottoms: Characteristic Suite for the Piano*. Chicago: Clayton F. Summy Co.

Dewey, John. 1908. "Does Reality Possess Practical Character?" In *Essays, Philosophical and Psychological, in Honor of William James, Professor in Harvard University, by His Colleagues at Columbia University*. New York: Longmans, Green, and Co.

Dickinson, Emily. 1999. *The Poems of Emily Dickinson: Reading Edition*. Edited by R. W. Franklin. Cambridge, MA: Belknap Press of Harvard University Press.

Dingle, Christopher. 2000. Liner notes. *Stravinsky: Piano Music*. Peter Hill, piano. Naxos 8.553871.

Distler, Jed. n.d. "Fazıl Say: Tchaikovsky 1, Liszt Sonata." Review of Fazıl Say, *Tchaikovsky: Piano Concerto No.1, Liszt: Sonata in B Minor*, Teldec Classics 8573 87009-2, Classicstoday.com. Accessed July 13, 2022. https://www.classicstoday.com/review/review-7074/.

Distler, Jed. 2020. "Beethoven through Say's Eyes." Review of Fazıl Say, *Beethoven: Complete Piano Sonatas*, Warner Classics 0190295380243, *Gramophone*, March 2020.

Donizetti, Gaetano. 1906. *Una furtiva lagrima (Romanza from "L'Elisir d'amore")*. New York: G. Schirmer.

Drott, Eric. 2010. "Fraudulence and the Gift Economy of Music." *Journal of Music Theory* 54 (1): 61–74.

Dunsby, Jonathan. 2009. "Roland Barthes and the Grain of Panzéra's Voice." *Journal of the Royal Musical Association* 134 (1): 113–32.

Eargle, John M. 1983. "Chopin: Fourteen Waltzes." Review of *Claudio Arrau, Chopin: Fourteen Waltzes*, Philips 400 025 2, *Audio* 67 (8), August 1983.

Ebert, Alan. 1980. *Intimacies: Stars Share Their Confidences and Feelings*. New York: Dell Publishing.

Edel, Leon. 1984. "Walter Berry and the Novelists: Proust, James, and Edith Wharton." *Nineteenth-Century Fiction* 38 (4): 514–28.

Eidsheim, Nina Sun. 2019. *The Race of Sound: Listening, Timbre & Vocality in African American Music*. Durham, NC: Duke University Press.

Ekman, Paul. 2003. *Emotions Revealed*. New York: Henry Holt.

Ekman, Paul. 2009. "Darwin's Contributions to Our Understanding of Emotional Expressions." *Philosophical Transactions: Biological Sciences* 364 (1535): 3449–51.

Elkan, Sophie. 2022. "Review: The Ivy Brasserie." *Ox Magazine*, May 2, 2022.

Ernst, Wolfgang. 2016. *Sonic Time Machines: Explicit Sound, Sirenic Voices, and Implicit Sonicity*. Amsterdam: Amsterdam University Press.

Ewell, Philip. 2020. "Music Theory and the White Racial Frame." *Music Theory Online* 26 (2).

Fanning, David. 2018. "Messiaen: *Catalogue d'oiseaux* (Aimard)." Review of Pierre-Laurent Aimard, *Catalogue d'oiseaux*, Pentatone PTC5186 670, *Gramophone* Awards Shortlist Edition, July 2018.

Farnsworth, Ward. 2011. *Farnsworth's Classical English Rhetoric*. Boston: David R. Godine.

Fava, Maria Cristina. 2003. Liner Notes. *Music for Velvet*. Velvet Brown, tuba. Crystal Records CD693.

Feste. 1923. "Ad libitum." *Musical Times* 64 (969): 764–68.

Field, Allyson Nadia. 2015. *Uplift Cinema: The Emergence of African American Film and the Possibility of Black Modernity*. Durham, NC: Duke University Press.

Fine, Elaine. 2003. "Casals Festival at Prades." Review of *Casals: Festival at Prades*, Music & Arts 1113, *American Record Guide* 66 (3), May/June 2003.

Fischer, William Arms. 1926. *Seventy Negro Spirituals*. Boston: Oliver Ditson & Co.

Fish, Stanley. 1980. *Is There a Text in This Class?: The Authority of Interpretive Communities*. Cambridge, MA: Harvard University Press.

Fisk, Charles. 2001. *Returning Cycles: Contexts for the Interpretation of Schubert's Impromptus and Last Sonatas*. Berkeley: University of California Press.

Floros, Constantin. 1993. *Gustav Mahler: The Symphonies*. Translated by Vernon Wicker and Jutta Wicker. Portland, OR: Amadeus Press.

Fludd, Robert. 1617. *Utriusque cosmi maioris scilicet et minoris metaphysica, physica atque technica historia in duo volumina secundum cosmi differentiam diuisa*. Oppenheim: Aere Johann-Theodori de Bry, typis Hieronymi Galleri.

Fouzas, Sotirios, Michael B. Anthracopoulos, and Abraham Bohadana. 2019. "Clinical Usefulness of Breath Sounds." In *Breath Sounds: From Basic Science to Clinical Practice*, edited by Kostas N. Priftis, Leontios J. Hadjileontiadis, and Mark L. Everard, 33–52. Cham, Switzerland: Springer International.

François, Jean-Charles. 1992. "Writing without Representation, and Unreadable Notation." *Perspectives of New Music* 30 (1): 6–20.

Frost, Thomas. 1965. Liner notes. *Glenn Gould Plays Beethoven Sonatas, Opus 10 Complete*. Glenn Gould, piano. Columbia Masterworks MS 6686.

Gannon, Frank. 1997. "The Nine Habits of Highly Effective Proustians." *New York Times*, June 15, 1997.

Gee, James Paul. 1999. *An Introduction to Discourse Analysis: Theory and Method*. London: Routledge.

Gelatt, Roland. 1977. *The Fabulous Phonograph: 1877–1977*. 2nd rev. ed. London: Cassell.

Gerson-Kiwi, Edith. 1953. "Exact Transcription of Tone-Relations." *Acta Musicologica* 25 (1/3): 80–87.

Giombini, Lisa. 2020. "The Challenge of Authenticity. Music, Plagiarism, and the Digital Age." *De Musica* 24 (2): 106–35.

Goebl, Werner. 2001. "Melody Lead in Piano Performance—Expressive Device or Artifact?" *Journal of the Acoustical Society of America* 110: 563–72.

Goehr, Lydia. 2010. "How to Do More with Words: Two Views of (Musical) Ekphrasis." *British Journal of Aesthetics* 50 (4): 389–410.

Gomez, Alice. 2013. *Bonampak for Tuba and Piano*. Anniston, AL: Potenza Music Publishing.

Gooley, Dana A. 2004. *The Virtuoso Liszt*. New York: Cambridge University Press.

Gould, Glenn, and Tim Page. 1984. *The Glenn Gould Reader*. New York: Alfred A. Knopf.

Gracyk, Theodore. 1996. *Rhythm and Noise: An Aesthetics of Rock*. Durham, NC: Duke University Press.

Gracyk, Theodore. 1997. "Listening to Music: Performances and Recordings." *Journal of Aesthetics and Art Criticism* 55(2): 139–50.

Grainger, Percy. 1915. "The Impress of Personality in Unwritten Music." *Musical Quarterly* 1 (3): 416–35.

Granados, Enrique. 1915. *El Pelele: Goyesca*. New York: G. Schirmer.

Grimley, Daniel M. 2019. "Form." In *The Oxford Handbook of Critical Concepts in Music Theory*, edited by Alexander Rehding and Steven Rings, 346–68. New York: Oxford University Press.

Guck, Marion. 1984. "A Flow of Energy: *Density 21.5*." *Perspectives of New Music* 32: 334–47.

Guck, Marion. 1997. "Music Loving, or the Relationship with the Piece." *Journal of Musicology* 15 (3): 343–52.

Gutman, David. 1992. "Richard Strauss: Tone Poems." Review of Guiseppe Sinopoli, *Richard Strauss: Ein Heldenleben, Don Juan,* Staatskapelle Dresden, Deutsche Grammophon 435 790-2, *Gramophone,* November 1992.

Haggard, Ernest, and Kenneth Isaacs. 1966. "Micro-Momentary Facial Expressions as Indicators of Ego Mechanisms in Psychotherapy." In *Methods of Research in Psychotherapy,* edited by Lewis Gottschalk and Arthur Auerbach, 154–65. New York: Appleton-Century-Crofts.

Hagood, Mack. 2011. "Quiet Comfort: Noise, Otherness, and the Mobile Production of Personal Space." *American Quarterly* 63 (3): 573–89.

Haigh, Caroline, John Dunkerly, and Mark Rogers. 2021. *Classical Recording: A Practical Guide in the Decca Tradition.* London: Routledge.

Hainge, Greg. 2013. *Noise Matters: Towards an Ontology of Noise.* New York: Bloomsbury.

Hamilton, Kenneth. 1996. *Liszt: Sonata in B minor.* Cambridge: Cambridge University Press.

Harris, Stephanie. 2006. "Exposures: Rilke, Photography, and the City." *New German Critique* 99: 121–49.

Hast, Dorothea E., James R. Cowdery, and Stanley A. Scott. 1997. *Exploring the World of Music.* Dubuque, IA: Kendall Hunt.

Haydn, Joseph. 2009. *Streichquartette, Opus 33.* Edited by Georg Feder and Sonja Gerlach. München: G. Henle Verlag.

Hayes, Roland. 1948. *My Songs: Aframerican Religious Folk Songs Arranged and Interpreted.* Boston: Little, Brown & Co.

Headington, Christopher. 1992. "Mozart: Piano Works." Review of Claudio Arrau, *Wolfgang Amadeus Mozart,* Philips Arrau Edition 432 306-2PM7, *Gramophone,* March 1992.

Hegarty, Paul. 2007. *Noise/Music: A History.* Cambridge, MA: MIT Press.

Hiebert, Elfrieda. 2013. "Listening to the Piano Pedal: Acoustics and Pedagogy in Late Nineteenth-Century Contexts." *Osiris* 28 (1): 232–53.

Heller, Eric J. 2013. *Why Do You Hear What You Hear: An Experiential Approach to Sound, Music, and Psychoacoustics.* Princeton, NJ: Princeton University Press.

Hemans, Felicia. 1836. *The Poetical Works of Mrs. Felicia Hemans: Complete in One Volume.* Philadelphia: Thomas T. Ash.

Henehan, Donal. 1986. "Ligeti in 'Horizons' Opening." *New York Times,* May 22, 1986.

Hilewicz, Orit. 2018. "Reciprocal Interpretations of Music and Painting: Representation Types in Schuller, Tan, and Davies after Paul Klee." *Music Theory Online* 24 (3).

Hisama, Ellie M. 2021. "Getting to Count." *Music Theory Spectrum* 43 (2): 349–63.

Holland, Bernard. 2007. "The Continuing Cult of Glenn Gould, Deserved or Not." *New York Times,* November 24, 2007.

Holloway, Robin. 1993. "Sugar and Spice: Robin Holloway Celebrates the Tchaikovsky Centenary." *Musical Times* 134 (1809): 620–23.

Horn, Geoffrey. 1985. "Beethoven: Symphony No. 3, etc." Review of Leonard Bernstein, *Ludwig van Beethoven: Symphonie No. 3 "Eroica" and "Egmont" Overture,* Wiener Philharmoniker, Deutsche Grammophon 413 778-2, *Gramophone,* April 1985.

Isbin, Sharon. 1999. *The Classical Guitar Answer Book.* San Anselmo, CA: String Letter Publishing.

Iverson, Jennifer. 2015. "Mechanized Bodies: Technology and Supplements in Björk's Electronica." In *The Oxford Handbook of Music and Disability Studies,* edited by Blake

Howe, Stephanie Jensen-Moulton, Neil William Lerner, and Joseph N. Straus, 155–75. New York: Oxford University Press.

Ivey, Donald. 1982. "Willis Patterson's 'Anthology of Art Songs by Black American Composers.'" *Black Music Research Journal* 1981–1982 (2): 106–26.

iZotope. n.d. "RX 7 Features." *iZotope.com*. Accessed January 15, 2020. https://www.izot ope.com/en/products/rx/features.html.

Jackson, H. J. 2001. *Marginalia: Readers Writing in Books*. New Haven, CT: Yale University Press.

James, William. 1907. *Pragmatism, A New Name for Some Old Ways of Thinking*. New York: Longmans, Green, & Co.

Jameson, Michael. 1992. "Britten: Cello Suites." Review of *Benjamin Britten: Three Suites for Cello Solo*, Globe GLO 5074, *Gramophone*, August 1992.

Janczewska-Sołomko, Katarzyna, and Michał Pieńkowski. 2021. *Dyskopedia poloników do roku 1918: Suplement*. Warszawa: Wydawnictwo Naukowe i Edukacyjne.

Johnson, James Weldon, and J. Rosamond Johnson. 1925. *The Book of American Negro Spirituals*. New York: Viking Press.

Jones, Alisha Lola. 2020. *Flaming? The Peculiar Theopolitics of Fire and Desire in Black Male Gospel Performance*. Oxford: Oxford University Press.

Judkins, Jennifer. 2014. "Silence, Sound, Noise, and Music." In *The Routledge Companion to Philosophy and Music*, edited by Theodore Gracyk and Andrew Kania, 14–23. London: Routledge.

Kajikawa, Loren. 2019. "The Possessive Investment in Classical Music: Confronting Legacies of White Supremacy in U.S. Schools and Departments of Music." In *Seeing Race Again: Countering Colorblindness across the Disciplines*, edited by Kimberlé Williams Crenshaw, Luke Charles Harris, Daniel Martinez HoSang, and George Lipsitz, 155–74. Oakland: University of California Press.

Kania, Andrew. 2006. "Making Tracks: The Ontology of Rock Music." *Journal of Aesthetics and Art Criticism* 64 (4): 401–14.

Kania, Andrew. 2020. *Philosophy of Western Music: A Contemporary Introduction*. London: Routledge.

Karpeles, Maud. 1968. "The Distinction between Folk and Popular Music." *Journal of the International Folk Music Council* 20: 9–12.

Kassinger, Ruth. 1999. *U.S. Census: A Mirror for America*. Austin, TX: Raintree Steck-Vaughn Publishers.

Keiles, Jaime Lauren. 2019. "How A.S.M.R. Became a Sensation." *New York Times*, April 4, 2019. https://www.nytimes.com/2019/04/04/magazine/how-asmr-videos-became-a-sensation-youtube.html.

Kemp, Lindsay. 1992. "Purcell: Airs and Instrumental Music." Review of Skip Sempé, *Henry Purcell: Airs and Instrumental Music*, Capriccio Stravagante, Deutsche Harmonia Mundi 05472 77419 2, *Gramophone*, September 1992.

Kernodle, Tammy L. 2020. "'When and Where I Enter': Black Women Composers and the Advancement of a Black Postmodern Concert Aesthetic in Cold War–Era America." *Journal of the American Musicological Society* 73 (3): 770–78.

Kim, David Hyun-Su. 2012. "The Brahmsian Hairpin." *19th-Century Music* 36 (1): 46–57.

Kimmerer, Robin Wall. 2003. *Gathering Moss: A Natural and Cultural History of Mosses*. Corvallis: Oregon State University Press.

Kittler, Friedrich. 1999. *Gramophone, Film, Typewriter*. Stanford, CA: Stanford University Press.

Klein, Hermann. 1990. *Herman Klein and the Gramophone: Being a Series of Essays on the Bel Canto (1923), the Gramophone and the Singer (1924–1934), and Reviews of New Classical Vocal Recordings (1925–1934), and Other Writings from the Gramophone*. Portland, OR: Amadeus Press.

Kodály, Zoltán. 1921. *Sonate, Op. 8*. Wien: Universal Edition.

Kramer, Jonathan. 1988. *The Time of Music*. New York: Schirmer Books.

Kremer, Aleksandra. 2021. *The Sound of Modern Polish Poetry: Performance and Recording after World War II*. Cambridge, MA: Harvard University Press.

Kresky, Jeffrey. 1984. "A Path through 'Density.'" *Perspectives of New Music* 32: 318–33.

Kromhout, Melle. 2021. *The Logic of Filtering: How Noise Shapes the Sound of Recorded Music*. Oxford: Oxford University Press.

Laitz, Steven G. 2016. *The Complete Musician: An Integrated Approach to Theory, Analysis, and Listening*. 4th ed. New York: Oxford University Press.

Large, Duncan. 1993. "Proust on Nietzsche: The Question of Friendship." *Modern Language Review* 88 (3): 612–24.

Laskier Martin, Adrienne. 2021. *Cervantes and the Burlesque Sonnet*. Berkeley: University of California Press.

Lechleitner, Franz. 1997. Liner notes. *Historische Stimmen aus Wien*, Vol. 5: *Brahms spielt Klavier, Aufgenommen in Hause Fellinger 1889, The Re-recording of the Complete Cylinder*. Wien: Verlag der Österreichischen Akademie der Wissenschaften OEAW PHA CD 5.

Lechleitner, Gerda. 1985. "Der Brahms Zylinder—Kuriosität oder musikalisches Vermächtnis." In *Bruckner Symposion: Johannes Brahms und Anton Bruckner*, edited by Othmar Wessley, 225–35. Linz: Anton Bruckner Institut.

Ledbetter, David. 2009. *Unaccompanied Bach: Performing the Solo Works*. New Haven, CT: Yale University Press.

Lehrer, Jonah. 2007. *Proust was a Neuroscientist*. Boston: Houghton Mifflin.

Lerdahl, Fred. 2001. *Tonal Pitch Space*. New York: Oxford University Press.

Levitan, Harold L. 1978. "The Significance of Certain Dreams Reported by Psychosomatic Patients." *Psychotherapy and Psychosomatics* 30 (2): 137–49.

Lewin, David. 1986. "*Auf dem Flusse*: Image and Background in a Schubert Song." In *Schubert: Critical and Analytical Studies*, edited by Walter Frisch, 126–52. Lincoln: University of Nebraska Press.

Li, Ang. 1986. *The Butcher's Wife*. Translated by Howard Goldblatt and Ellen Yeung. San Francisco: North Point Press.

Lim, Liza. 2020. "Program Note for *Sex Magic*." Accessed July 14, 2022. https://www.dens ity2036.org/liza-lim.

Lim, Liza. 2021. *Sex Magic*. Berlin: G. Ricordi & Co.

Liszt, Franz. 1949. *Sonate en si mineur*. Edited by Alfred Cortot. Paris: Editions Salabert.

Little, Meredith, and Natalie Jenne. 2009. *Dance and the Music of J. S. Bach*. Bloomington: Indiana University Press.

Lorde, Audre. 2004. *Conversations with Audre Lorde*. Edited by Joan Wylie Hall. Jackson: University Press of Mississippi.

Lucas, Olivia. 2018. "'So Complete in Beautiful Deformity': Unexpected Beginnings and Rotated Riffs in Meshuggah's *obZen*." *Music Theory Online* 24 (3).

Luong, Vivian. 2017. "Rethinking Music Loving." *Music Theory Online* 23 (2).

Lysenko, Mykola. 1952. *Zibrannja tvoriv, Tom XI*. Kyiv: Mystectvo.

Magix Computer Products International Company. n.d. "Magix Sequoia 12." Accessed January 15, 2020. https://www.magix.com/us/music/sequoia/audio-restoration/.

Magnus, Cristyn, P. D. Magnus, and Christy Mag Uidhir. 2013. "Judging Covers." *Journal of Aesthetics and Art Criticism* 71 (4): 361–70.

Mahler, Gustav. 1963. *Symphonie Nr. 4*. Wien: Universal Edition.

Mahler, Gustav. 1969. *Symphonie Nr. 9*. Edited by Erwin Ratz. Wien: Universal Edition.

Malawey, Victoria. 2020. *A Blaze of Light in Every Word: Analyzing the Popular Singing Voice*. New York: Oxford University Press.

Malin, Yonatan. 2010. *Songs in Motion: Rhythm and Meter in the German Lied*. New York: Oxford University Press.

Maltese, John Anthony, and Gregor Benko. 2009. Liner notes. *The Dawn of Recording: The Julius Block Cylinders*. Marston 53011–2.

Marrington, Mark. 2021. *Recording the Classical Guitar*. London: Routledge.

Marston, Ward. 2000. Liner notes. *Enrico Caruso: The Complete Recordings, Volume 1*. Naxos Historical 8.110703.

Marston, Ward. 2008. Liner notes. *The Dawn of Recording: The Julius Block Cylinders*. Marston 53011-2.

Martin, Nathan John, and Steven Vande Moortelle. 2014. "Formal Functions and Retrospective Reinterpretation in the First Movement of Schubert's String Quintet." *Music Analysis* 33 (2): 130–55.

Mastromatteo, Francisco. 2015. "Kodály's Sonata Opus 8: Transformation of Hungarian Lament." *International Journal of Musicology* 1: 101–36.

Meijering, Chiel. 2013. *La vengeance d'une femme*. Rijswijk, The Netherlands: Stichting Donemus Beheer.

Melbye, Hasse. 2019. "Nomenclature." In *Breath Sounds: From Basic Science to Clinical Practice*, edited by Kostas N. Priftis, Leontios J. Hadjileontiadis, and Mark L. Everard, 75–82. Cham, Switzerland: Springer International.

Melville, Herman. 1979. *Moby-Dick; or, The Whale*. Berkeley: University of California Press.

Millard, Andre. 2005. *America on Record. A History of Recorded Sound*. 2nd ed. New York: Cambridge University Press.

Miller, Richard. 1997. "Nose or Mouth Breathing?" *Journal of Singing: The Official Journal of the National Association of Teachers of Singing* 53(3): 37–40.

Monglond, André. 1930. *Le préromantisme français*. Grenoble: B. Arthaud.

Morrison, Bryce. 1997. "Liszt/Schumann Piano Works." Review of Evgeny Kissin, *Piano Works by Liszt and Schumann*, Revelation Records RV10031, *Gramophone*, June 1997.

Morrison, Toni. 1987. *Beloved*. New York: Alfred A. Knopf.

Moseley, Roger. 2009. "Between Work and Play: Brahms as Performer of His Own Music." In *Brahms and His World*, rev. ed., edited by Walter Frisch and Kevin C. Carnes, 137–66. Princeton, NJ: Princeton University Press.

Moseley, Rowland. 2018. *The Art of Gigue: Perspectives on Genre and Formula in J. S. Bach's Compositional Practice*. Printed by the author, 2018. Revised edition of doctoral dissertation (PhD diss., Harvard University, 2014).

Moses, Paul J. 1974. *The Voice of Neurosis*. New York: Grune & Stratton.

Myers, Arnold. 1997. "Design, Technology, and Manufacture since 1800." In *The Cambridge Companion to Brass Instruments*, edited by Trevor Herbert and John Wallace, 115–30. Cambridge: Cambridge University Press.

Nainby, Keith. 2019. "Not Just Literature: Exploring the Performative Dimensions of Bob Dylan's Work." In *Polyvocal Bob Dylan*, edited by Nduka Otiono and Josh Toth, 67–83. London: Palgrave Macmillan.

Native Instruments. n.d. "Symphony Series—Brass." Accessed June 30, 2022, https://www.native-instruments.com/en/products/komplete/cinematic/symphony-series-brass/.

Nattiez, Jean-Jacques. 1982. "Varèse's *Density 21.5*: A Study in Semiological Analysis." *Music Analysis* 1: 243–340.

Neuhaus, Heinrich. 1983. *The Art of Piano Playing*. Translated by K. A. Leibovitch. London: Kahn & Averill.

Nicholas, Jeremy. 2004. "Kissin at His Mercurial Best and Laboured Worst." Review of Evgeny Kissin, *Schubert: Piano Sonata In B-flat, Op. Posth., Schubert-Liszt: Four Songs, Liszt: Mephisto Waltz No. 1*, RCA Red Seal 82876-58420-2, *Gramophone*, July 2004.

Nichols, Roger. 2000. "A Disappointing Recording—with Few Redeeming Features—of Fairly Familiar French Repertoire." Review of Yutaka Sado, *Chabrier and Ravel: Hommage à L'Orchestre Lamoureux*, Erato 3984-27321-2, *Gramophone*, August 2000.

Niles, Laurie. 2019. "Viola Masterclass with Kim Kashkashian." Violist.com. Published February 4, 2019. Accessed July 9, 2021. https://www.violinist.com/blog/laurie/20192/27639/.

O'Connell, Dennis G., Martha R. Hinman, Kevin F. Hearne, Zach S. Michael, and Sam L. Nixon. 2014. "The Effects of 'Grunting' on Serve and Forehand Velocities in Collegiate Tennis Players." *Journal of Strength and Conditioning Research* 28 (12): 3469–75.

Ohriner, Mitchell. 2019. "Expressive Timing." In *The Oxford Handbook of Critical Concepts in Music Theory*, edited by Alexander Rehding and Steven Rings, 369–94. New York: Oxford University Press.

Ólafsson, Víkingur. 2022. Liner notes. *From Afar*. Deutsche Grammophon 486 1681.

Oliver, Michael. 1985. "Shostakovich Piano Quintet; Piano Trio No 2." Review of Borodin Trio, *Shostakovich: Piano Quintet in G minor and Piano Trio No. 2 in E minor*, Chandos CHAN8342, *Gramophone*, April 1985.

Oliveros, Pauline. 1984. *Software for People: Collected Writings 1963–1980*. Kingston, NY: Pauline Oliveros Publications.

Oliveros, Pauline. 2013. *The Witness*. Kingston, NY: Deep Listening Publications.

Osborne, Richard. 1984. "Mahler: Symphony No. 4." Review of *Mahler: Symphony No. 4*. Chicago Symphony Orchestra, Georg Solti, conductor, Decca 410 188-2, *Gramophone*, August 1984.

Osborne, Richard. 2000. "Highly Unpredictable, Hélène Grimaud Plays Beethoven in a Way That Will Either Thrill or Infuriate." Review of Hélène Grimaud, *Beethoven Piano Concerto No.4; Piano Sonatas Op.109 & 110*, Teldec (Warner Classics) 3984-26869-2, *Gramophone*, February 2000.

O'Toole, Michael. 2020. *John Williams: Changing the Culture of the Classical Guitar*. London: Routledge.

Paganini-Ambord, Maria. 1994. *Reading Proust: In Search of the Wolf-Fish*. Translated by Caren Litherland with Kathryn Milun. Minneapolis: University of Minnesota Press.

Page, Denys. 1955. *Sappho and Alcaeus: An Introduction to the Study of Ancient Lesbian Poetry*. Oxford: Oxford University Press.

Palmer, Caroline. 1989. "Mapping Musical Thought to Musical Performance." *Journal of Experimental Psychology: Human Perception and Performance* 15 (12): 331–46.

Palmer, Tony. 1982. *Julian Bream: A Life on the Road*. London: MacDonald.

Parkening, Christopher, and Kathy Tyers. 2006. *Grace Like a River: An Autobiography*. Carol Stream, IL: Tyndale House Publishers.

Pasco, Allan H. 1994. "Reading the Age of Names in *A la Recherche du Temps Perdu*." *Comparative Literature* 46 (3): 267–87.

Peirce, Charles Sanders. 1998. *The Essential Pierce: Selected Philosophical Writings (1893–1913)*. Bloomington: Indiana University Press.

Peles, Stephen. 2010. "'Was Gleichzeitig Klingt': The Schoenberg-Schenker Dispute and the Incompleteness of Music Theory." *Music Theory Spectrum* 32 (2): 165–71.

Pérez Firmat, Gustavo. 1994. *Life on the Hyphen: the Cuban-American Way*. Austin: University of Texas Press.

Philip, Robert. 1992. *Early Recordings and Musical Style: Changing Tastes in Instrumental Performance*. Cambridge: Cambridge University Press.

Philip, Robert. 2004. *Performing Music in the Age of Recording*. New Haven, CT: Yale University Press.

Pirrotta, Nino. 1984. *Music and Culture in Italy from the Middle Ages to the Baroque*. Cambridge, MA: Harvard University Press.

Plack, Rebecca. 2008. "The Substance of Style: How Singing Creates Sound in Lieder Recordings 1902–1939." PhD. diss., Cornell University.

Platt, Russell. 2017. "The Recordings of Toscanini: Learning to Love the Maestro." *New Yorker*, August 11, 2017.

Poudrier, Ève, and Bruno Repp. 2013. "Can Musicians Track Two Different Beats Simultaneously?" *Music Perception: An Interdisciplinary Journal* 30 (4): 369–90.

Pressnitzer, Daniel, Clara Suied, and Shihab A. Shamma. 2011. "Auditory Scene Analysis: The Sweet Music of Ambiguity." *Frontiers in Human Neuroscience* 5: 1–11.

Proust, Marcel. 2010. *À la recherche du temps perdu*. Originally published between 1913 and 1927. Paris: Gallimard.

Putnam, Hilary. 1995. "A Reconsideration of Deweyan Democracy." In *Pragmatism, a Contemporary Reader*, edited by Russell B. Goodman. New York: Routledge.Ratliff, Ben. 2019. "We Are an Instrument." *Affidavit*. Cultural Counsel, July 30, 2019. Accessed February 12, 2022. http://www.affidavit.art/articles/we-are-an-instrument.

Rehding, Alexander. 2005. "Wax Cylinder Revolutions." *Musical Quarterly* 88 (1): 123–60.

Reid, Cornelius. 1983. *A Dictionary of Vocal Terminology: An Analysis*. New York: Joseph Patelson Music House.

Rilke, Rainer Maria. 1987. *Rilke and Benvenuta: An Intimate Correspondence*. Edited by Magda von Hattingberg. Translated by Joel Agee. New York: Fromm International.

Rilke, Rainer Maria. 2000. *Briefwechsel mit Magda von Hattingberg » Benvenuta «*. Herausgegeben von Ingeborg Schnack und Renate Scharffenberg. Frankfurt am Main: Insel Verlag.

Rings, Steven. 2011. "Riemannian Analytical Values, Paleo- and Neo-." In *The Oxford Handbook of Neo-Riemannian Theories*, edited by Edward Gollin and Alexander Rehding, 487–511. New York: Oxford University Press.

Rings, Steven. 2019. "Tonic." In *The Oxford Handbook of Critical Concepts in Music Theory*, edited by Alexander Rehding and Steven Rings, 106–35. New York: Oxford University Press.

Riva, Douglas. 1986. "Enric Granados: Composer, Performer, and Teacher." *Catalan Review* 1 (2): 101–14.

Riva, Raymond T. 1968. "Marcel Proust: An Immodest Proposal." *Criticism* 10 (3): 217–24.

Rochester, Marc. 1997. "Saint-Saëns Symphony No. 3, etc." Review of Saint-Saëns: Symphonie No. 3 "Avec Orgue," Cyprès et Lauriers, La Foi, Toulouse Capitole Orchestra, conducted by Michel Plasson, EMI Classics 7243 5 55584 2 8, Gramophone, December 1997.

Rodzinski, Artur. 1947. "'The Master Builder.'" Time 49 (February 17, 1947): 73–74 and 76–78.

Roeder, John. 1994. "Interacting Pulse Streams in Schoenberg's Atonal Polyphony." Music Theory Spectrum 16 (2): 231–49.

Romano, John. 1978. "Beckett without Angst." American Scholar 47 (1): 95–102.

Rorty, Richard. 1982. Consequences of Pragmatism. Minneapolis: University of Minnesota Press.

Sachs, Harvey. 1995. Rubinstein: A Life. New York: Grove Press.

Salter, Lionel. 1993. "Arthur Friedheim: The Complete Recordings." Review of Arthur Friedheim, Alexander Siloti, and Emil von Sauer, Complete Recordings, Pearl GEMM CD 9993, Gramophone, August 1993.

Salter, Lionel. 1996. "Arriaga String Quartets." Review of Guarneri String Quartet, Arriaga: The String Quartets, Philips 446 092-2, Gramophone, July 1996.

Sanden, Paul. 2009. "Hearing Glenn Gould's Body: Corporeal Liveness in Recorded Music." Current Musicology 88: 7–34.

Sanden, Paul. 2013. Liveness in Modern Music: Musicians, Technology, and the Perception of Performance. London: Routledge.

Sanden, Paul. 2019. "Rethinking Liveness in the Digital Age." In The Cambridge Companion to Music in Digital Culture, edited by Nicholas Cook, Monique M. Ingalls, and David Trippett, 178–92. Cambridge: Cambridge University Press.

Saraswati, Swami Niranjanananda. 1994. Prana, Pranayama, Prana Vidya. India: Bihar School of Yoga.

Schenker, Heinrich. 1906. Harmonielehre. Wien: Universal Edition.

Schmalfeldt, Janet. 2019. "Phrase." In The Oxford Handbook of Critical Concepts in Music Theory, edited by Alexander Rehding and Steven Rings, 295–345. New York: Oxford University Press.

Schmidt Horning, Susan. 2015. Chasing Sound: Technology, Culture, and the Art of Studio Recording from Edison to the LP. Baltimore: Johns Hopkins University Press.

Schoenberg, Arnold. 1922. Harmonielehre. Wien: Universal Edition.

Schoenberg, Arnold. 1983. Theory of Harmony. Translated by Roy E. Carter. Berkeley: University of California Press.

Schubert, Franz. 1953. The Complete Piano Sonatas, Volume II. Edited by Erwin Ratz. Wien: Universal Edition.

Schubert, Franz. 2006. String Quintet C major, D. 956. Edited by Egon Voss. München: G. Henle Verlag.

Schumann, Robert. 1995. Concerto for Violoncello and Orchestra in A minor, Op. 129. Edited by Joachim Draheim and Heinrich Schiff. Wiesbaden: Breitkopf & Härtel.

Schusterman, Richard. 1999. "Somaesthetics: A Disciplinary Proposal." Journal of Aesthetics and Art Criticism 57 (2): 299–313.

Scriabin, Alexander. 1968. Ausgewählte Klavierwerke (1967–1972), Volume 3. Edited by Günter Philipp. Leipzig: Edition Peters.

Senn, Olivier. 2007. "Die Analyse von Tonaufnahmen." PhD diss., University of Zürich.

Senn, Olivier. 2010. "'… mieux citron que jamais': Thelonious Monk Plays 'Body and Soul.'" In Five Perspectives on Body and Soul: And Other Contributions to Music Performance

Studies, edited by Claudia Emmenegger and Olivier Senn, 77–91. Zurich: Chronos Verlag.

Senn, Olivier, Marc-Antoine Camp, and Lorenz Kilchenmann. 2009. "Expressive Timing: Martha Argerich Plays Chopin's Prelude Op. 28/4 in E Minor." In *Proceedings of the International Symposium on Performance Science 2009*, edited by Aaron Williamon, Sharman Pretty, and Ralph Buck, 107–12. Utrecht: European Association of Conservatoires.

Senn, Olivier, Lorenz Kilchenmann, and Marc-Antoine Camp. 2012. "A Turbulent Acceleration into the Stretto: Martha Argerich Plays Chopin's Prelude op. 28/4 in E minor." *Dissonance* 120: 31–35.

Service, Tom. 2012. "Glenn Gould: A Willfully Idiotic Genius?" *The Guardian*, September 20, 2012.

Sévigné, Marie de Rabutin-Chantal, marquise de. 1811. *Letters of Madame de Sévigné to Her Daughter and Her Friends, Volume II*. London: J. Walker et al.

Sévigné, Marie de Rabutin-Chantal, marquise de. 1862. *Lettres de Madame de Sévigné de sa Famille et de ses Amis*, Tome III. Paris: Librairie de L. Hachette et Cie.

Singer, Mark. 2007. "Fantasia for Piano." *New Yorker*, September 17, 2007, 66–81.

Smith, Charlotte. 2007. "'I Did It for My Wife'—Joyce Hatto Exclusive, William Barrington-Coupe Confesses." *Gramophone*, February 26, 2007. Accessed March 16, 2022. https://www.gramophone.co.uk/features/article/i-did-it-for-my-wife-joyce-hatto-exclusive-william-barrington-coupe-confesses-february-26-2007.

Smith, Harriet. 2005. "This Superb Team Have the Full Measure of These Russian Trios." Review of Boris Berezovsky, Dmitri Mahktin, and Alexander Kniazev, *Rachmaninov and Shostakovich: Piano Trios*, Warner Classics 2564 61937-2, *Gramophone*, April 2005.

Smith, Peter H. 2016. "Schumann's A-minor Mood: Late-Style Dialectics in the First Movement of the Cello." *Journal of Music Theory* 60 (1): 51–88.

Stahl, Anita. 2021. "Somaesthetics of the Grunt: Policing Femininity in the Soundscapes of Women's Professional Tennis." In *Somaesthetics and Sport*, edited by Andrew Edgar, 142–63. Leiden: Brill.

Sterne, Jonathan. 2003. *The Audible Past: Cultural Origins of Sound Reproduction*. Durham, NC: Duke University Press.

Sterne, Jonathan. 2012. *MP3: The Meaning of a Format*. Durham, NC: Duke University Press.

Stiochita, Victor, and Anna Maria Coderch. 1999. *Goya: The Last Carnival*. London: Reaktion Books.

Stravinsky, Igor. 1975. *An Autobiography*. London: Calder & Boyars.

Strohm, Reinhard. 1992. "Unwritten and Written Music." In *Companion to Medieval and Renaissance Music*, edited by Tess Knighton and David Fallows, 228–33. Berkeley: University of California Press.

Talbot, John. 2004. "Tennyson's Alcaics: Greek and Latin Prosody and the Invention of English Meters." *Studies in Philology* 101 (2): 200–31.

Tárrega, Francisco. 1985. *Collected Guitar Works: The Early Spanish Editions*. Frankfurt am Main: Edition Chanterelle im Allegra Musikverlag.

Tchaikovsky, Pyotr Ilyich. 1982. *Casse-Noisette, Op. 71, L'arrangement soulagé pour piano par l'auteur*. Leningrad: Muzyka.

Terry, Mickey Thomas, Ingrid Monson, and George Walker. 2000. "An Interview with George Walker." *Musical Quarterly* 84 (3): 372–88.

Thompson, Marie. 2017. *Beyond Unwanted Sound: Noise, Affect, and Aesthetic Moralism*. New York: Bloomsbury.

Treitler, Leo. 1991. "Medieval Improvisation." *The World of Music* 33 (3): 66–91.

Varèse, Edgard. 1946. *Density 21.5*. Milan: Casa Ricordi.

Vernallis, Carol. 2013. *Unruly Media: YouTube, Music Video, and the New Digital Cinema*. New York: Oxford University Press.

Vickers, David. 2011. "Success and Failure in Oratorio Stagings." Review of Georg Frideric Handel, *Belshazzar*, Festival d'Aix-en-Provence, conducted by René Jacobs, Harmonia Mundi DVD HMD9909028.29, *Gramophone*, October 2011.

Volioti, Georgia. 2021. "Rethinking Classical Sound Recordings: Creativities beyond the Score." In *Remixing Music Studies: Essays in Honour of Nicholas Cook*, edited by Ananay Aguilar, Ross Cole, Matthew Pritchard, and Eric Clarke, 61–75. Oxford: Routledge.

Waldman, Katy. 2012. "Long Live the Tennis Grunt!" *Slate*, June 28, 2012. https://slate.com/human-interest/2012/06/grunting-and-tennis-why-the-case-to-ban-women-from-making-loud-noises-on-court-is-crazy.html.

Walther-Hansen, Mads. 2020. *Making Sense of Recordings: How Cognitive Processing of Recorded Sound Works*. New York: Oxford University Press.

Waves. n.d. "DeBreath Vocal Plugin." Waves.com. Accessed June 25, 2021. https://www.waves.com/plugins/debreath#removing-vocal-breaths-with-debreath.

Weingarten, Gene. 2007. "Pearls before Breakfast: Can One of the Nation's Great Musicians Cut through the Fog of D.C. Rush Hour? Let's Find Out." *Washington Post*, April 8, 2007. https://www.washingtonpost.com/lifestyle/magazine/pearls-before-breakfast-can-one-of-the-nations-great-musicians-cut-through-the-fog-of-a-dc-rush-hour-lets-find-out/2014/09/23/8a6d46da-4331-11e4-b47c-f5889e061e5f_story.html.

Wellmann, Janina. 2017. *The Form of Becoming: Embryology and the Epistemology of Rhythm, 1760–1830*. Translated by Kate Sturge. Brooklyn, NY: Zone Books.

Wen, Eric. 2016. "Schubert's *Wiegenlied*: The Andante sostenuto from the Piano Sonata in B-flat, D. 960." In *Schubert's Late Music: History, Theory, Style*, edited by Lorraine Byrne Bodley and Julian Horton, 134–48. Cambridge: Cambridge University Press.

West, Cornel. 1989. *The American Evasion of Philosophy: A Genealogy of Pragmatism*. Madison: University of Wisconsin Press.

West Marvin, Elizabeth. 1991. "The Perception of Rhythm in Non-Tonal Music: Rhythmic Contours in the Music of Edgard Varèse." *Music Theory Spectrum* 13: 61–78.

Wheelock, Gretchen. 1992. *Haydn's Ingenious Jesting with Art: Contexts of Musical Wit and Humor*. New York: Schirmer Books.

Work, John W. 1940. *American Negro Songs and Spirituals*. New York: Bonanza Books.

Zbikowski, Lawrence. 2011. "Music Theory, Music History, and Quicksand." *Music Theory Spectrum* 33 (2): 226–28.

Zöllner, Frank. 2011. *Leonardo da Vinci 1452–1519*, Vol. 1: *The Complete Paintings*. Köln: Taschen GmbH.

Zuffi, Stefano. 2019. *Leonardo in Detail*. Brussels: Ludion.

Index

For the benefit of digital users, indexed terms that span two pages (e.g., 52–53) may, on occasion, appear on only one of those pages.

Figures are indicated by *f* following the page number.